Also by T

THE BANK HOLIDAY MURDERS

The True Story of the First Whitechapel Murders

This award-winning* work of literary archeology digs deep into the archives of the Victorian police and press and offers a goldmine of revelatory material never before seen in Ripper literature. Travel back to 1887 to meet the earliest known Whitechapel victim for the first time. Discover the truth about 'Leather Apron' and the plot of one policeman to frame an innocent man. Follow the trail of lies as a well-known witness's false evidence is exposed for the first time in more than a century. Learn the shocking truth that links Emma Smith and Martha Tabram to two other brutal assault victims – and to the Ripper himself.

This is Jack the Ripper's Origin Story

AVAILABLE NOW IN PAPERBACK & KINDLE
AMAZON.COM
AMAZON.CO.UK
AMAZON.CA
AMAZON.FR

*Best True Crime Book 2014 – Indie Reader, Best History Book 2014 - IPPY

RIPPER
CONFIDENTIAL

New Research on the Whitechapel Murders

Tom Wescott

CrimeConfidentialPress

www.RipperBook.com
www.Facebook.com/RipperBooks
Twitter: @Ripperbook
E-mail author: tom@ripperbook.com

Ripper Confidential by Tom Wescott
Cover image design: SelfPubBookCovers.com/Shardel

This book is dedicated to the great Editors who helped me along the way: Paul Begg, Christopher-Michael DiGrazia, Christopher T. George, Adrian Morris, Dan Norder, Ally Ryder, Don Souden, and Adam Wood.

To Stephen P. Ryder of Casebook.org for giving a generation of Ripperologists a place to call home.

And to my friends for whom there's no longer any mystery: Christopher Scott, Paul 'Nemo' Kearney, Linda 'Celesta' McAuliffe-Roderick, Richard Whittington-Egan, David Radka, Adrian Phypers, Des McKenna, and Karen Dunlop. You are missed.

Acknowledgements

It's said that a book is never finished, only abandoned. Such is doubly so for the acknowledgements page. After more than 15 years learning from and exchanging with Ripper scholars the world over, any attempt at acknowledging everyone who's helped me along the way would only end in failure. But there are certain individuals without whom this book would have been absolutely impossible.

A very special thank you goes to Debra Arif for all the outstanding original research of hers that appears in this book. I'm far from the only person in the field who stands in awe of her historical wizardry, but I must surely be among the most grateful.

A special thank you to Adrian Phypers, Chris Scott, and all others who have over the years contributed to that most venerable and (thanks Spry!) available of resources for Ripper writers – the Casebook Press Project. And to Howard Brown for the astounding repository of unique contemporary reportage that is Jtrforums.com. He does the work of 10 men for which I'm grateful tenfold.

It is my pleasure and honor to express my sincerest gratitude to the following awesome individuals:

Glenn Andersson, Maria Birbili, Adam Bird, Burl Barer, Gary Barnett, David Barratt, Paul Begg, Neil Bell, David G. Bennett, John Bennett, Adam Bird, Gavin Bromley, Lynn Cates, Ron Chepesiuk, Jane Coram, Alex Daniels, Elaine Dutton, DYLAN, Ivor Edwards, Justin Evans, Stewart P. Evans, David Gates, Penniemarie Gibson, Christopher T. George, Aaron Habel, Ann Smalley Hargis, Jonathan Hainsworth, Howard

Hammick, Ben Holme, Christer Holmgren, Rob House, Pete Howard, Ellen Jamett, Michael Richards, Tracy I'anson, Dave James, David Knott, Rowan Lennon, Robert Charles Linford, 'Magpie', John Malcolm, Harry Mann, Jonathan Menges, Karen Morgan, Caroline Morris, Dan Norder, Richard Nunweek, David O'Flaherty, Adrian Phypers, Stan Reid, Mark Ripper, Stephen Russell, Ally Ryder, Stephen P. Ryder, Chris Scott, Gene Simmons, Jon Simons, Jennifer Shelden, Neal Shelden, Don Souden, Paul Stanley, Edward Stow, Heather Swartz, Wolf Vanderlinden, Alan Warren, David White, Ken Whiteway, Gareth Williams, A.P. Wolf, Adam Wood, Simon Wood, 'Yazoo', Dan Zupansky.

Contents

21st Century Ripperology

MY APOLOGIES TO any readers for whom this is your first Ripper book. It shouldn't be. My sincere advice would be to place *Ripper Confidential* snuggly and safely on your shelf and go get yourself a copy of the excellent *Jack the Ripper: CSI Whitechapel* by Paul Begg and John Bennett. Following this, I'd suggest you read any five or six other Ripper books. Once you've accomplished this, the myriad of names and streets that populate Ripperland will begin to click into place in your head. You'll know Buck's Row from Dorset Street. You'll remember that Elizabeth Stride was probably a Ripper victim but might not have been, and that Martha Tabram probably wasn't a Ripper victim but might have been. You'll still be hazy about the police officials (Was it Anderson or Warren who erased the graffito? Who was the boss of whom? Where does Henry Smith fit in?), but you'll probably know your memoranda from your marginalia.

Maybe your curiosity about the Ripper case will be satisfied and you'll be off to read about the Zodiac killer, or find out who killed JonBenet Ramsey; or, if classic British crimes are more your fair, you'll dive into the 'did he/didn't he' debate of chess enthusiast-cum-widower William Wallace.

If this is the case, consider yourself lucky. You're immune to the powerful bug that infected me back in the late 90s when a used paperback copy of

Dr. David Abrahamsen's *Murder & Madness: The Secret Life of Jack the Ripper*, misplaced in the horror section, spoke to me and said 'Take me home. I've been waiting for you.' I practically lived at the library for the next several months, hunting down books and reading every post on this new website called *Casebook: Jack the Ripper*, started by a college kid after he became intrigued by the infamous Ripper 'Diary'.

The message boards were positively brimming with thoughts and opinions and reams of contemporary reportage. I couldn't keep up, so I would print pages out to take home and study. I eventually worked up enough courage to write my own posts. Not under my own name, at first (I went by Red Demon), but my profile informed the curious who I really was. Tom Wescott, a single guy in his 20s, living in Tulsa, Oklahoma, USA.

When my meager income would allow, I'd reach out to local book dealers to order books that the library system couldn't provide me. Words can't describe the pleasure of the hunt and the anticipation of arrival. Such pleasures have since been lost in the name of progress. That library is gone, too. And the bookstores have closed.

But Ripperology appears timeless.

Writers have never had it better than we have it now. And that can only be good news for readers. We can publish with full control and compete at the same level as most other books in our niche. We no longer have to abide by the tired formula that for too long has had Ripper readers flipping with malaise through obligatory 2,000 word chapters on East End history and one each for the victims - seemingly copied from one book to the next - just to get to the 'good stuff'. This good stuff – the promised 'new information' or 'final solution' - all too often amounts only to an overhyped suspect who was probably in Paris during the murders anyways.

But times they are a changin'. It's a new century (though not as new as it once was) and a new generation of researchers are poised to give the world's greatest murder mystery a much overdue facelift.

What does this mean? What it *doesn't* mean is more poorly constructed revisionist theory or conspiratorial 'fringe' Ripperology which might put a few pounds (or dollars) in the author's pocket but otherwise serves no purpose to the field. There will be such works, to be sure, but I believe they'll find their support and audience dwindling as readers realize they do not need to turn to alternative history for exciting new finds and ideas. *Real* history still has plenty to offer, even in the most studied crime series of all time. Which brings us to the book in your hands (or phone, or Kindle, as the case may be).

In 2014 I published *The Bank Holiday Murders: The True Story of the First Whitechapel Murders*. The approach I took in researching and writing the book was part historian/part investigative reporter. The reception of the book was far beyond anything I could have expected. So, if I sound optimistic about the present state of Ripperology, it's because I have good reason to be.

BHM focused on the Whitechapel murders prior to that of Polly Nichols, where most books begin their narrative in earnest. A wealth of new information was presented and the lodging house keepers or 'Lords of Spitalfields', as I termed them, were put under the microscope. Sergeant William Thick was indicted (some say unfairly, but I'll let you be the judge) for fitting up John Pizer as Leather Apron. Using contemporary evidence I demonstrated the probability that Mary Ann 'Pearly Poll' Connelly fabricated the story about having spent August Bank Holiday in the company of Martha Tabram and two soldiers. The evidence in this instance is so strong that it must, for the sake of accuracy, become part of the narrative from this point forward.

I also utilized the available medical evidence in a way that it had not been presented before and demonstrated the likelihood that Martha Tabram was violated in a manner nearly identical to that of Emma Smith on the previous Bank Holiday. Going further back I discussed - for the first time in a Ripper book - the similar murder of Emily Horsnell, discovered by Debra Arif in 2008 but ignored in literature for six years. I drew attention to the fact that Polly Nichols's death certificate has her living in the same house as Annie Chapman in the days prior to her death. This was also a fact ignored by Ripper literature, despite a scanned image of the death certificate appearing on Polly's profile at *Casebook.org* for at least a decade prior.

I mention these things not to toot my own horn but to draw additional attention to the facts themselves. One of the negatives about writing a book where so much of the information is new and in some cases rather sensational is that some of the most important bits get lost in the shuffle. This is why I feel only those already versed in the widely accepted narrative of the Ripper murders, but who have not been at it so long as to give the old school ideas time to petrify, could appreciate *The Bank Holiday Murders* and *Ripper Confidential.*

For the young minds who've caught the Ripper bug in recent years who are curious – or even confused about – where they should start their personal research, I'd recommend starting from the very beginning and not taking for granted anything you're told by an author, including yours truly. In ten years you'll have access to information and databases that are not available right now, just as I've been able to take full advantage of a wealth of material that would not have been possible 20 or even 10 years ago. My hope is that some of you will prove me wrong on some of the stuff I present in this book. I can take it, because that will mean you've turned up something I didn't, or couldn't have, and that's how we keep this old hansom cab running along the cobbles. If anyone should happen to prove some of my suppositions correct then, hey, I'll take that as well.

For all of the new material I presented in *The Bank Holiday Murders*, the one thing I would like to see remembered above all else, and that I feel should be taken on board by the next generation of Ripperologists, is the undisputed fact that between November of 1887 and August of 1888, no less than four women were murdered or severely assaulted in a particularly brutal manner and each of these women, at the time of their assault, lived at one of two neighboring houses on George Street. In other words, imagine any two houses next door to each other, either in your neighborhood or another. Now, imagine that in a 9 month period four of the women who live in these houses are brutally assaulted and murdered. Would law enforcement in your area see that as a coincidence? Would you? Should it make a difference that it happened in a century other than our own? I don't think it should and this is why I believe this might be the single best lead developed in the hunt for Jack the Ripper since the Macnaghten memoranda came to light well over 50 years ago.

The book in your hands is not a sequel to BHM but more a continuation of my research and a return to those aspects of the mystery that most intrigue me. I cut my teeth writing for the Ripper journals back when they were all still in print form. My first article was for *Ripperologist* #34 in April 2001 and it wasn't particularly good. If memory serves, Editor Paul Begg had to cut swathes through it to make it printable. The next one was a little better, but only just. I've spared my readers the republication of these well-intentioned misses.

I had subscriptions to both *Ripperologist* and *Ripper Notes*, but as a writer I was more or less a *Ripper Notes* mainstay until the magazine folded after 2007. I then found myself scribing for the digital journals of Don Souden, an exceptional writer, editor, and human being. Two years after the last of his journals ceased publication I switched my focus to writing in book form. But over the years people would read about my essays on old threads on the message boards and ask me where they might find them. I decided it was time I pull the best (or at least my favorite) of the essays I'd written for now-defunct journals together, polish them up a bit, and present them to a new generation.

One distinct advantage that an essay has over a book is that it allows a writer the freedom to take a single aspect they're intrigued by, no matter how small, and magnify it as big as they'd like or dissect it down to its atoms. In my experience, this is how discoveries are made. You've got to first ask the question and then look for the answer. If you get a hunch about something you should work hard to prove yourself wrong. If you can't prove yourself wrong, then it's time to publish, and odds are someone else will be up to the task. If they can't prove you wrong, then you've got something. I've taken this same approach with my books. BHM is essentially a long essay. But *Ripper Confidential* is something a little different.

The book you hold is separated into three sections. The first section, 'The Buck's Row Murder', is a mini-book devoted entirely to mysteries orbiting the murder of Polly Nichols. The medical evidence is looked at in more depth and detail than is usual and new insights are presented. For instance, we find two separate pools of blood under Polly when her body is moved – the one we'd expect to find where her butchered neck had been, but also a second pool under where her legs had been. And yet her skirts aren't bloodied. What might this tell us? We later join a journalist who found himself in the dead house as the autopsy of Nichols was under way and we learn that we do *not* know for certain that the Ripper had failed in his presumed mission of organ thievery. We then take a turn down Brady Street and are introduced to a woman we've never met before who might have been the Ripper's first intended victim that night. Sound unbelievable? It did to me. Still does. But when you have 'suspicious' blood stains, screams of murder, a woman with a serious wound to her arm, and reports a few weeks later describing just such an event, you might agree it is worthy of consideration.

The second section entitled 'The Berner Street Mystery' is, as you might expect, all about the colorful characters and goings-on in and around Dutfield's Yard. This section is comprised of eight separate essays, some from the archives and some written brand new for this book. The older essays are followed by an 'Author's Note' giving a brief history of the influence and circumstances that led to its composition. It's no fair skimming or skipping these essays as tucked into each one are numerous nuggets that I hope you find new and interesting.

Perhaps of particular significance is the material relating to the various witnesses. Using sources not available to earlier authors and taking advantage of exceptional research produced by some of my fellow journal contributors, I've been able to construct a more accurate and reliable timeline of events than we've ever seen before. Of paramount importance is the impact this new information has on our understanding of the role played by Israel Schwartz, long considered as one of the most crucial witnesses in the Ripper case.

Because these essays were written across the span of a decade and often discuss the same events and individuals, certain source material is repeated at different points throughout the book. I apologize for any annoyance this causes, but I found it necessary to revisit material when considering a different perspective. I also believe some points are worth repetition (i.e. 2 neighboring houses, 4 women, 9 months).

In the final section, whimsically titled 'Curios & Oddities', I present three essays that did not fit into the framework of the earlier sections. Admirers of Mary Kelly or those who enjoy discovering connections between suspects and victims might enjoy 'Mary Kelly and the Decadents'. Readers of *The Bank Holiday Murders* yearning to again see Kelly's landlord at his firebrand best should read 'The McCarthys of Dorset Street'. But the highlight of this section would be 'The Ghoul of Goulston Street', a brand new composition in which we take a long and long overdue objective look at the mysterious chalked message and consider what it might mean, what the investigators thought of it at the time, and why so many modern experts dismiss it as mere happenstance.

Plenty of authors tell you who the Ripper was. Or, if we're to be truthful, who they want him to have been. I'm not one of those authors, at least not yet. I can no longer say that I believe the case will ever truly be solved – That is to say that a single candidate will emerge whom most of us agree must have been the Ripper. But I do believe that if there's even to be hope of such a revelation, then more effort needs to be put towards understanding the crimes themselves. More research needs to be undertaken on the world these women inhabited, such as the houses in which the lived and near which they died. And closer consideration given to the people who moved in and around these houses. Maybe Emily Horsnell was the first victim, and maybe Emma Smith was. Maybe that tragic honor belongs to a name yet uncovered.

What I do know – beyond any and all doubt – is that there is much yet to be discovered. I hope some will see this book as a testament to that and will believe, as I most assuredly do, that the hunt for history is a worthwhile pursuit.

Tom Wescott
Jan. 29th, 2017

SECTION ONE

The Buck's Row Murder

CHAPTER 1

3:40am, Friday, August 31ˢᵗ, 1888

ELECTRICITY EXISTED IN 1888. So did telephones and automobiles. The oldest surviving examples of recorded music and motion picture come to us from that year. The world as it had been for centuries was morphing into the world we know today and it must have been exciting times for London's West Enders who were still grappling with the idea that you could speak into a tube and someone miles away could hear you. Just as we are today, they would have been confronted with the thought both frightening and comforting that 'anything is possible'.

Such were not the burdens in London's East End, where things were as they had always been and very little that was good seemed possible. For all intents and purposes, they were a people lost in time.

But someone from the future was about to step into the shadows of the East End and bring with him a new kind of darkness; something the people of Whitechapel had never seen before.

Gas light glowed dimmer than electric light and cut much smaller swathes through the dark, more like beacons in the distance than sources of illumination. But gas and the moon were all Charles Cross[1] had to light his way as he made his normal early morning trek to Pickford's on Broad Street, where he worked as a delivery driver.

As the oft-told story goes, it was about

3:40am when Cross found himself about halfway along Buck's Row and something on the other side of the road caught his eye. It was dark, large, and resting in front of stable gates. An abandoned tarpaulin, he thought, as he stepped across the road for further inspection. But it occurred to him as he got closer that something wasn't right. So he stopped. He stood. He stared.

It wasn't a tarpaulin.

Buck's Row was a narrow, cobbled street that ran east to west from Brady Street to Baker's row.[2] The Northeastern Railway line ran through it and the sound of the rattling rails were audible to all who lived there. In 1892 the street was renamed Durward Street in an effort to remove the stigma that followed from Jack the Ripper's visit there. It didn't work.

As Charles Cross stood in the road, coming to terms with what he was seeing, he heard footsteps approaching.

Robert Paul was also a car man on the way to his work in Corbett's Court off of nearby Hanbury Street. As he made his way along the dimly lit thoroughfare he noticed a man standing in the road ahead of him. Paul would later describe this moment to a reporter: "He came a little towards me, but as I knew the dangerous character of the locality I tried to give him a wide berth. Few people like to come up and down here without being on their guard, for there are such terrible gangs about. There have been many knocked down and robbed at that spot. The man, however, came towards me and said, 'Come and look at this woman.'"[3]

The 'spot' Paul referred to was the recess created by the gateway that led into Brown's stable yards. Paul joined Cross in kneeling beside the unmoving mass on the sidewalk. Cross thought she was dead but Paul thought he felt a movement. It was too dark for them to see the condition of her throat and the men were fortunate not to have made contact with the pool of blood streaming along the incline of the pavement and toward the street.

Both Cross and Paul needed to get to their jobs and were no doubt anxious not to be found hovering over a body. They decided to be on their way and inform the first constable they came to. Paul first attempted to lower the woman's skirts.

As the men approached Hanbury Street they found PC Jonas Mizen of H Division 'knocking up'[4] residents of Hanbury Street. The exchange that took place between the three men is open for debate. If you believe the car men, they informed PC Mizen that a woman was either dead or drunk in Buck's Row and walked on, annoyed that Mizen continued knocking on doors instead of hustling to the scene. If you believe Mizen, the men told him that he was wanted by another constable because a woman was found dead. Mizen acknowledged knocking one more person up because he thought a PC was already at the scene and so the need for his presence wasn't immediate. The men denied stating that there was already a PC present, and all things considered, they were probably telling the truth.

As fate would have it, there was in fact a policeman waiting at the scene when Mizen got there. PC John Neil had discovered the body on his own after the car men had left.

PC John Neil, a 'tall, fresh-coloured man, with brown hair, and straw coloured moustache and imperial'[5], was 38 at the time and had spent the last thirteen of those years policing Bethnal Green with the Metropolitan Police J Division. At approximately 3:45 am, on August 31st, he was walking his eastward beat along Buck's Row when he came upon the body on the sidewalk. He opened the flap on his bulls-eye lantern, thrust the light forward and illuminated a horrendous gash circling the woman's neck. It still oozed blood. He touched the arm, found it warm, and noticed that the eyes were still open. His first thought was that he'd discovered a suicide.[6] Protocol dictated that he could not leave the side of the body, nor could he blow his whistle in a residential neighborhood if it could be avoided, so he opened and closed the flap on his lantern, creating a light signal.

Answering the silent alarm was fellow J Division man, PC John Thain, whose beat took him along Brady Street which intersected Buck's Row. Neil dispatched Thain to summon Dr. Rees Ralph Llewellyn from his home and practice at nearby 152 Whitechapel Road. PC Mizen eventually found his way to Buck's Row and was sent to fetch an ambulance.

Neil was once again left alone in the dark with the corpse. He used this time to search the area for clues but found none. The recent rains had softened the grime and soil on the roads, allowing Neil to see if any carriage had recently passed, but no such tracks were visible. He stepped across the road and rang the bell of Essex Wharf, a narrow, three-storied office building that also served as the living quarters for its manager, Walter Purkiss, and his family. Walter's wife, Mary Ann, endured a sleepless night, and although her windows overlooked the murder site, she'd seen and heard nothing.

While still waiting for the doctor, Neil found himself flanked by three large men who would have smelled not so different from the corpse at his feet. Harry Tomkins, Charles Bretton, and James Mumford worked as horse slaughtermen in Winthrop Street, the next street over from Buck's Row. Their slaughterhouse was colloquially known as Barber's Yard and was apparently a place where constables on the beat could expect a warm cup of coffee, a dry roof, and a few words of friendly conversation.

PC John Thain, who had been the first to join his colleague Neil in Buck's Row, had come to know the men of Barber's Yard, and the story they told was that after Neil had dispatched him to Dr. Llewellyn's house, Thain first went out of his way to Barber's Yard to fetch his coat and tell the men about the body in Buck's Row. This seemingly minor indiscretion on Thain's part would become significant in the coming days.

Dr. Llewellyn arrived in the street shortly after 4am, pronounced the woman dead, noted the cut throat, and ordered her body removed to the mortuary. He then returned home and likely went back to bed.

The Lady in the Shell

Polly Nichols was born Mary Ann Walker on August 26th. Her age is given as between 42 and 44 at the time of her death, making the year of her birth between 1844 and 46. She was 5'2" with brown eyes, brown hair turning grey, a dark complexion, and missing some of her front teeth, the remainder of which were somewhat discolored at the time of her death.

As with almost all of the Ripper's victims, Polly was an alcoholic who had remained estranged from her family in the final years of her life, having separated from her husband for the final time in 1881.

William Nichols married Polly Walker in 1864 and together they bore five children. In 1882, only one year following their separation, William found out that Polly was living as a prostitute and ceased all support payments. The Parish authorities came after him for money but he argued that she had abandoned him with five children. He won the case when he was able to prove that she'd been earning her living as a prostitute.

It appears that she also had been living with Thomas Drew, a smith living in Walworth, who had been her sweetheart before William. The rekindled flame with Drew was snuffed quickly when he discovered that she had been stealing his belongings and selling them for money to buy alcohol.[7]

Without Drew providing for her and no further support from her husband, Polly had no choice but to drift into the workhouse system, becoming a ward of the Lambeth Workhouse from April 4th, 1882 to March, 1883, when she went to live with her father, Edward Walker, in Camberwell.

Mr. Walker did the best he could for his daughter and her children but found her to be a drunkard of 'dissolute character' and let her know how he felt about the way she chose to live. One morning he found her bed empty and did not see her again until 1886 when the two met at the funeral of one of her brothers who had burned to death in the explosion of a paraffin lamp. Mr. Walker remarked that on this day his daughter was dressed respectably.

Whatever good turn Polly's life had taken would plummet to an all-time low by October of 1887 when she was found sleeping rough in Trafalgar Square. This event was reported in the press and gives us valuable new insight into Polly's character:

At the Bow-street police-court, Mary Ann Murphy, 50, Mary Duncan, 60, James Foley, 19, Joseph Drew, 16, Elizabeth Pegrim, 65, Elizabeth Lawrence, 30, Margaret German, 32, Mary Ann Nichols, 36, Annie Bates, 16, and Flora Isabelle Cadman, 18, were charged with wandering abroad without any visible means of subsistence. The accused presented a very dejected appearance. Inspector Bullock deposed that at half-past 10 o'clock on Monday night a gentleman attended in Trafalgar-square and gave bread and coffee to 170 outcasts, and gave them tickets for admission to lodging houses. Several returned, and said the lodging-houses were full. The witness offered to admit them to the casual ward. They nearly all refused. Thirty were sent to the casual ward, and nineteen were admitted. The other eleven ran away. The prisoners were taken into custody. Mr. Bridge: Does not the distribution of coffee and food induce these people to go to the square? – Inspector Bullock: Yes, sir, it does; but it is distributed at 11, and there is plenty of time for them to get lodgings, or to go to the casual ward. Passers-by throw money from the terrace, and when they see a respectable person pass they will take off their shawls and shake themselves as if they were cold, in order to invite sympathy.[8]

This unhappy moment offers us a window into the lowest period of Polly's life when she was sleeping rough in parks and depending on hand-outs to both survive and feed her drinking habit. The *Daily News* of the same day offered similar coverage with the additional detail that Nichols and her fellow 'outcasts' 'presented a woeful aspect, being dirty and very ragged'. Also provided was her statement:

Nichols said she had a ticket for a lodging-house, and went there, but it was full. The reason why she would not go to the casual ward was because they were kept there in the morning, and so lost any work they had to go to. She had no friends, and no home; but was born in the City. Her father lived in Walworth, but where she did not know. Mr. Bridges said he would take her recognisances to appear when called upon.

It's been stated in other works that Nichols spent December in the square, but it seems this was not the case. What is certain is that she was once again admitted to Lambeth Workhouse on December 2nd. At some point in April of 1888, Nichols, who pitifully described herself in October as having no friends and no home, did indeed make a friend in the person of Mary Ann Monk, a young woman with 'a haughty air and flushed face'. Monk would be the first to provide the police with Polly's full and proper name.

Her final stint at the Lambeth Workhouse - which spanned from April 16th to May 12th - seems to have been well-spent as on the 12th of May Polly was sent to Wandsworth to work in service for Samuel and Sara Cowdry. It is doubtful the workhouse would have recommended Polly's services if they hadn't seen some marked improvement in her character. It is also pos-sible that she'd done a turn as a confidential informant for the police, as Mr. Cowdry was the Chief of Works for the local police department.

Once settled at her new address, the proud Polly wrote her father a letter:

'I just right to say you will be glad to know that I am settled in my new place, and going all right up to now. My people went out yesterday and have not returned, so I am left in charge. It is a grand place inside, with trees and gardens back and front. All has been newly done up. They are teetotallers and religious so I ought to get on. They are very nice people, and I have not too much to do. I hope you are all right and the boy has work. So good bye for the present.

from yours truly,

Polly

Answer soon, please, and let me know how you are.[9]

Edward Walker wrote back but never received a reply. By the end of July, Polly's demons had gotten the best of her and she abandoned her position in the idyllic home, making away with 3 pounds, ten shillings worth of clothes stolen from her benefactors. She's next found in the registry of the Gray's Inn Workhouse on the nights of August 1st and 2nd.

After the brief stay at Gray's Inn, Polly seems to have drifted back into the abyss of the East End lodging houses. Her movements during the final month of her life are shrouded in mystery and will be discussed later after we consider more evidence about Polly herself.

An important observation about Polly Nichols's character comes from the *Standard* of October 26th, 1887, when she was brought into custody for 'wandering abroad' and sleeping in Trafalgar Square. The report noted that 'Nichols was stated to be the worst woman in the square and at the police-station was very disorderly.' This is a very dramatic statement and stands in stark contrast to how she's generally portrayed in Ripper literature.

In October of 1887 a political storm was brewing in Trafalgar Square and the unemployed, the homeless, and the burgeoning socialist movement assembled in the thousands to protest the government. The growing tension between the poor and the establishment culminated in a micro war between the Metropolitan Police and the disenfranchised that resulted in two dead and over one-hundred injured. It occurred on Sunday, November 13, less than three weeks after Nichols had been arrested in the square, and from that moment forward was referred to as 'Bloody Sunday'. Considering the amount of trouble the police had with squatters and protestors in Trafalgar square throughout the month of October, for Polly to have been 'the worst woman in the square' speaks volumes about her behavior.

Another recently discovered item entitled 'A Victim', from the September 27th, 1894 edition of *The Woman's Signal*, paints a similarly dark picture of Polly:

> The introduction of a superior class of paid nurses, which has become the rule in Workhouse Infirmaries, renders it possible to employ workhouse girls in little tasks among the sick and suffering. Workhouse tempers become subdued in those corridors of pain, where girls of their own age lie dying. One of the most violent of this class, who was in the habit of secreting table-knives, and who had been imprisoned for attempting to stab an official, became completely tamed under the influence of kindness. Change of residence having removed me from the neighbourhood, she was lost sight of, and relapsed into vice, finally meeting with a violent end as the first victim of the Whitechapel outrages.[10]

If Polly was in the habit of secreting knives and used one to stab a workhouse official, one can only wonder at what she might have done to earn the moniker of 'worst woman of the square'.

The murdered women of Whitechapel have become romanticized to the point that they're often portrayed as anything but what they were. That is not to say they deserved their fate. Nobody does. But if we're to hunt Jack the Ripper, we must observe his victims in the same context in which he observed them, and for all intents and purposes, they were addicts and criminals. Prostitution would have been only one of their illegitimate means of earning money and the most obvious. The older they became the less money they could demand and the less interest they would be able to attract. As a result, many resorted to thievery, pick pocketing, or working with a male accomplice to lure men to a secluded spot and mug them. This is certainly not true of all lodging house women, but it's true of many, and such criminal connections should be kept in mind.

A pitiful and often retold story of Polly's life is that while she was sick and confined her husband began an affair with her nurse and inevitably abandoned his wife for the woman. Another oft-told tale about William

Nichols is that he had not spoken to his eldest son in years prior to seeing him again at the inquest. These rumors were spread by Polly's father and have become part of her biography, but William Nichols denied the allegations at the inquest and even wrote a letter to *Lloyd's Weekly Newspaper* to set the record straight. The following was published on Sept. 9th, 1888:

'To the Editor of Lloyd's Newspaper –

Dear Sir,

I hope you will correct an error in your Sunday Edition in reference to the Whitechapel murder. It is stated that I did not know my own son. That is not so. He left home of his own accord two and a half years ago, and I have always been on speaking terms with him. Only two or three months ago I saw him, and last week received two letters from him, asking me if I knew of any work for him. I did not leave my wife during her confinement and go away with a nurse girl. The deceased woman deserted me four or five times, if not six. The last time she left me without any home, and five children, the youngest one year and four months'. I kept myself with the children where I was living for two and a half years before I took on with anybody, and not till after it was proved at Lambeth police-court that she had misconducted herself.

Yours respectfully,

W. Nicholls' (sic)

While William Nichols was taking the time to defend his honor in the press, he was also apparently attempting to profit from the death of his wife. Word got around and made it into the press that the firm in which Nichols worked had, like many businesses, a benefit fund to which the employees contributed and could draw from in times of emergency. The members were permitted to draw money from the fund upon the death of a spouse or child to cover funeral expenses. Although Nichols was entitled to such benefits, it was well known that Polly's father and William's own son had covered most of the funeral expenses (although William contributed some as well), so it was to the chagrin of his colleagues that Nichols applied to receive remuneration for the whole of the expense.[11]

Polly's last days and hours are as much a mystery as is the name of her killer. The few surviving police reports available to us erroneously put her final address as either 55 Flower & Dean Street (Helson) or 18 Thrawl Street (Swanson). Polly is not known to have ever lived at 55 Flower & Dean Street and her tenure at 18 Thrawl Street ended weeks prior to her murder. In fact, just hours prior to her murder she had applied to the keepers of her old bed to see if she could gain admittance on credit. She was refused and went away cheerfully, optimistically stating that she'd likely earn the money soon enough on account of her 'jolly new bonnet' that was actually a rusting old thing recently acquired, probably on or around her birthday five days earlier.

Ripper books tell us that her final address was a lodging house known locally as the 'White House', located at 56 Flower & Dean Street. This is because some of the newspapers stated this as fact, citing Ellen Holland, Polly's friend and former lodging mate. However, as I revealed in *The Bank Holiday Murders*, this was merely a guess on Holland's part, based on Polly's description of a house in which men and women lived together. In truth, her final address as recorded on her death certificate was 35 Dorset Street.

Ellen Holland was described in the press as 'an elderly woman in a brown dress, with a dolman and bonnet, whose naturally pale face was flushed with excitement, and who gave her address in a frightened manner, which necessitated the coroner frequently urging her to speak up'. Ellen stated that she believed Polly had briefly lived in Boundary Street[12] but told her in their final conversation, only an hour before her murder, that she'd recently changed lodgings and did not like her new house. Holland's impression was that 'some trouble was weighing upon her,'[13] giving rise to the possibility that the trouble weighing upon Polly had something to do with her recent lodgings at 35 Dorset Street. One of her fellow lodgers, Annie Chapman, would be the next to fall to the Ripper's blade, also around the time of her own birthday.

Polly was buried at the City of London Cemetery on the afternoon of Thursday, September 6th. The procession set off from the office of the undertaker in Hanbury Street. Her killer may have been there watching from the crowd. He would certainly be in Hanbury Street in two days' time.

CHAPTER 2

Sifting the Medical Evidence

INSPECTOR SPRATLING WAS called to Buck's Row at 4:30am. By the time he arrived the body had been removed to the mortuary and James Green, a neighbor's son, had washed most of the blood away. Finding little to investigate at the murder scene, Spratling headed to the mortuary on Old Montague Street where he found the body lying unguarded on a stretcher in the yard.

John Spratling joined the Metropolitan Police in 1870 at the ripe old age of 30 and was promoted to Divisional Inspector J Division (Bethnal Green) in 1887, apparently replacing Edmund Reid who'd moved over to H Division. He lived to the very ripe age of 94 and boasted that he smoked blacker tobacco and drank blacker tea than anyone else on the Met force but lived so long that he drew more money in pension than in pay.[14]

While waiting for the mortuary attendants, Inspector Spratling made notes about the appearance of the deceased, which will be referenced in part as well as presented in whole throughout the following chapters. At about 5:00am, two attendants, Robert Mann and James Hatfield, arrived and moved the body inside the small room; they then went for breakfast, again leaving Spratling alone with the body. The inspector continued his observation, raising the clothing and peaking under the loose stays. He had not been feeling well that day and what he saw under the stays did little to settle his stomach. He stepped into the yard and threw up.[15]

There was a large gash running from her chest all the way down to her pubes; a loose flap of flesh was pushed out and folded over by her protruding intestines. He at once sent a constable to summon Dr. Llewellyn.

The doctor prepared himself for a long morning and left with the constable on a dark trek to the shack in Old Montague Street where he set about performing his post mortem. While no doubt an excellent general practitioner and a more than capable surgeon, Llewellyn's powers of deduction left much to be desired. Among the howlers he put forth as evidence are:

- The killer was left-handed
- Nichols was murdered elsewhere and her body dumped in Buck's Row
- The killer had inflicted the horrendous and certainly fatal abdominal wounds *before* cutting her throat.

Llewellyn had his reasons for reaching these conclusions, but they were not very good ones, and the police almost immediately saw the errors apparent in his findings. To the doctor's credit, he admitted his mistakes. But leaving aside Llewellyn's flawed interpretation of the evidence, we move on to the evidence itself.

A report carried in the press, but not confirmed by extant police reports, describes impressions on Polly's fingers that suggested she had recently worn rings. It was speculated that her killer may have taken them from her. The *Times*[16] astutely observed that 'if the police are right in believing that certain flash rings[17] were torn from Nichols's finger, this is a circumstance which slightly disconcerts the idea that the murderer was a simple maniac.' In other words, if robbery was a sub-motive, then the killer had his wits about him. Polly may have pawned or traded her rings, but there's no question that the next victim, Annie Chapman, was mugged by her killer, so it's probable Nichols was as well; or else the Ripper got the idea from reading news reports about Polly's rings and brought a rumor to vivid life in Hanbury Street.

How the killer subdued Nichols remains a matter of conjecture. There was a laceration to her tongue which probably occurred as the killer gripped her face to steady her neck in order to cut it. The fact that Nichols was lying on her back with her tongue protruding between her teeth strongly suggests that her breathing was interfered with in some way, although any tell-tale bruising would have been obliterated by the deep throat wound. As with Tabram, her fists were clenched, so there's a likelihood that she was partially strangled or placed into a chokehold until unconscious and then lowered to the pavement.

Missing Links

There has long been a debate as to whether Martha Tabram was a Ripper victim or not and the dividing line between both sides is inevitably the medical evidence: Martha was stabbed and Polly was ripped. Many Ripperologists find it difficult to reconcile the frenzied stabs inflicted upon Tabram with the more deliberate incisions practiced upon Polly Nichols. In spite of the fact that the two women were almost identical in terms of victimology, I personally saw it as unlikely that a killer's methodology could 'mature' so dramatically in such a short period of time. This is because I assumed the murders were perpetrated in the way they're portrayed in all the books written over the years.

Ripper books can vary greatly in their conclusions but rarely veer from the path in their portrayal of the injuries inflicted upon the women. However, in researching the Tabram murder for my first book I was surprised to learn a number of new things, such as the fact that she had been laid out, half nude, with her legs spread apart as though the killer sought access to her private area. Digging further, I found evidence that she had been violated in a manner similar to that endured previously by Emma Smith who managed to survive briefly before succumbing to her injuries.

Making these discoveries opened my eyes to the fact that there was still more to learn about these murders and how they were committed. This left me with an open mind as I reconsidered the murder of Mary Ann Nichols for this book.

Although Llewellyn could not be accused of being a brilliant forensic examiner, we should assume he was capable of at least the most fundamental aspects of his trade, such as making determinations about the sort of blade used to murder a woman. Regarding the knife, he opined that it was long-bladed and moderately sharp[18], and although he couldn't say whether it was a clasp or butcher's knife, he was certain the blade was strong.

On the surface, it seems contradictory that wounds so deep as to reach the bone could be inflicted with a knife only 'moderately' sharp. However, if Nichols had been stabbed and ripped, as opposed to cut, then it makes perfect sense.

An unnamed journalist for *People* who visited the mortuary and saw the corpse of Nichols with his own eyes recorded the injuries as he saw them. He noted there were two wounds to the throat and '...in the first instance the knife had been thrust into her neck behind the left ear, and a horrible wound inflicted. Then, thrust in, in a similar position behind the right ear, it was wrenched round with such force [as to almost decapitate her].'[19] This is an unambiguous description of two deep stab wounds. The same article goes on to record the journalist's impression of the abdominal wounds thusly: 'The knife had been thrust into the lowest point of the body, and the woman deliberately ripped open to the breast, causing almost complete disembowelment. Again the knife had been thrust into the body under each breast, and drawn down to the thighs in a zig-zag fashion.'

This first-hand description is impressive but it is nevertheless an unqualified opinion from an unofficial source. Coverage of Dr. Llewellyn's evidence at the inquest provides more illumination. The *Daily Telegraph*[20] reported that 'there were no injuries about the body until till just about the lower part of the abdomen. Two or three inches from the left side was a wound running in a jagged manner. It was a very deep wound, and the tissues were cut through. There were several incisions running across the abdomen. On the right side there were also three or four similar cuts running downwards. All these had been caused by a knife which had been used violently and been used downwards. The wounds were from left to right, and...had been done by the same instrument.'

The *East London Advertiser* similarly recorded that the injuries 'had been caused by a knife which had been used violently, and in a downward direction. The injuries were from left to right...'

These statements have confused readers and commentators over the years because if we're facing the body a cut cannot run left to right and downwards at the same time. This is yet another seeming contradiction that exists only if we assume all the injuries were cuts in the classic sense. What Llewellyn is actually describing when he says that the knife was 'used downwards' and 'violently' are deep stab wounds inflicted by Nichols's killer who would then pull the blade in whichever direction he wanted the wound to go, leaving in its wake the tell-tale 'rip' that would inspire the name by which he would always be known.

In fact, the *East London Observer* wrote that 'on the abdomen there were some severe cuts and stabs, which the witness described in detail.'[21]

Polly Nichols, like Martha Tabram, was a victim of multiple stabs. This understanding of the source material marked a crucial breakthrough in my research because it provided for the first time a legitimate 'bridge' in the medical evidence between Martha Tabram and Polly Nichols; instead of two killers with markedly different M.O.s, we appear to be looking at a multiple stabber who upgraded his hardware and 'graduated' from stabbing to stabbing *and* ripping. He would again upgrade his hardware prior to meeting Annie Chapman, confirming that he was progressing in his methods with each victim.

The next piece of medical evidence to consider is an intriguing mention in Inspector Spratling's report of 'two small stabs on private parts'. Like Dr. Killeen before him, Llewellyn omitted mention of genital injuries at the inquest, and if not for Spratling's notes, any knowledge of them would not have survived in the record. These small stabs have received some comment over the years with the assumption being that they were inflicted unintentionally as the Ripper clumsily worked to get his knife under Polly's stays. But there might be a better explanation if the same man who took the lives of Emma Smith and Martha Tabram was also responsible for the dark deed on Buck's Row.

Emma Smith was raped with an unidentified 'blunt instrument' and Martha Tabram was similarly assaulted with a long-bladed weapon.[22] I wondered if perhaps Polly didn't suffer the same fate, so I trawled back through the reports in search of answers. Because Dr. Llewellyn's reports are no longer extant and he followed tradition by avoiding any discussion of injury to genitalia at the inquest, the surviving official documents offered no further clues. Fortunately, the coroner, as well as Charles Cross, and one of the constables who moved the body, were not so tight-lipped and made some rather suggestive observations.

Charles Cross testified at the inquest that when he found Nichols her legs were spread wide open and her toes pointed outward[23], identical to how Tabram had been found. He also testified that before they left in search of a constable, Robert Paul attempted to pull Polly's skirts down, but 'they did not seem as though they would come down.'[24] This suggests that Polly's body had been lifted by her killer and her skirts tucked underneath her with a purpose.

Inspector Spratling, called as a witness at the first session of the inquest, described for the coroner the various throat and abdominal injuries. Of interest is this piece of testimony:

> There were no blood marks between the groin and the knees, except, perhaps, very slight ones. He did not feel very well at the time and the sight "turned him up," so that he did not make a very precise examination. The skin of the deceased was clean, but he could not say that it bore evidence of blood having been recently washed from it.[25]

Many newspapers would record only the answers given by witnesses at an inquest, leaving readers to infer what the questions were. The question as to whether or not the victim had been washed by her killer was an important one at the time because it was not yet clear to all concerned that the murder had occurred where the body was found. Dr. Llewellyn speculated that she had been taken elsewhere, undressed, murdered, redressed, and dropped in Buck's Row. What's most intriguing here is why the coroner expected there to have been blood between the groin and the knee when her legs had not been injured in any way.

Spratling did not notice any blood on the exposed surfaces of Polly's legs, although he admitted he felt sick and did not pay special attention. However, a policeman closer to the action told a different story. PC John Thain, who it will be remembered was sent by PC Neil to fetch Dr. Llewellyn, was also on hand to move Polly's body from the pavement to the police ambulance. The *Times* of Sept. 18th reported on his inquest statement and recorded what he saw:

> He helped to put the body on the ambulance, and the back appeared to be covered with blood, which, he thought, had run from the neck as far as the waist. He got blood on to his hands. There was also blood on the ground where the deceased's legs had been.

Thain's observations are very specific in that they describe two separate areas of blood: one soaked into the clothing under her back which terminated at the waist, and another, probably smaller area, under where her legs had rested. He was doubtlessly correct in supposing that the greater volume of blood had been produced by the fatal neck injuries, but what might have caused the other stain is not addressed publicly at the inquest.

My first thought was that, in spite of Thain's apparent certainty, he had been mistaken and the blood under Polly's legs had also originated from her neck flow. To prove or disprove this I turned my attention to the discussion of Polly's clothing, of which there was more than would usually be the case, due to the initial suspicion that she might have been murdered elsewhere, redressed, and abandoned in Buck's Row.

Inspector Joseph Helson went to the mortuary a few hours after discovery of the murder and inspected the body while it was still clothed. He testified that there was no blood on the back of the skirts[26], which is a crucial and telling detail because any blood that passed from under her back and into the area under her legs must have first passed under her skirt and stained it. Apparently, this point was not lost on coroner Baxter in his questioning of Inspector Spratling, who replied that 'there was no evidence of the skirt having been washed.'

Based on the statements of inspectors Helson and Spratling, we can conclude that the blood in the region of Polly's legs did not originate from the neck wound and must therefore have had another source. I could think of only two possibilities, both of which challenge our modern understanding of the Buck's Row murder.

The first and (to my mind) most likely explanation is that the killer repeated himself from the previous two murders and brutally raped Nichols with the blade of his knife. This is further supported by the 'two small stabs to privates' as noted by Inspector Spratling, which would be the byproduct of a knife thrusting in and out and occasionally missing its mark.

Missing Pieces

Another and more controversial explanation for the blood pool under Polly's legs is that the Ripper succeeded in his attempt to make away with a portion of his victim. The evidence for this is minimal but compelling. According to the papers, Dr. Llewellyn began his post mortem at 10am on the morning of Saturday, Sept. 1st, in the presence of his assistant, Dr. Samuel Hubert Seccombe.[27] The results are described by Dr. Llewellyn (sans injuries to 'private parts') at the inquest and in written reports from Inspector Spratling and Chief Inspector Donald Swanson (quoting Spratling). What's lacking from these sources is any indication that an examination of the internal organs took place. There could be good reason for this: the policemen would have no need to quote extraneous detail about the health of Nichols's liver and perhaps Llewellyn likewise felt such information was superfluous for the intentions of the inquest. In contrast, Dr. Killeen spoke in detail about the condition of Tabram's organs, as would Dr. George Bagster Phillips at the later inquest into the murder of Annie Chapman.

I questioned for some time whether a post mortem of any sort had taken place when proof of it surfaced in an *Evening Post* report from the day following the murder. The journalist was an eyewitness to the actual autopsy and his report offers a rare first-hand account of a Ripper victim's post mortem:

> During the greater part of this morning, Dr. Llewellyn and his assistant was engaged in making a minute examination of the body and the wounds. For this purpose it was taken from the shell in which it had lain all night in the mortuary, and placed upon a slab in the adjoining building, erected specially for post-mortem examinations. It is a lean-to-shed in the vestry yard, glazed along the entire front with large windows that open outwards towards the bottom in order to let a current of air through the room. Closely-drawn blinds of yellow material kept out the inquisitive

rays of the sun, and prevented the atmosphere from becoming close and obnoxious.

When the Evening Post reporter arrived, about 11 o'clock, he found some half-dozen detectives in the yard, and a couple of men waiting to identify the body. Advancing to the open door, he saw a gaseous spectacle. The stripped body of the murdered woman lay upon the slab, with the flesh of that peculiarly yellow and ghastly tint usual in deaths from violence. As the doctor was engaged in examining the fearful wound in the abdomen – which looked like nothing so much as that which would be inflicted by an Eastern fanatic perishing from self-disembowelment – the head fell back over the slab, revealing the deadly gash in the throat. The windpipe, completely severed, stood but prominently in the centre of a maze of blood-clotted flesh. It looked as though a touch would make the head fall back upon the floor. The body, which was fairly clean, was exceedingly well-proportioned, and showed that the deceased was a woman of unusually good figure for her class in life. The surgeon was in his shirt sleeves, drawing out the intestines and their covering, and minutely examining them for traces of injury. Now and again he would pause in the examination, and, still holding a portion of the internal anatomy of the woman in his hand, would dictate something in a low tone to his assistant, who stood on the other side of the slab with a book supported on a piece of wood, and wrote it down. The calm scientific demeanour counteracted somewhat the awful nature of the spectacle. He looked as though he was delivering a lecture on anatomy, or posing for one of those gruesome "old masters" who appall spectators by the awful nature of their realism and anatomical accuracy.

The terrible nature of the abdominal injuries had not been in the least exaggerated in the early accounts of the murder. They enabled the surgeon to make a post-mortem examination of the whole of the internal organs of the woman below the breasts, and he found that not only was she well-nourished, but a fairly healthy subject. Beyond the gashes already described, there were no marks upon the body except the bruises on the face. It was upon the face, after surveying the wounds, that the gaze lingered for some moments. Distorted in death as it was, the sight was unpleasant; but after a moment's look, one could readily imagine that the deceased had been a pleasant sort of woman. The hair, of the darkest brown, though wet with the perspiration of the mortal agony, stood out from the head, instead of lying limp and dank as in a case of natural death. The eyes were closed, and the skin around them loose and wrinkled. The nose approached the aquiline. The mouth looked capable of a pleasant smile, did it not display the teeth broken in the deadly struggle and carry a look of pain. Deceased was a sharp featured woman, of a by no means degraded type.'

This report puts to rest the notion that Dr. Llewellyn did not perform a post mortem, but raises new questions in the process, such as why a reporter was allowed access to such a sensitive location, and how thorough the examination could have been if the doctor had only gotten as far as the intestines by 11am when the inquest was to start at 1pm. The answer to the former is probably a simple matter of a reporter greasing the palm of the doctor as well as the inspector on duty in the yard. As for the latter, it was likely a passable but not particularly thorough examination of only the vital organs, as there would not have been sufficient time for much else.

Aside from the distraction of entertaining a pressman during the autopsy, the doctor was also interrupted by the police so that two potential witnesses could make an attempt to identify the body.[28]

Further proof that the post mortem was rushed came at the third session of the inquest when Dr. Llewellyn stated that since the first session he had made a 'second examination' of the body and confirmed that the victim had a small forehead scar, which Polly's father, Edward Walker, had mentioned as an identifying mark.[29] A second examination should not have been necessary, and if the good doctor missed a visible surface scar, what might he have missed under the surface?

Keeping in mind that as none of the victims prior to Polly Nichols had been eviscerated, there was no reason for Dr. Llewellyn to assume or even consider that Polly's killer might have made away with any portion of her anatomy. Therefore, it may not have occurred to him to inspect anything outside of the vital organs. He would have had no special reason to examine her uterus. However, following the discovery of Annie Chapman's body – *sans* uterus – in the backyard of 29 Hanbury Street on Sept. 8th, it would have occurred to him that he'd made a terrible error.

Chapman's murder occurred between the second and third session of the Nichols inquest and two days following Polly's funeral, so any certainty about the full extent of the Ripper's depravity in Buck's Row was now buried under six feet of dirt at City of London Cemetery. Coroner Baxter was aware of the question mark now hanging over the Nichols murder and so queried Dr. Llewellyn, who sheepishly responded that he 'did not believe that any portion of the body was missing.'[30]

It seems odd that Dr. Llewellyn could only remark as to his 'belief' and could not state with certainty that the entirety of Polly Nichols was present and accounted for at the time of his presumably thorough autopsy. To recap, a possible explanation for this is that he confined his study to only the most vital of organs and failed to observe the condition or even the presence of a uterus. It will be remembered that he did not even begin the post mortem until 10am on the morning of the inquest, which started early in the afternoon, and he failed to note an identifying forehead scar. Polly had been buried by the time Annie Chapman was murdered and it was observed that her uterus had been removed and taken away, so it was not possible to go back and do a more thorough examination on Nichols.

It should not be assumed that the Ripper had succeeded in removing Polly's uterus, or even that this was his intention. However, we can't be any more or less certain than was the doctor who should have known but didn't, so the possibility remains that some portion of Nichols – uterus or otherwise – left with her killer.

Another clue comes to us in the form of a newspaper report appearing two days after the murder:

> Shortly after noon on Friday some men while searching the pavement in Buck's-row, above the gateway, in a different direction

to that which the woman came, or was brought, found two large spots of blood, and each about the size of a shilling. The first was about 25 feet from the gateway and the second 10 feet beyond. Both were a few inches from the kerb in the roadway and clearly defined. It was at once agreed they came either from the hands or clothing of the murderer as he went away, and that they resulted from the squeezing out some blood-soaked clothing.

The information that blood spots were found 25 and 35 feet from the murder site[31] is not something discussed in modern literature, perhaps because it defies explanation; the one offered by the investigating reporter – that a blood soaked killer stopped twice to ring his clothes out – is not wholly convincing. The blood may have dripped from the push-cart ambulance as the police removed the body. However, if we speculate that the Ripper made off with a gory specimen from his kill, such stains some yards from the body might be expected. Indeed, one newspaper believed that the blood drops were 'probably caused by something in the hands of the murderer as he walked away.'[32]

There is some medical evidence to support this possibility. When Polly's abdominal injury was discovered at the mortuary, it was noted by Inspector Spratling that 'the flesh was turned over from left to right and the intestines exposed.'[33] When the body was lifted from the ground to be placed on the ambulance the body would have heeled in the middle and may have forced a portion of the intestine out through the ripped flesh. Or, perhaps, the body was left in this state by the Ripper, as suggested by Inspector Spratling, who noted in an official report that the victim had been 'disemboweled'.

Llewellyn's reports and notes do not survive, so we'll have to rely primarily on his inquest testimony as reported in the newspapers. Perhaps the most significant document pertaining to Nichols's mutilations comes from Inspector Spratling. The notes he took at the mortuary as Llewellyn detailed the wounds are preserved in a report submitted the day of the murder. Authors Stewart Evans and Keith Skinner painstakingly transcribed all surviving reports of the Ripper crimes for their indispensable reference work, *The Ultimate Jack The Ripper Companion*. They had their work cut out for them in transcribing Spratling, who was prone to use only commas as punctuation and would truncate words in a style that was apparently only supposed to make sense to him. Evans and Skinner, both experts on Victorian handwriting and police vernacular, were able to flesh out the details as represented in the bracketing:

Upon my arrival there and taking a description I found that she had been disemboweled, and at once sent to inform the Dr. of it, l[latter?] arrived quickly and on further examination stated that her throat had been cut from left to right, two disti[nct] cuts being on left side. The windp[ipe] gullet and spinal cord being cut through, a bruise apparently of a th[umb] being on right lower jaw, also one o[n] left cheek, the abdomen had been [cut] open from centre of bottom of ribs a[long] right side, under pelvis to left of the stomach, there the wound was jag[ged], the omentium [sic], or coating of the stomach, was also cut in several places, and tw[o] small stabs on private parts, apparently done with a strong bladed knife, supposed to have been done by some le[ft] handed person, death being almost instantaneous.

Spratling's statement that the woman had been 'disemboweled' refers to the fact that her intestines were partially protruding. The statement that her spinal cord had been 'cut through' might leave the impression that she'd been decapitated, but what it's meant to convey is that the knife had cut so deeply into the flesh of the neck that it nicked the bone.

Spratling next observes that the throat was cut not once, but twice, and that her face was bruised on either side. This is sometimes assumed to be proof that the Ripper used his hand either to silence or suffocate Polly into unconsciousness. I believe this is a mistake. Regardless of which hand you use or whether you stand in front of or behind a person, if you cover their mouth with your hand your thumb will be well above the jaw line. If we disregard the notion that the Ripper stood Polly up and delivered a 'one-two' punch on the right jaw and left cheek then what we're left with as the most plausible explanation is that he kneeled to her right, next to her head and grabbed her face with his left hand, applying great pressure to hold it steady as he inflicted the second and deepest of his throat wounds. For the first stab she would have been turned away from him so that he was not hit with arterial spray, but after a few moments she was turned on her back again and the second throat wound was inflicted.

As the blade was described as only 'moderately' sharp but reached all the way to the vertebrae, great force must have been applied by the killer as he stabbed it in deep and pulled it back towards himself, ripping the flesh and tissue and nicking the bone. The necessary downward pressure applied to the face by his left hand in order to achieve such bruising might also have broken Polly's nose, explaining the odd bend to her nose evident in the mortuary photograph.

The most important part of the inspector's notes is also the least clear. It is sometimes written that there was a single primary wound to Nichols's abdomen that was surrounded by small superficial cuts, but when Spratling writes 'the abdomen had been [cut] open from centre of bottom of ribs a[long] right side, under pelvis to left of the stomach, there the wound was jag[ged],' he is describing two separate but primary wounds. The first wound commenced, according to Spratling (recording Llewellyn's observations), from the center of the bottom rib toward the right side and reached all the way down the abdomen. The killer **se**ems to have intentionally intersected the two wounds to meet over the abdomen, creating a flap of flesh that could be lifted for access to the internal organs. The most obvious and logical reason for this is that he intended to remove something.

Corroborating my interpretation is an exclusive report published in the *Star* of August 31st, the same day of the murder. The reporter had access to the mortuary and was able to personally view the body and provide a detailed description of the wounds. Here is how the two sources compare:

First Wound

Spratling: 'The abdomen had been [cut] open from the centre of bottom of ribs a[long] right side.'
The Star: 'went straight upward, along the centre of the body, and, reaching to the breast-bone.'

Second Wound

Spratling: 'under pelvis to left of the stomach, there the wound was jag[ged].'
The Star: 'veered to the [killer's] right, slitting up the groin, and passing over the hip.'

Two large wounds intersecting over the abdomen in such a way suggests Nichols's killer was cutting with a purpose. Llewellyn's observation that the omentum - or protective layer of peritoneum surrounding the organs - was cut in several places is interesting. Spratling's wording might suggest these cuts were intentional, but they may have been incidentally caused by the deep ripping. It's now impossible to be certain of how successful the Ripper was in his objective in Buck's Row, but the only conceivable purpose for such ghoulish behavior is that he was attempting to engage in a bit of organ thievery.

CHAPTER 3
The Brady Street Puzzle

THE BUCK'S ROW blood stains were not the only mysterious marks reported following the Nichols murder. Numerous newspapers reported that there was actually a series of bloodstains – or, at least, stains that appeared to be blood – running haphazardly along Brady Street, a thoroughfare that intersected with Buck's Row. According to the press, the blood stains started at Honey's mews[34], a stable yard located in Brady Street approximately 150 yards from the top of Buck's Row and 170 yards from the murder spot. There the stains were described as 'large' and looking 'as if the bleeding person had fallen against the wall and lain there'.[35] From Honey's mews 'there would be drop after drop every two or three feet, and sometimes six feet apart for a distance, and then a larger pool or splash.'[36] The mysterious stains came to an abrupt end at the top of Buck's Row.

The reporter observed these stains around noon on the day of the murder (about 8 hours following the discovery of Polly's body) and noted that although it had rained the stains were still visible. Six hours prior to this, 39 year-old Detective-Sergeant Patrick Enright, on orders from Inspector Spratling, searched the neighborhood for signs of blood. His findings are not clear, but Spratling performed his own search around noon the same day (perhaps bumping heads with the investigative reporter) and stated at the inquest that no blood at all was discovered.[37]

On one hand we have the press telling us there was a substantial amount of blood zig-zagging along Brady Street towards the turn into Buck's Row, and on the other hand we have Inspector Spratling assuring us there was no blood at all to be seen. Confusing matters further is 43 year-old Inspector John Helson, who stated in a press interview two days after the murder that he searched Brady Street in the company of Sgt. Enright on Friday morning, the result being that 'neither bloodstains nor wheel marks were found,'[38] but only a day later, at the inquest, would admit to a single 'suspicious mark' in Brady Street that 'might have been blood.'[39] Helson's admission at the very least allows us to conclude that the finding of blood in Brady Street was not a journalistic fantasy, and if that's the case, then it might prove relevant to our inquiry.

Two Brady Street residents, Caroline Coldwell[40] and her 11 year-old daughter, Charlotte, claimed to have heard a series of disturbing nighttime events that they believed correlated to the blood stains on their street.

The Coldwells lived about midway along Brady Street at #72[41] and were available to speak with a *Lloyd's Weekly* reporter on the same day of the murder when their memories were fresh. Young Charlotte was the most candid, stating "early this morning, before it was light, I heard terrible cries of 'Murder! Murder! Police! Police! Murder!' They seemed a good way down Brady Street to the right, where the marks of bloody hands are. Then the sounds came up the street towards our house, and I heard a scuffling and a bumping against our shutters. I got out of bed and woke my mother. The woman kept on calling out 'Murder! Police!' and the sounds went on in the direction of Buck's Row, where the body was found. I am sure the first sounds seem to come from where the bloodstains of hands are on the wall."[42]

Mrs. Coldwell said that her daughter woke her with the news that a woman was trying to break into their house, and heard with her own ears a female voice screaming 'Murder! Police!' five or six times, then fading in the direction of Buck's Row.[43] She added that she 'only heard the steps of one person,'[44] a curious detail that suggests the distressed woman was not pursued or that her pursuer wore silent footwear.

Early speculation was that the blood in Brady Street belonged to Polly Nichols, who either was assaulted in Brady Street and ran screaming to her eventual murder in Buck's Row, or who was murdered in Brady Street and carried to Buck's Row. Once the blood and clothing evidence had been gathered and interpreted it was clear that neither of these explanations were possible; the lack of blood on the legs and most areas of the clothing made it clear that Nichols was murdered where found and the first cut was inflicted after she had been placed on her back. The only injuries to her exposed flesh were the two deep and instantly fatal throat wounds that severed her windpipe and would have made it impossible for her to either run or cry out. Likewise, her hands were void of blood and could not have been responsible for the bloody handprints mentioned by Charlotte Coldwell.

The Brady Street bloodstains do not receive much modern commentary, largely due to a mistaken belief that the Coldwell incident occurred hours before the murder of Polly Nichols. This assumption arises from an early news report: 'In Buck's Row, naturally, the greatest excitement prevails, and several persons in the neighborhood state that an affray occurred shortly after midnight, but no screams were heard, nor anything beyond what might have been considered evidence of an ordinary brawl.'[45] This report has become part of Brady Street lore and seems to fix a time for the Coldwell incident. However, it becomes clear when reading the report of the 'affray' that it is describing a completely unrelated incident that occurred in Buck's Row (not Brady Street) in which no screams were heard and there's no mention of a female participant. The words 'ordinary brawl' suggest that it was little more than a fight between men.

The Coldwells did not give a specific time for what they witnessed and were probably incapable of doing so, as most people did not own time pieces. The best Charlotte could say was that it was early morning and 'before it was light'. Sunrise came that day at 5:13am, and if we can reasonably assume that it transpired before the discovery of Polly's murder at 3:45am, then it's probable that what the Coldwell's witnessed occurred closer to 3:45am than midnight. One report gives a time of the attack. The *New York Times* had a correspondent in London who reported the following:

The victim was a woman, who, at 3 o'clock, was knocked down by some man, unknown, and attacked with a knife. She attempted to get up, and ran a hundred yards, her cries for help being heard by several persons in the adjacent houses. No attention was paid to her cries, however, and when found at daybreak she was lying dead in another street, several hundred yards from the scene of the attack. (Sept. 1st, 1888 edition.)

This early report seems to be melding the murder of Polly Nichols with the earlier assault upon a different, unnamed woman. If the Brady Street attack occurred at 3am, then the attacker would have had ample time to scurry back to Whitechapel Road and make the acquaintance of Polly Nichols by 3:45am.

The question of how severe the bloodstains in Brady Street actually were can never be answered with any certainty, but I do believe that a careful reading of the evidence can give a reasonable idea of what awaited investigators and reporters that Friday morning. Inspector Helson emerged as our primary police source, so his various statements are presented here in sequence:

Aug. 31st: The matter is being investigated by Detective Inspector Abberline, of Scotland Yard, and Inspector Helson, J Division. The latter states that he walked carefully over the ground soon after 8 o'clock in the morning, and beyond the discolourations ordinarily found on pavements, there was no sign of stains.' *Daily News*, Sept. 1st, 1888.

Sept. 2nd: "The report that blood stains were found leading from Brady Street to Buck's Row was not true. The place was examined by Sergeant Enright and [myself] on Friday morning, and neither bloodstains nor wheel marks were found to indicate that the body had been deposited where found, the murder being committed elsewhere." *Daily News*, Sept. 3rd

Sept. 3rd: "The only suspicious mark in the neighbourhood of the place where the body was found was one spot, which might have been blood, in Brady Street." *Lloyd's Weekly Newspaper*, Sept. 9th, 1888

Helson's testimony of a 'suspicious mark', made at the resumed inquest, seems to contradict his earlier statements, but a closer reading reveals that this is not the case. His earliest observations make it clear that there were indeed 'discolorations' on the pavement, presumably as described by the press, but at this time he did not accept that any were blood. In his press statement on the 2nd, which appears to have been officially sanctioned and prepared, the impression is left that no blood stains were found, but this not what he actually said. All he specifies is that it's not true that blood stains were found *which led from Brady Street to Buck's Row*, nor were any bloodstains (or wheel marks) discovered which indicated that Polly Nichols had been murdered in Brady Street. In other words, there were blood stains on Brady Street, but they did not lead to Buck's Row and did not appear to have any direct connection to the murder of Polly Nichols.

As for the bloodstains in Brady Street, what can we learn about them from Inspector Helson? For starters, we can conclude that some or all of the stains on the roadway that appeared to create a trail towards Buck's Row were in all likelihood produced by something other than blood and were noticed only as a result of the microscope the neighborhood was put under following discovery of the murder. Support for this is found in a *Daily Chronicle* report that appeared the same day Helson gave his evidence at the inquest: 'The conclusion now arrived at is that the woman met with her dreadful fate where her body was found. What were at first supposed to have been pools of blood for some distance upon the pavement cannot be relied upon as such, owing to the darkness of the stains.' The source for this was presumably a member of the police force (possibly Helson) and as it jibes with what Helson alluded to the day before, we can conclude that the zig-zagging stains on the street were possibly not blood.

If we eliminate the stain trail and assume that a small drop of blood would not be looked upon as "suspicious", then we're looking for a stain of some substance that was not part of the zig-zagging trail, and that would be the Honey's mews stain. The newspapers placed the stain in front of the gates of the mews, and Charlotte Coldwell puts them on the 'wall', so they must have been on the wall on either side of the gateway. The cryptic markings left one reporter with the impression that a bleeding person had fallen against the wall and lain there, leaving what Charlotte Coldwell described as the "bloody marks of hands". It makes sense that this would be the suspicious blood mark referenced by Inspector Helson.

On the day following the murder the *Echo* reported that 'several of the police investigating the case declare that very few bloodstains were seen when they first visited the spot [i.e. Brady Street]', but surely even a few bloodstains are too many on a street where no crime is known to have occurred?

The only explanation offered for any of the anomalous blood stains found in the neighborhood on that cloudy, damp August morning came from *Lloyd's Weekly News*: 'Our representative discovered, on making inquiries the same night, that at a house near where the blood spots were a man, early on the morning of the tragedy, had made a murderous assault on his wife and cut her throat. She was carried to the London hospital, and it is very probable some blood dripped from her.'

This story related specifically to the Buck's Row blood spots but could conceivably apply to the Brady Street stains as well, particularly if a bleeding woman other than Polly Nichols was running the streets that night. But is the story true? If so, it's remarkable that no other mention of it was made in the press, in spite of the intense interest in all matters related to Buck's Row. It's possible that someone on the staff of the paper confused an event that had occurred on the very day this issue went to press, which was the violent assault of one Henry Hummerston, a 32 year-old laborer living in the neighborhood at Thomas Street, upon his common-law wife, Eliza Smith.

A fight in the house led out into the backyard where Henry beat and kicked Eliza, finally falling on top her with a large-bladed table knife in his hand, threatening to make a "second Buck's Row murder" of her, and nearly delivering on the promise with a cut along her throat that fortunately was not deep enough to cause serious injury. The theory that such an episode might have produced some or all of the suspicious stains in Buck's Row and Brady Street would be immensely reasonable if not for the fact that the assault occurred a full two days after the blood stains were first noticed and written about.

CHAPTER 4

The One That Got Away

WORKING ON THE assumption that anyone bleeding so freely would seek immediate medical attention, I reached out to the London Hospital archives in search of the original registration records still retained on file. I requested copies of all individuals who registered between the hours of 10pm on August 30th and the time of the Nichols murder the next morning.

There was no woman admitted with a cut throat, but looking at the entries for men and women, in both the 'Physicians' and 'Surgeons' rolls, I discovered one woman whose injury suggested she might have been the Brady Street victim.

'Margaret Millous' gave her address as 59 Old Nichol Street, Bethnal Green; her age as 35; her profession as 'hawker'; and stated she was married. 'Millous' is possibly a phonetic misspelling of 'Millhouse', or something similar.[46] Her reason for admission was listed as 'wound of radial artery' and she was sent to Dr. John Couper for surgery. The radial artery is the primary artery of the forearm. Millhouse must not have been very far from the London Hospital when she sustained the injury or else she likely would have bled to death. Her home address is a good distance from the hospital whereas Brady Street was practically across the road from it.

It would be too broad a generalization to

suggest that any East End woman identifying herself as a 'hawker' or seller of small goods was a casual prostitute, but it is accurate to state that prostitutes would hawk items to support their income or at least would identify themselves as a hawker (if not a charwoman) when required to provide their profession. It is possible that Millous was hawking items on Whitechapel Road, though the time of night supports the supposition that she was prostituting herself.

The hospital registries are tragically filled with failed suicide attempts, either obvious or self-confessed, and they're duly marked as 'suicide', but Millous's was not. This leaves the possibility that her injury was either accidental or else inflicted by another party. It's not outside the realm of possibility that she accidentally cut herself while using a sharp knife, but such a wound also lends itself quite well to a defensive wound sustained while fending off a would-be murderer.

Somebody with a bloody hand was in Brady Street in the hours prior to Polly Nichols's murder and it's logical to suspect that a person bleeding so freely would go across the road to the hospital. A bloody hand could come about from a number of causes, including a relatively minor head wound that one instinctively puts their hand to. However, around the same time of night we also have a woman running along Brady Street screaming 'Murder!' If the two events (blood stains and screaming woman) are connected, then we'd expect someone very much like Margaret Millous with an injury such a deep cut to the forearm/hand palm, seeking medical attention at London Hospital. That we should find such a person is an extraordinary coincidence.

If Margaret Millous was attacked by a man with a knife then she may have chosen not to report it to the police. Emily Horsnell and Emma Smith, the first two Whitechapel Murder victims, both initially survived their injuries but chose not to report the attacks. Police only became aware of them after they died and the doctors, as a matter of course, reported the deaths to the coroner. Doctors were not obliged to report any suspicious injuries to the police and apparently did not do so. However, as we shall soon see, there's reason to believe the police may have known about the Millous assault.

It's impossible to say for certain if Margaret was attacked by a man in

Brady Street, or, if she were, that her attacker was Jack the Ripper, but the location of the blood stains is quite suggestive. Polly Nichols was murdered in front of stable yard gates and later victim, Liz Stride, was murdered just inside of identical gates. Likewise, the Brady Street blood stains were found in the dark recess of the Honey's mews gates. Such recesses were perfect places for prostitutes to take their clients for quick intercourse and were no doubt popular at night for that purpose.

The material collected here confirms from two credible sources (Inspector Helson and resident Charlotte Coldwell) that there were unexplained blood stains on Brady Street, which Coldwell describes as a hand print and places in front of the gates to Honey's mews. These stains must have been left at the scene on the same night that a woman was heard running from near that spot, screaming bloody murder. Following that trail we end up at London Hospital where a woman fitting the Ripper's victimology is being treated for a cut sharp and deep enough to have wounded her radial artery. Without a victim statement or an eye witness account we cannot say that Margaret Millous was a survivor of Jack the Ripper, but the possibility that she was is intriguing and worthy of consideration.

Contrary to how he's often portrayed, the Ripper was not a perfect killing machine. We should not be shocked to learn that he attempted to murder a woman and failed. On the contrary, we might expect that such a thing happened and perhaps happened more than once. It would have been very risky for him to procure a second victim and return to almost the same location without knowing if the authorities had been communicated with, but then everything the Ripper did was extraordinarily risky. After murdering Liz Stride on September 30th he walked a mere ten minutes away and claimed a second victim. This has become popularly known as the 'double event', but it's possible his first 'double event' occurred a month earlier and remained undiscovered for 128 years.

As it would happen, a fellow researcher named Adam Bird, wholly unaware of my Brady Street research, posted a newspaper find to a Ripper Facebook page I belong to and innocently asked if anyone might know anything about the incident described. This article is from the *Daily Telegraph* and was published on October 3rd, 1888:

An alarming story was told to a detective yesterday, and it is understood that the Metropolitan police have for some time been cognizant of its details. If this statement be true, and there appears to be no reason to question it, then some time between the date of the Hanbury-street murder and last Sunday the blood-thirsty maniac who is now terrifying Whitechapel unsuccessfully attempted another outrage. The woman who so narrowly escaped death is married, but she admits having entered into conversation with a strange man for an immoral purpose. She alleges that he tripped her up, so that she fell upon the pavement. He made an effort to cut her throat, but she shielded herself with her arm, and in doing so received a cut upon it. Alarmed by his failure, and fearing her shrieks, the would-be murderer ran off, and the woman, when discovered, was removed to the hospital. She has since been discharged, and the wound upon the arm is still to be seen. The occurrence is alleged to have taken place ten days ago, in a bye-turning off Commercial-street. Unfortunately the woman was so much in liquor when she was assaulted that she cannot recollect the man's face or dress, and has been unable to give a description of him, which may account for the secrecy which has been maintained in regard to the attack.

In the same edition, but apparently written by a different journalist, I discovered the following:

There is reason to believe that the monster of whom policemen and 'Vigilants' are still eagerly but fruitlessly in quest attempted another outrage upon a woman of loose conduct some time between the date of Annie Chapman's murder and last Sunday morning. As we are informed, the metropolitan police have for several days past been in possession of every detail of this woman's startling narrative, a full account of which will be found in another column. Here we will merely observe that she was admitted ten days ago to a London hospital, in which a serious cut on her arm was treated; and that she has solemnly declared that she received the injury in question whilst protecting her throat from an attempt made to cut it by a man who, having engaged her in conversation and struck an immoral bargain with her, tripped her up, threw her heavily on the pavement, and attacked her, knife in hand, with murderous intent.

I was to learn that some years ago researcher Stephen Willments looked at the London Hospital registers for this time frame and the only person he could find that fit the description was a woman named Susan Ward, and it was believed she must have been the victim described. However, in 2008, Debra Arif uncovered the following in the Sept. 16th edition of *Lloyd's Weekly Newspaper*:

> Yesterday Susan Ward, aged 64, a labourer's wife, of Nicholas-road, Old Bethnal Green Rd. was admitted to the London Hospital with a dangerous lacerated wound on the arm, through falling on a broken bottle which she let fall.

That seemed to settle it as far as most researchers were concerned. If Susan Ward cut her arm on a bottle, then she could not be the woman described in the article. But if not her, then who? I decided I'd have to look for myself and so ordered scans of all the women registered into London Hospital between Sept. 8th and Sept. 24th. To be thorough – since the newspaper article did not specify the London Hospital – Debra Arif scoured the register of the Whitechapel Infirmary for a candidate but could find none. I discovered, just as Stephen Willments had, that Susan Ward was the only person who'd been admitted with a cut arm. I thought it curious that a leading London newspaper would find an elderly pauper cutting her arm on a bottle to be newsworthy, but as it would happen, *Lloyd's* made a regular feature of publishing the names and details of some of the people admitted to hospitals a day or so before they went to press, and in that particular edition Ward was one of a long series of similar entries.

As *Lloyd's* was only a weekly publication, it's by no means an exhaustive list, but still a worthy source of information, and at times delivers information not present in the registers such as how the person received their injury. Following is the information as it appears in the hospital register, and as can be seen it's obviously the source for the biographical information present in the *Lloyd's* blurb:

> Sept. 15th (She's the first entry in the Surgeon's register, so it must have been in the early hours)
>
> Susan Ward
>
> 4 Nicholas Rd, Old B.G. Rd. B.G.
>
> 64 (age)
>
> M (married)
>
> Labrs Wife
>
> Mary (name of the ward she was admitted to)
>
> Incised Wound over elbow
>
> Treves (the attending surgeon)
>
> Sep. 28 88 (Date released)

We can rule Susan out as the would-be Ripper victim only if we accept at face value the assertion that she fell on a bottle and broke it. That may be what happened, but as Ward would have been the source for the information, it's not inconceivable that she provided the bottle excuse upon admission and when probed more fully by a doctor, opened up about her assault. However, there are reasons to suppose Ward was not the victim: she was 64 at the time of her injury, and while that by no means rules her out as a streetwalker, it makes it somewhat less likely. Also, if we're intent on holding to the 'ten days earlier' timeframe set forth by the Oct. 3rd *Daily Telegraph* report, Ward is a poor fit, her admission being on Sept. 15th and not on the 22nd or 23rd.

There is one candidate in the registers closer to the prescribed date of admission, and that is Alice Morrison, who was admitted to the hospital on Sept 21st with a 'lacerated hand'. Morrison was a 17 year-old girl gainfully employed as a servant, and her injury was apparently quite minor, as she was treated and released the same day, so what seemed a good lead at first glance quickly fizzled out. In fact, the *Lloyd's* of Sept. 23rd provided information that she had cut her hand while forcibly opening a bottle of lemonade.

This leaves us with a few possibilities: the mystery victim was, in fact, Susan Ward, and the broken bottle episode was the explanation she provided for her injuries upon admission but later changed her story; the entire incident in the newspaper story was a fabrication; or, the story was true but the paper's source (the unnamed detective) was mistaken on some of the details.

In my research I discovered another possible explanation for Ward's injuries – they may have been inflicted by her crazy knife-wielding brother.

Susan's husband, James, passed away in early 1891, and she subsequently lived with her invalid brother, George Hopkins, who previously worked for Pickford's and may have known witness Charles Cross. Also residing in the house at 12 Bradstock Road, South Hackney, was Susan's adult son, William Ward, as well as 58 year-old William Hopkins – the much younger brother of George and Susan and the bane of their existence.

Early on the morning of April 7th, William Ward heard a disturbance coming from his Uncle George's room on the second floor. Going up to investigate, he found his Uncle William and a woman of questionable character named Martha Arnold causing a ruckus and annoying poor, helpless George. Mr. Ward insisted the two leave his uncle alone, but Uncle William would have none of it. Ward removed Martha from the room as his uncle yelled threats. Uncle William then left the room, returning shortly thereafter with a weaver's knife – a folding penknife with a wide razor-sharp blade with which he would use to shave – and went to work on William Ward's face and neck.

Susan was next door in her own room and heard Uncle William and Martha Arnold abusing her older brother. She went to intercede when she heard her son's voice join the mix. She testified at trial that her son ordered Martha to leave and when she refused he pushed her against a wall, at which time she left. When Uncle William returned with the knife and began slashing at her son it was Susan who put herself in harm's way to stop her mad brother and take his knife. She then went to the street and called for a constable.

Constable 384J, Jonathan Wilson, was on duty nearby and answered the call. He followed Susan up to the back bedroom and found the bloody group waiting. Uncle William swore to the constable "I will murder him." Not giving him the chance, Constable Wilson took William Hopkins into custody, procured the weapon from Susan, and marched the group to the Victoria Park station where they were met by an inspector.

Inspector George Collett charged William Hopkins with the felony of wounding William Ward with the intent to murder him, and a second count of intent to do grievous bodily harm. Dr. James Turtle, the police surgeon for J Division at Hackney, took charge of the seriously injured Ward, and reported his wounds thusly:

> One incised wound on the right side of the neck three and a half inches long, extending half an inch from the jaw, and a quarter of an inch deep; another incised wound two inches long, half an inch deep, extending across the neck below the preceding one; a superficial incised wound one inch long and two and a half inches above the right ear—on the left side of the head an incised wound of the scalp half an inch from the fore part of the left ear, and upwards and backwards three inches; the hemorrhage from this was considerable, a small artery being divided; another incised wound two and a quarter inches above the left eyebrow, extending backwards two inches; another one running into that half an inch backwards and upwards; the two middle fingers of the right hand and one on the left were cut across.

Dr. Turtle stitched the wounds and had Ward transported to the infirmary. He was lucky to be alive. As he was being stitched, Uncle William raged at the inspector and his own family, proclaiming "I am sorry he is not dead and I was going to be hung tomorrow for it." Turning to young William, he vented "You ain't got so much as I thought you had. I will settle you; you are twenty years younger than me; you struck me and challenged me to fight." After Ward was escorted to the infirmary, Uncle William poured his venom onto Susan: "If I get two years for it I will give him and you worse than he has got this time. I will use a 'b— belt' for both of you. I am sorry his head is not off his shoulders. This is only a start on him; if I get two years I will finish him when I come out; I said I would murder him, I will murder your son, God blind me, I will murder the lot of you."

Inspector Collett testified at trial that although Hopkins had been drinking, he was not drunk; an observation supported by William Ward's testimony. Ward also observed that he was staying in the house only to protect his mother from her evil brother, so the violence of this day was not an isolated incident.

Hopkins was found not guilty of attempted murder, but guilty on the second count of intending to cause grievous harm, and was sentenced to a mere six months hard labor.[47]

This episode raises the possibility that, three years earlier, Susan's incised arm had been caused not by a murderous stranger, or a broken bottle, but by a wayward brother whom she was eager to protect. If nothing else, this new glimpse into the life of Susan Ward further weakens the argument that she was haunting the dark alleys of Whitechapel in search of illicit custom, because the 64 year-old was married to a working man and had at least one brother and an adult son gainfully employed who were eager to keep her from the streets and provided her with a home when her husband passed away. It is even less likely that a 'respectable' woman would fabricate a story in which she was a prostitute, so unless it can be shown that Susan Ward was indeed a streetwalker, we have to conclude it's highly unlikely that she was the victim described in the *Daily Telegraph* report.

The search of the records has failed to turn up a woman with an injured arm who meets all the qualifications listed in the Oct. 3rd *Daily Telegraph* articles, but there is one woman who sought medical attention in September for a serious cut to her arm for whom we do not have a mundane explanation – Margaret Millous. Her injury also happened to coincide with a woman running from a bloody scene in Brady Street, screaming 'Murder!' and 'Police!' The seriousness of the wounds she received is underlined by the fact that she spent 2 ½ weeks in the hospital and was not released until Sept. 17th. It might be that her story did not become known to police until after her release and this gave rise to the misinformation that it had occurred after and not before the murder of Annie Chapman.

There was another attack reported in September that may or may not be related to Millous and/or the *Daily Telegraph* story. The *Pall Mall Gazette* of Sept. 25th published a short piece describing an event that does not appear to have been reported in any other newspaper:

A report has been made to the London police of another outrageous

attack upon a woman in Vine-street, Whitechapel, the circumstances of which up to a certain point, resemble the cases recently
reported. The only difference is that in this case it was an attempted
murder only. The woman was of the same class, the locality was
Whitechapel, and the man is not in custody. The woman describes
him as being about 35 years old, 5ft 8in in height, with a black moustache, dressed in a brown coat. He struck her in the face, inflicted a
wound with a knife on the shoulder, and then decamped.[48]

A date for the attack is not provided but it could be presumed to have
occurred sometime in September. However, as already noted, no woman with
such a wound was admitted to the London Hospital or Whitechapel Infirmary
at that time; even Margaret Millous would not fit this description, since her
wound was to the radial artery, which runs through the forearm but not the
shoulder. It's possible that this report as well as the Oct. 3rd *Daily Telegraph*
report were the result of 'Chinese whispers' leaking out of the hospital about
Millous, the patient who may have been a Ripper victim. This would explain
the discrepancies as well as the lack of another viable candidate.

The woman with the wounded shoulder makes a second appearance in
one of the first book-length non-fictional treatments of the Ripper murders,
published in December of 1888. I would hesitate in accepting it as an independent source as the author drew much of his material from the papers
and might here have been dressing up what he'd read in the *Pall Mall Gazette*.

There was found in a London Hospital a disreputable woman, suffering from a wound in the shoulder, who stated that she had been
approached by a strange man, who drew her to a lonely spot on a
cross street, and, drawing a knife, attempted to kill her. She, stout
and agile and by a tremendous display of strength, succeeded in
breaking from him, and escaped. The wound on her shoulder
seemed to give proof to her story.[49]

Whether or not these various snippets relate to the assault upon Margaret
Millous or are describing separate events must remain a matter of conjecture. A study of the ones that got away might not tell us who the Ripper was,
but it might give us a better idea of how he thought and operated.

In an effort to be as thorough as possible, I returned to the London Hospital archives and ordered scans going all the way back to September 1st in an effort to see if there was any other viable candidate for the mysterious unknown victim described in the press. There was not, and Margaret Millous, whose injury happened concurrently with the leaving of blood stains in Brady Street, shortly before the murder of Polly Nichols in nearby Buck's Row, emerges as the best if not only candidate and a possible example of a woman who met and survived an assault by Jack the Ripper.

CHAPTER 5

Lost Clues & Missed Opportunities

WHEN THE PUBLIC filed into the coroner's court on the first day of the Nichols inquest, there was among their number a man who attended out of sheer curiosity. He would later write a letter about his experience to the *Evening News*[50], identifying himself as A.D.V.

A.D.V. didn't go into the evidence presented or testimony given – that had already consumed enough newspaper print. He instead described what happened when he slipped out of his chair and walked behind the jury on their way to the mortuary to view the body. He thought he'd have a look to see if he recognized the woman, but he was thwarted at the door. It was explained to him that as the body had been positively identified it was no longer available for public viewing. He was gob smacked by this and pointed out, quite logically, that identifying the victim was only half the battle; there was also the matter of identifying the killer, and if a person might recognize the body as a woman they'd seen at a pub or out and about with a man near the time of her death, then the police would have a legitimate start towards tracking the murderer.

Similar complaints would crop up after

later murders, but nowhere are the failings of the Metropolitan Police more evident than in the Nichols murder investigation. It is not my objective to disparage the police unfairly, but if we're to be fair and accurate, their errors must be taken on board and acknowledged.

Inspector Edmund Reid had been the head of Bethnal Green's J Division until late 1887 when he was moved over to H Division. Judging from his lightning-speed approach to investigating the Martha Tabram murder, it boggles the mind that the comedy of errors that followed the discovery of Polly's murder were acted out by a troupe that had once served and learned under Reid.

PC Jonas Mizen was an H Division constable, not J, but his beat was in the same area, and it will be remembered that he was found by witnesses Charles Cross and Robert Paul knocking up residents at the junction of Hanbury Street and Baker's Row. There was nothing wrong with constables making a little extra money and serving the public by acting as a human alarm clock, but the complaint lodged against him in this instance is that after he was notified of an emergency in Buck's Row, he continued his knocking up instead of hurrying to the scene. Surprisingly, of all the constables that figure into the Nichols story, he might be considered to have been the least lax in his duties.

PC John Thain had apparently been hanging out with the three slaughtermen of Barber's Yard on Winthrop Street on the night of the murder. This may have been a coffee and gossip stop for many of the constables in the area, but it was Thain who got caught out when he found himself standing without cape over a corpse on Buck's Row. PC Neil sent him to fetch Dr. Llewellyn, but knowing that it was against policy for him to be without his full wardrobe, he swung back by Barber's Yard to fetch his cape and couldn't resist sharing news of the murder with the three horse slaughterers: Charles Bretton, James Mumford, and Henry Tompkins.

Thain would later deny fetching his cape and informing the slaughtermen, who predictably made a beeline to Buck's Row to view the body. This natural curiosity would put the men in hot water. Although it should have been obvious to police superiors that they were telling the truth about how they learned of the murder, police culture dictated that they believe their own over others, so they accepted Thain's denial and thrust the spotlight of suspicion onto the men with sharp knives and bloody aprons who possessed seemingly prescient knowledge of the murder in their neighborhood. They would become the first suspects and suffer the consequences of this, as we'll see later.

PC Neil is generally given a clean bill of service as far as the Nichols murder is concerned: he discovered the body, solicited the help of nearby constables, and inspected the scene for any clues. The one exception was his failure to question a man passing through Buck's Row after Dr. Llewellyn and PC Thain returned. They all watched the man walk by and did not think to question him as to who he was, what he was doing there, and if he might have seen or heard anything. Odds are he was just a man going to work and would have been of no assistance, but the failure of the constables to do their duty raised the ire of coroner Wynne Baxter and leaves us today with one more unanswered question. There's another episode that occurred that night that might suggest PC Neil was negligent in his duties.

Patrick Mulshaw was an older man employed as a night watchman for the Whitechapel Board of Works and was in charge of watching some water works only 30 yards (his estimate) from the murder site. He'd been on duty since 4:45pm, so he must have been quite tired by 3:30am, and while he admits he may have nodded off from time to time, he states he was fully awake in the crucial hour from 3am to 4am at which time he heard and saw no one. However, around 4:40am he said a man walked by him and said "Watchman, old man, I believe someone is murdered down the street." At this time he went to the scene where he saw three or four policemen and five or six working men standing around, and a doctor (Llewellyn) working on the deceased.

Many Ripperologists believe that the man who spoke to Mulshaw was Charles Bretton, one of the three slaughtermen from Barber's Yard who lagged behind the other two. It might be assumed that Mulshaw would have been familiar with the butchers and would have recognized him, but if the watchman were in his tent at the time and did not see the passerby, it would make sense. Bretton presumably would have been asked if he made such a statement and denied it. Mulshaw probably did spend the evening and morning in his heated tent but with the front flap open; this is suggested by his statements regarding sightings of the constables in the area, and it's here we come to the most interesting but overlooked element of Mulshaw's inquest testimony.

The fact that Mulshaw timed the incident at more than an hour after the murder had taken place casts doubt on its relevance, but what might be relevant to our understanding of the Brady Street attack, the Buck's Row murder, and the killer's ascribed ability to murder silently and disappear with supernatural alacrity, is Mulshaw's comments on police movements on the night of the murder. The following exchange[51] occurred between Mulshaw and Coroner Baxter at the third session of the inquest:

Coroner: Was there a man running away?

Mulshaw: No, sir. It is very quiet after eleven o'clock, and I should have noticed anyone running away. You don't see a policeman very often in that quarter.

Coroner: Did you see any that night?

Mulshaw: I think I saw two that night.

At this point, PC John Neil was asked to stand and Mulshaw identified him as one of the two constables he'd seen that night. A juror asked Mulshaw how often he saw constables pass, and Mulshaw's response was "About once in two hours, I suppose."

This is of critical importance since Neil's beat should have taken him around every 30 minutes and not every couple of hours. Mulshaw, with his occasional dozing, is not the most reliable witness, but he stood his post every night and his observation that 'you don't see a policeman very often in that quarter' suggests that as a rule the constables did not stick to schedule.

PC Neil's version of events was that upon discovery of the body he used his lantern to signal PC Thain, who was passing on Brady Street where it crossed Buck's Row. The timing was certainly fortuitous, as Neil might have found himself standing by for up to half an hour waiting for Thain to pass. Longer if Thain was spending time with the butcher boys. It must be considered at least possible that Neil either broke protocol and abandoned the body to flag down his comrade or that the two were already together and walking off their beat when they discovered Nichols. Thain, as we know, had already broken protocol by leaving his cape with the slaughtermen.

The rather slack behavior of bored constables in an area that was typically quiet and routine is unfortunate if understandable; less understandable is what happened after the murder had been discovered.

At the fourth and final session of the Nichols inquest, Inspector Spratling gave evidence and surprised the coroner by admitting that the police had not done any door knocking in Buck's Row since the discovery of the murder, save for speaking with the Purkiss family of Essex Wharf, the Greens, and the watchmen on duty at Schneider's tar factory and the Great Eastern Wharf. The coroner replied "then that will have to be done", but there's no evidence the advice was heeded, and as three weeks had passed and memories faded, it's unlikely it would have proved to be of any value.

The Inspector's remarkably naive reason for not undertaking this most basic of investigative measures was that the residents of the area would have taken it upon themselves to communicate with the police if they had anything worth reporting.[52] Even a novice knows that a civilian wouldn't necessarily know if the information they possess is significant and might not share it unless approached and asked. It was through door-knocking by the City Police after the Mitre Square murder that Joseph Lawende – considered by many as the witness most likely to have seen the Ripper – was discovered.

To the chagrin of the contemporary investigator and the delight of the modern day researcher, the press was tight on the heels of the police, speaking to witnesses and picking up information where they could. Many times they uncovered witnesses the police had missed. If not for a relentless press we'd know far less than we do today and we'd be completely ignorant of the Brady Street bloodstains, the evidence of a screaming woman from the Coldwells, or the intriguing ear-witness evidence of Buck's Row resident, Harriett Lilley.

Lilley was a 47 year old woman living at 7 Buck's Row with her husband, William, a Brewer's car man.[53] Her statement appeared in numerous newspapers, the fullest account in the *Echo* of Sept. 6th:

> I slept in front of the house, and could hear everything that occurred in the street. On that Thursday night I was somehow very restless. Well, I heard something I mentioned to my husband

in the morning. It was a painful moan - two or three faint gasps - and then it passed away. It was quite dark at the time, but a luggage [train] went by as I heard the sounds. There was, too, a sound as of whispers underneath the window. I distinctly heard voices, but cannot say what was said - it was too faint. I then woke my husband, and said to him, "I don't know what possesses me, but I cannot sleep to-night." Mrs. Lilley added that as soon as she heard of the murder she came to the conclusion that the voices she heard were in some way connected with it. The cries were very different from those of an ordinary street brawl.

Harriett Lilley receives little attention in Ripper books and doesn't even warrant a listing in the latest edition of *The Jack the Ripper A-Z* (The Complete Jack the Ripper A-Z, Messrs. Begg, Fido, and Skinner (2010)), but has been regularly debated and discussed over the years on Ripper message boards. Lilley's evidence is often discounted for lack of relevance or reliability, it being argued that someone being awakened out of their sleep could be unreliable as to what they heard and at what time. Some of the newspaper reports that featured Lilley's story were not as detailed as the *Echo*'s, which is why I've isolated it here. A careful reading makes it clear that Lilley had not slept at all and was wide awake at the time she heard the painful moans, two or three gasps, and the simultaneous sound of the train passing. She does not say if the sound of people whispering was at the same time as, prior to, or after the gasps, but it was likely either the killer and Nichols she heard or (if after) Cross and Paul.

Lilley's evidence, *prima facie*, tells us nothing we don't already know – a woman was murdered and people whispered. However, if it can now be appreciated that she was indeed awake at the time and mere feet from the murder when it happened, her statement should be given full consideration, and it does tell us a couple of things that without a witness we could not know. For instance, there's little doubt but that the moans and gasps she heard were the sound of Polly Nichols being rendered unconscious and murdered. Perhaps most significant is the timing of the train passing as the murder was occurring.

The *Echo* followed up its story by providing this information about the train heard by Lilley: 'It has been ascertained that on the morning of the date of the murder a goods train passed on the East London Railway at about half-past three - the 3.7 out from New-cross - which was probably the time when Mary Ann Nicholls (sic) was either killed or placed in Buck's-row.' The significance of the 3:30am time is that it is 10 minutes earlier than the time usually assumed to have been Nichols' time of death. It's also ten minutes prior to the time Charles Cross would have entered Buck's Row, when it was assumed he interrupted the killer at work.

If this timing is to be trusted then Charles Cross was certainly not the killer himself (as argued in a recent documentary and on Internet boards) and there's no reason to suppose the Ripper was kept from completing his task, lending further to the possibility that he may have taken something with him from the victim's body.

Inspector Frederick Abberline of Scotland Yard's Criminal Investigation Department (CID) was present on the first day of the inquest and from that moment forward Scotland Yard was involved, melding the investigation into the still active inquiry into the Martha Tabram murder. Uniform constables were pulled from the case which was now firmly in the hands of the detectives.[54]

But problems for the police were only starting.

So were the murders.

The Great Ripper Hunt had begun.

CHAPTER 6

The Great Ripper Hunt

THE MURDER OF Emma Smith passed with little comment from the press or public. When the murder of Martha Tabram followed and the police were unable to identify her slayer, the East End found itself gripped with fear and embroiled in a true mystery. When a third body turned up the fear and paranoia spread like a virus across London and people from all classes, quarters, and walks of life looked to the police and demanded results.

The police responded by going on vacation.

In 1884 James Monro was appointed the first Assistant Commissioner of Police in London and was in charge of the Criminal Investigation Department (CID). In 1886, Sir Charles Warren was appointed Commissioner, a position that Monro coveted; in that same year, Henry Matthews, 1st Viscount Llandaff, was appointed Home Secretary. It would be an understatement to say that Matthews and Warren didn't get along and Monro, whose duties required that he answer to both men as his superiors, was caught in the middle. The politics of the situation are beyond the scope of this book, but suffice it to say that both Warren and Monro were threatening to tender their resignation by August of 1888 and Monro took advantage of Warren leaving on holiday that month to make good on his threat. His last day in office was August 31st, the day of

Polly Nichols's murder. With Warren out of the country and Monro out of office, both the police and the CID were left without a man in charge at the very moment that the first in the 'Ripper' series of murders was dropped into their lap.

To make matters worse, Superintendent Thomas Arnold, the head of H Division, as well as his star detective, Edmund Reid, were on annual leave. Reid headed the investigation into the two previous murders, so his input would be invaluable to the detectives taking up the Buck's Row inquiry. Fortunately, he agreed to offer whatever assistance he could, presumably by post, until his return later in the month of September.

Monro's replacement was Robert Anderson, who'd barely taken time to warm his chair before he was allowed to go on a month's sick leave. He's one of the most quoted sources in Ripper literature, and the only police official to claim the Ripper's identity was definitely known, but he was only in office and in London for one of the canonical murders, that being the obliteration of Mary Kelly.

The press delivered gossip about the police – truths, half-truths, and outright lies – by the bushel, reporting in the days before Nichols's murder that Police Commissioner Charles Warren's resignation was imminent; in what was perhaps a bit of self-serving local propaganda, the *Manchester Courier* went so far as to announce erroneously that his resignation had already been tendered and that his replacement was likely to be Manchester's own chief constable, Malcom Wood. But aside from the usual slings and arrows one might expect from a competitive press, there was no escaping the fact that London's Metropolitan Police was in a state of flux. The *Morning Advertiser* of Sept. 1st offered this ultimatum:

> All eyes are now turned upon the London police. The air is rife with rumours of discord and discontent in the force and of cross purposes among the controlling authorities of it. All this must be brushed ruthlessly aside. The public does not want to know of it. If it exists it must be buried by those responsible for it, in the face of the terrible necessity of tracking out the undiscovered murders that have lately shocked society. This much the public demands of the police. The detective department is on its trial. It must be

judged not only by its acts, but by what it fails in. It must justify itself by bringing the criminals in this and in other brutal murders to the scaffold. Otherwise it will stand condemned.

The pressure on police to catch the Ripper was immense and no one felt it more acutely than did the men on the ground.

Frederick Abberline had for many years been the Local Inspector for H Division before being promoted to Inspector First-Class in early 1888 and transferred to Scotland Yard. He was succeeded in H Division by Reid, who in turn appears to have been succeeded by Spratling in the position of Local Inspector for J Division.

It was Inspector Helson and not Spratling who worked closest with Abberline in the investigation into Nichols's murder. Had Inspector Reid not been on his annual leave at the time he would have been an adviser to the investigation and an active official participant a few weeks later when the Annie Chapman murder happened on his patch and that inquiry was merged with the Nichols case.

The Original Suspects

Many new leads and theories were merged with holdovers from the Tabram investigation. Notably missing in the countless press reports is the 'soldier' theory that briefly enjoyed prominence after Mary Ann Connelly aka 'Pearly Poll' identified the George Yard victim as her lodging mate 'Emma' and offered up a story of having shared the final evening of 'Emma's' life in the company of two soldiers. As detailed in my book, *The Bank Holiday Murders: The True Story of the First Whitechapel Murders*, Inspector Reid would come to determine that Pearly Poll had fabricated her story.

The first suspects that had to be dealt with were the three slaughtermen – Henry Tompkins, James Mumford, and Charles Bretton. They were the first civilians to attend the murder scene following the discovery of the body by PC Neil. The slaughtermen gave a simple and believable explanation for their knowledge of the murder – they'd been informed of it by PC Thain, presumably when he retrieved his cape on his way to fetch Dr. Llewellyn. Had Thain admitted to the relatively minor delinquency in duty he may have received a reprimand but would have spared his acquaintances a lot of heartache. However, since Thain denied informing them of the murder, they were assumed liars and worse.

The policemen in the neighborhood vouched as far as they could for the character of the Barber's Yard men, but it wasn't enough to protect them from official scrutiny and public suspicion. The newspapers were bursting with hints that the police knew who committed the murders and were on the verge of obtaining a confession from an associate of the mysterious killer. The *Echo* of Sept. 4th carried the story under the headline 'Expected Confession and Arrest':

> The authorities now investigating this mysterious case assert that they now have a clue, but in what direction they are not permitted to make the faintest allusion. "If we did," remarked one of the officers "justice would be undoubtedly frustrated." But the chain of evidence is, it is alleged, being fast drawn around the persons implicated – for it is believed there are more than one concerned – but the persons watched will not at present be arrested unless they make an effort to leave the district. The reason of this is explained by the fact that further sworn evidence which might be lost by precipitate action is likely to reveal the criminal at the forthcoming Coroner's inquiry. To complete the investigation no steps are being left unturned by Inspector Abberline, Inspector Helson, Inspector Spratling, Detective-sergeant Enright, and the numerous other officers engaged in making the necessary inquiries. It is not improbable that one man, not immediately concerned in the crime, but who has a knowledge of the circumstances, may make a confession, and thus shield himself from serious consequences which might otherwise ensue.

Although this story was carried in a number of papers, none dared openly state or even speculate as the identity of the alleged suspects, but in this excerpt the *Echo* puts forth that more than one person were involved in the murder and yet another person 'not immediately concerned in the crime, but who has a knowledge of the circumstances' was suspected to make a confession. Other papers stated this revelation would occur at the next session of the inquest.

Without explicitly stating that the slaughtermen were the suspects and opening themselves up to a slander lawsuit, the *Echo* did the next best thing and segued from the above article into an interview with James Mumford, auspiciously titled 'Police Have Some Clue':

The murder of Mary Ann Nicholls [sic] still excites the keenest interest in Whitechapel. Some malicious persons have actually chalked a libelous statement on the gate of the slaughterhouse where the three men were engaged on the night of the tragedy, one of whom gave evidence at the adjourned inquest yesterday, while the states of his two comrades – Brittain [sic] and Mumford – were reserved for the concluding hearing before Mr. Wynne Baxter, the Coroner. These three slaughter-house men are considerably annoyed at the slanderous insinuations conveyed in the expression written on the gate as stated.

Our reporter visited this slaughter-house – a block of extensive premises – this afternoon, where he was courteously shown over by a representative of the firm, who wish him to give publicity to the reiterated statements of the men as to their utter abhorrence of the crime in Buck's-row. The business carried on at the place is mainly confined to the killing of horses and boiling their flesh, which is afterwards sold to cat's-meat men. There are two descriptions of knives used in the killing and cutting-up process, one having a long tapering blade, while the other has one about five inches in length, with a strong wooden handle – a weapon, in fact, very similar to those originally employed for killing pigs.

'THE SLAUGHTERMAN'S STORY

James Mumford, one of the men engaged here, who was left in charge of the premises the night of the murder while his two comrades went out for an hour's walk, made the following statement this afternoon: "I am at work here all hours of the night, and don't go out of the premises until I am done. My time to come in of an evening is quarter-past eight o'clock. Then I am here until the governor comes down in the morning, which is sometimes six and sometimes half-past." Then Mr. Mumford, indignant, suddenly burst forth, "I don't know why that should be wrote on the gate against our chaps."

"What is written on the gate?" asked the reporter.

"Why, 'This is where the murder was done,'" exclaimed Mr. Mumford, "which is a great untruth; and if you can put it right, as you say, I don't mind telling you what our work is."

"No one, of course, even hints anything against you men," remarked the interviewer; "but did you hear any screams that night?"

"Screams! I never heard no screams. I never took one step out of the yard; never one step all that night – except when my mates heard from a policeman that there had been a murder committed. Why don't the police go to some of the lodging-houses so well known about here, instead of coming down to Winthrop-street?"

"They are, I hear, making inquiries in the district," was interposed.

"And so they ought. Well, my mates, when they heard that, went off at once. They were gone ten minutes before I left because I had the water turned at the boiler, and could not leave. My work is to boil the meat."

"Is that all? Don't you kill horses?"

"We all kill horses, but I'm left to attend the boilers when my mates are away at night. They always go up the top to the Grave Maurice" (a public house half a minute's walk from the slaughter-house, and about a minute's walk from the gateway of Essex Wharf).

"What time?"

"About twenty minutes after twelve they usually start."

"But the house closes then, does it not?"

"No, not till half-past. They go there and have their refreshment, and bring me some back. I am not supposed to leave the place, and I don't do so. They take a crust of bread-and-cheese with them, and if they haven't time to eat it in the house they keep outside and have a blow. These chaps are very upset about what the police are doing."

"Do they take their knives with them?"

"Knives! No, they don't take em."

"What sort are they?"

"Well, large and small; the same as butchers use."

"How many horses did you kill altogether on Thursday night?"

"I can't tell – three or four, perhaps. I helped to do the killing 'em with my mates before they went. Then I attended to the boilers, as I tell you, and did not leave until they came back; and not then, not till after the constable came, and said a murder had been committed in Buck's-row. Let the police to the lodging-houses. They are five or six about this part, and they are known well."

The *Echo* reporter wormed his way into an interview by pretending to believe in Mumford's innocence and by offering him an opportunity to 'put it right', but the way the questions were formed and the overall tone of the article's construction suggests this was contrary to the paper's true motives.

Mumford's statement that his two cohorts were off on their own for an hour was corroborated by Henry Tompkins at the inquest when he stated that he and Bretton had been gone from their work from 12:40am to 1am on the night of the murder. Given that these men were quite near the murder site and were accustomed to the use of sharp instruments, the police would have been remiss if they hadn't fully investigated them. Not helping matters was the fact that at least one of them was an unapologetic misogynist.

Henry Tompkins, a 'roughly dressed young fellow of low stature', gave evidence at the inquest on September 3rd and received no quarter from either the coroner or the jurymen, who 'badgered' him about his 'midnight ramble'.[55] Much of his testimony elicited laughter from those present, and the following exchange would have been no exception:

Coroner: Is yours noisy work?

Tompkins: No, sir: very quiet.

Coroner: Was it all quiet on Friday morning? – say after two o'clock?

Tompkins: Yes, sir: quite quiet. The gates were open, and we heard no cry.

Coroner: Did any one come to the slaughter-house that night?

The witness replied that nobody passed except the policeman.

Coroner: Are there any women about there?

Tompkins: Oh, I know nothing about them. I don't like them.

Coroner: I don't ask whether you like them. I ask whether there were any about that night?

Tompkins: I did not see any.

Coroner: Not in Whitechapel-road?

Tompkins: Oh yes, there, all sorts and sizes. It's a rough neighbour-hood, I can tell you.[56]

After being grilled by an openly suspicious coroner and jury, Tompkins was excused and went away 'rather angry and somewhat relieved.'[57] One inconsistency is that Tompkins states he went to the murder site with James Mumford and it was Bretton who came along some minutes later. However, Mumford stated in his interview that it was he who remained behind approximately ten minutes to tend to the meat boiler.

The accusatory graffiti left on the door of the slaughterhouse is proof that public opinion had turned against the slaughtermen, due in part to their own reputations. Writing to City Police Commissioner Sir James Fraser, in response to an early October newspaper announcement of a reward being offered by the City Police for information leading to the capture of the murderer, a Mr. Longley from Yalding shared the following piece of gossip:

Oct. 3, 1888

Col Fraser,

Sir, seeing your name in the daily paper I take the liberty to write to you to inform you that I heard yesterday that there has be [sic] down here some of the Whitechaple [sic] people hoppicking who knew one of the women that has been murdered, I also heard that they said they should not be surprised to hear that the murderer is one of the slaughter men that work at the publick slaughter house close bye, as there is one man there that cannot bare the sit of a woman and hates them. Please keep this private as is only a hear-say as I was passing through our village.

It seems inescapable that this refers to one of the three Barber's Yard men, and probably Henry Tompkins.

The women who'd gone hop picking in Mr. Longley's village had evidently already shared their suspicions with police, who investigated the men thoroughly before dismissing them as suspects. Chief Inspector Swanson summarized their efforts in an Oct. 19th, 1888 report:

> The absence of the motives which lead to violence and of any scrap of evidence either direct or circumstantial, left the police without the slightest shadow of a trace consequently enquiries were made into the history and accounts given of themselves of persons, respecting whose character & surroundings suspicion was cast in statements made to police.

> Amongst such are the three slaughtermen, named Tomkins, Britton and Mumford employed by night at Messrs. Harrison Barber & Coy. premises Winthorp [sic] Street. Their statements were taken separately, and without any means of communicating with each other, and they satisfactorily accounted for their time, being corroborated in some portions by the Police on duty near the premises.

Swanson, while writing this, was likely referencing a report prepared a full month earlier by Inspector Abberline who also noted 'no grounds appeared to exist to suspect them of the murders'. This, of course, is not the same as saying they'd been proved innocent of the crime, only that there was no direct evidence linking them to the crime, such as a confession or a witness. Tompkins would have fallen under much keener suspicion if not for the married and more respectable (and less openly misogynistic) Charles Bretton providing him an alibi for every moment of the evening. Bretton, then 29 years old, lived at 25 Buck's Row with his wife Annie but had moved by the time the 1891 census was taken, possibly because of the lingering suspicion against him.

At the same time the police were investigating the three horse slaughter-ers, they were also expending much needed resources towards a local phan-tom known as 'Leather Apron'. Numerous 'Leather Aprons' were found and – much like the slaughtermen – no proof of complicity could be attached to them. The intriguing saga of Leather Apron #1, John Pizer, is detailed in full in *The Bank Holiday Murders*, so instead of retreading that ground here, we'll look at some of the other suspects and theories that arose during the investigation.

Because the Nichols investigation was immediately merged with the now three-week old Martha Tabram inquiry, it's logical that suspects already developed were looked at and further investigated. There were two competing theories at that time, the 'blackmailing gang' theory and the 'madman' theory.

It was in conjunction with the gang theory that the word 'ripper' first enters the Whitechapel Murders lexicon. The *Evening News* of Sept. 1st mentioned the theory that a gang of 'high rippers' were responsible; 'high rippers' (or High Rip gangs as they were most commonly called) was a col-loquial term for blackmailing gangs that stemmed from a group of hood-lum youths in Liverpool. The *Evening News* of August 31st, published mere hours after the discovery of Polly Nichols's murder, sums up the theory:

> The officers engaged in the case are pushing their inquiries in the neighbourhood as to the doings of certain gangs known to frequent these parts, and an opinion is gaining ground amongst them that the murderers are the same who committed the two previous murders near the same spot. It is believed that these gangs, who make their appearance during the early hours of the morning, are in the habit of blackmailing these poor unfortunate creatures, and when their demands are refused, violence follows, and in order to avoid their deeds being brought to light they put away their victims. They have been under the observation of the police for some time past, and it is believed that with the prospect of a reward and a free pardon, some of them might be persuaded to turn Queen's evidence, when some startling revelations might be expected.

The next day, the *Echo* added, probably correctly, that 'though a 'High

Rip' gang is suspected of the deed, most of the detectives who are investigating the case believe that it was the work of a maniac.'

Inspectors Abberline and Helson made no secret that they were of the opinion that a lone murderer and not a gang was responsible for the crimes. Perhaps it was only those such as Reid and Walter Dew, who'd personally worked the Emma Smith case, who were still partial to the idea of a murderous gang. Reid would eventually come to the opinion that the murders were the work of a lone slayer but remained steadfast that Emma Smith and Martha Tabram were among his tally.

The police were successful in gaining permission to offer a pardon to an accomplice not involved in the murder itself who'd be willing to turn Queen's evidence and help convict the murderer.[58] This was most likely motivated by the slaughtermen, with the belief that only one or two would be involved in the crime itself but would have boasted to their mate of their deed. Although the pardon was to go unused, it was to the credit of Scotland Yard that they were keeping an open mind as to who or what might be behind the series of grisly murders haunting the East End.

One of the forgotten suspects looked at and quickly cleared was a man named James Spilsby who, so claimed one paper, was wanted for the stabbings of four or five women. His involvement was doubted when it was discovered that he'd been lying low and out of the way, attempting to avoid a warrant that had been put out for him.[59]

Another unknown suspect mentioned in passing was a 'seafaring man who has already stood trial for a crime not far short of murder'.[60] Perhaps if James Spilsby can be positively identified in the records and he's found to have been a sailor put on trial for a crime not far short of murder, two mysteries can be laid to rest at once.

Henry Birch & the Cambridge Heath Road Incident

On Tuesday, September 4th, four days after the murder of Polly Nichols, it was reported that another assault allegedly occurred the day after and mere yards from the location of the Buck's Row murder. An unnamed woman left Forester's Music Hall on Cambridge Heath Road, where she had been in the company of a sea captain, and once alone was approached by a well-dressed man who asked that she walk with him to meet a friend of his. When they reached an area close to Buck's Row he grabbed her by the throat and dragged her into a court where he was joined by a group of 'bullies', male and female, who set about robbing her of her necklace, purse, earrings, and brooch. She was also 'brutally assaulted', but in what manner it was not reported. Most ominously, when she tried to call for help, one of the ruffians put a knife to her throat and threatened "We will serve as we did the others." She was released and reportedly informed the police who prosecuted inquiries without result.[61]

Although muggings were common enough, this incident was significant because of where it occurred, when it occurred, and for the threat issued by the attacker. The notion of a gang was not a new one, but to cast the killer as a well-dressed man was a novel idea at this stage of the investigation. Doubt would soon arise as to whether or not an assault had occurred at all. The *Daily Telegraph*, which reported the original story, received a letter from the manager of Forester's Music Hall stating that he had contacted the police about the incident and was informed they'd received no such report. Following behind this, and perhaps in an effort to take a stab at their competition, the *East London Observer* called the story 'absolutely false and groundless'. This denouncement has been accepted as truth.

However, the police were under no obligation to confirm any reports they received to the manager of the music hall (the alleged assault did not occur on his property), and if the station he inquired at was not the one the woman reported the crime to, then it's possible, if not likely, that they would have been unaware of the event outside of what they might have read in the papers. The *Eastern Argus* speculated that the story was a muddled version of Henry Hummerston's attack on Eliza Smith, but this makes little sense as that story had already made the rounds and bore little resemblance to the tale of a well-dressed woman (presumably a higher class prostitute) approached outside a music hall.

The story disappeared from the papers but would be resurrected a month later when a man named Henry Birch emerged in the press as a potentially significant witness.

Birch was a milk seller with a small stand at 2 Little Turner Street and the story he sold the press was that on the night of the Cambridge Heath

Road incident a strange man with a shiny black bag ran into his shop and requested a glass of milk. He drank the milk hurriedly and proceeded to put a pair of overalls on over his clothes. Seeing Birch watching him incredulously, the man commented "That was a terrible murder last night wasn't it? I think I've got a clue." The man then snatched up his black bag and took off.

Birch claimed to have alerted authorities to the man at the time, but no record of this exists in the police or press reports. Depending on which paper he was talking to the man he saw was described as young and of clerkly appearance or as a sea-faring man.

There is no mention of Birch anywhere in the known record prior to October and it's likely his entire story was fabricated. A hint towards his motives might lie in the fact that he backed up the claims of discredited Berner Street witness, Matthew Packer, in early October and by November the two were in fast company together when they made the papers again. *The Northeastern Daily Gazette* of November 26th reported:

> Late on Friday night several of the witnesses who, there is no doubt, saw the man who is believed committed the murders, again saw him and quietly followed him to try and get on his track. After watching him for some time they saw him accost a woman, but on their crossing towards him he suddenly disappeared down a dark turning in the Commercial Road. These witnesses were Mr. Burch [sic], the milkman, and his son, and Matthew Packer, the fruitier [sic].

Birch's story doesn't pass the sniff test and his repeated pairing with the completely undependable Matthew Packer means we can set aside the story of the milk-drinking man of disguises. However, Birch's emergence in the press revived the story of the Cambridge Heath Road incident and new details emerged. The *Star* had police sources and may have tapped them for new information; or maybe they just wanted to give the impression that their speculations were something more. They reported that earlier stories that the unnamed woman had been set upon by a gang of ruffians 'proved to be false as far as the gang were concerned. The police ascertained, however, that a woman had been set upon by a man, and that her cries had attracted a number of others, whose efforts to capture her assailant led to the gang story. The miscreant escaped in the direction of Commercial-road.'

While the Cambridge Heath Road incident is more credible (or at least not as discredited) as the Birch story, there's still not enough for us to be able to take it on board as legitimate evidence, though I'd argue it might be wise for researchers to keep it in mind and not toss it in the bin just yet, as new information is being unearthed all the time.

Of the five canonical Ripper murders, the Buck's Row murder is unique for having been the only case that did not generate a suspect description. However, researcher Chris Scott discovered an intriguing find in an American newspaper published mere hours after the discovery of the murder:

> The police were called to a house in Whitechapel last night on an alarm of murder, in which they found a woman in great suffering. On examination it was found she had been horribly and indecently mutilated. She could not tell who inflicted the wounds save that he was a tall man with a black beard. The woman was taken to a hospital, and it is doubtful whether she can recover from her terrible injuries. This is the third case of the kind known to the police. It is believed the awful work is the crime of one man, and that he is a maniac.[62]

The newspaper industry was booming in 1888, and with the advent of the telegraph and telephone, communication was quicker than ever. As a result, most, if not all, major American newspapers had correspondents in London, the then-power center of the Western world. It is not uncommon to find information in American papers that for one reason or another was overlooked by or not provided to London papers.

On the surface this article from Illinois seems like a hopelessly garbled telling of the Nichols murder, but there's enough contrary detail that it makes one wonder if it's not describing an altogether different assault. In this description the victim lives, was transported to the hospital, and was able to provide a description of her attacker – a 'tall man with a black beard.' The author seems ignorant of Polly Nichols's murder, describing the assault as the 'third case known to police'; at this time Emma Smith and Martha Tabram were popularly considered the first and second of the Whitechapel mysteries.

Could the woman referred to in the article be Margaret Millous? There are similarities (violent assault, serious injury, gone to hospital), but there are also crucial differences, such as the mention that the police were called to a house. If Millous was successful in rousing a neighbor of the Coldwells and the police were then summoned, we might expect that word of this would have made it to the hungry London pressmen.

As with the Cambridge Heath Road story, this unnamed woman remains an enigma: possibly real, probably a concoction, or perhaps some combination of the two.

CHAPTER 7

Buck's Row – A New Perspective

WHAT MAKES FOR good history is, like most things, open for debate. I personally believe it consists of discovery, interpretation, and re-interpretation. History writers – academic or otherwise – should always be keeping an eye out for new discoveries, and when one is made, they should be in a position to rationally and Logically interpret the discovery within its proper historical context. Likewise, the 'old stuff', or accepted data, should continue to be re-interpreted and *must* be re-interpreted when new data is placed into the frame.

There are many new discoveries presented in this book and I think it would be wise now to put them into perspective and see what they might tell us about the man behind the mystery, who, for lack of a given name, we call Jack the Ripper.

But first, let's briefly consider what we now know about Polly Nichols. Her friends described her as quiet and keeping to herself, and there may have been a measure of truth to that, but it was not the whole truth. In the lodging house culture of the time you did not talk to the police, and if you did, you told them no more than you had to. People such as Ellen Holland , who was no doubt anxious to see the slayer of her friend brought to justice, was terrified to find herself in a coroner's court surrounded by men with titles before and letters after their names. Did she know Polly was a prostitute? Of course she did, but she would not be the one to say as much. She also probably knew Polly had recently moved into 35 Dorset Street but didn't want to get herself into possible hot water by pointing a finger in that direction, so she pretended not to be sure what house Polly had last gone to. For some reason Polly had not gotten along well at 35 Dorset Street, where lived and worked a rogue's gallery of characters who pop up elsewhere in the Ripper mystery: Pearly Poll, Annie Chapman, William Crossingham, Eliza Cooper, and Timothy Donovan among them. Had she remained alive to earn one more doss she might have taken Ellen Holland up on her offer to return to 18 Thrawl Street.

The reason Polly didn't get along well at Crossingham's remains obscured, but other new finds mined from contemporary sources raise the possibility that Polly herself was at the root of her troubles. She certainly had a problem with authority figures, proving as she did to be a problem for the police when she and others were prevented from Living rough in Trafalgar Square; and secreting knives which she once used to attack a workhouse official. Such information won't tell us who her killer was, but it might tell us something about him.

Polly was not a small woman. She was described as 'exceedingly well-proportioned' and a 'woman of unusually good figure for her class in life'; and with her fearlessness in defending herself against males whom she felt were a threat, she was by no means a wilting violet. If the Ripper's aim, as often suggested, was to choose the frailest, weakest victim available, then he missed wide of the mark in his selection of Polly. Nevertheless, he was able to subdue her, render her unconscious, and bring about her murder without attracting the attention of a single verifiable eye witness.

The Ripper was not without confidence, skill, and proficiency in his gruesome undertakings, but he was human, and therefore fallible. For all of his 'successes' it stands to reason that he would not be without his failures. If I'm correct in my interpretation of the data, then Margaret Millous was one such failure.

In the hours just prior to the murder of Polly Nichols and in front of a similar stable gateway mere yards away, somebody bled onto their hand

and left at least one significant bloody mark in front of Honey's mews in Brady Street. Around that same time a woman was heard running frantically from that spot, screaming 'Murder!' and 'Police!' There is no reason to suppose the Coldwells were lying about what they said they heard and the bloody hand prints they described were confirmed at least partially by a police inspector, so the fact that *something* occurred in Brady Street is not a matter of speculation. Nor is it speculation that around this same time Margaret Millous sought medical assistance at nearby London Hospital for a most unusual injury to her arm that cut deep enough to injure the radial artery. One possible interpretation is that these disparate facts are connected and point us to the name of a Ripper victim who survived and was lost to history until now.

Regarding the medical evidence, it is a fact overlooked by modern literature - but a fact nonetheless - that Polly Nichols was stabbed multiple times in the neck and abdomen, just as Martha Tabram had been three weeks prior; it is a fact that - like Tabram and Emma Smith before her - Nichols had been injured in her groin area and bled profusely between her legs; it is a fact that the overwhelming majority of contemporary opinion came down on Nichols and Tabram having been felled by the same hand. Dr. Haslip, who tended to Emma Smith in her final hours and provided the medical evidence at her inquest, felt that there was 'very little question that both murders (Nichols and Smith) were committed by the same person'[63], a sentiment shared by the investigators who worked the Smith case. Few things are absolute in our study of the Ripper murders, but if speculation and preconceived notions are placed to the side, we are faced with far more commonalities than discrepancies in the George Yard and Buck's Row tragedies and should consider it a likelihood that the crimes were part of the same series.

We might also show restraint in stating with certainty that the Ripper did not abscond from Buck's Row with any part of his victim. If the doctor who performed the autopsy could not be certain, than neither can we be. That's not to say I'm convinced the Ripper succeeded in his goal, but the location and depth of the cuts, the slices to the omentum, and his subsequent theft of Annie Chapman's uterus in Hanbury Street, leaves little doubt as to what his motives were in Buck's Row. Without firm reason for believing he was interrupted, we can't deny the real possibility that the Ripper did not leave Buck's Row empty-handed.

Before we go further, I should point out my belief that the Ripper used armed robbery as a ruse to gain the compliance of his would-be victims. He would pull his knife and assure his victim that if they did what he said they would not be hurt. Robbery being common enough, they would believe him, and go along with it, unaware that his intention was murder. The evidence for this is in the rings stolen from Nichols and Chapman prior to their murder (the clenched fists rule out a post-murder plunder), the cachous found in Liz Stride's hand (it would have lodged their as she went into her pocket for her coin currency), and the thimble next to Catherine Eddowes' hand (same scenario as Stride).

Bringing the new information together with what we already know, a new interpretation of what might have happened in the early hours of August 31st emerges: At some point in the wee hours the Ripper propositioned - or was propositioned by - Margaret Millous in the Whitechapel Road and they proceeded to the gateway of Honey's mews in Brady Street. The Ripper tripped her up and Margaret fell to the pavement, reacting just in time to scream and ward him off with an upheld arm. The Ripper struck out, injuring her arm severely, before running away. She instinctively puts her hand to her wound, bloodying it in the process, and then uses it for support to lift herself up, transferring a bloody handprint onto the wall. Terrified, in pain, and bleeding, she runs off into the dark in a blind panic, calling for help in case her attacker remained nearby in the shadows. She makes her way back to the light and safety of Whitechapel Road where she finds help and is taken to London Hospital. The Ripper may have been watching the main road at that moment and saw that she was going to the hospital and assumed he would have time enough to seek out another victim.

Whatever his sense of security or state of mind, we know that the Ripper met Polly, probably on Whitechapel Road, and that they went together to Buck's Row and into the shadows of Brown's stable yard's locked gates. At this point there would have been brief conversation, followed by the mugging of Polly where she would have surrendered her rings and any money she may have had. The Ripper would then have rendered her unconscious, possibly by means of what was then referred to as 'garroting' but that we today would call a carotid chokehold (for more discussion on this method, see 'A Murder in the Neighborhood' elsewhere in this book). Arthur Harding, an East End criminal, gave this description:

A lot of garrotting [sic] went on. Five years and a bashing you got for it – eighteen strokes with the cat. That was the penalty. But alot of it still went on, by Flowery Dean Street (Flower & Dean Street), and in the pubs at the back of Leman Street, and all down the Highway. Even at the 'Fleur de Lis' in Elder Street I've known it done. Not in Bethnal Green. I've never known it done in Bethnal Green. You had to be tall to do it. You would come up to a man from behind, put your arms round his throat, with your fists on his throttle. If it went on for more than a few seconds he would choke, so you had to be skilled. Some of them had a girl working for them – she would get a man well boozed, mix his drinks for him and they'd get him while he was drunk.[64]

Polly Nichols was murdered in the Bethnal Green district, lending a note of irony to Harding's observation, if indeed she had been 'garroted'. She had not been struck on the head and there's not sufficient evidence to suggest a straightforward strangulation, so 'garroting' in the sense described by Harding, and common amongst certain criminals of the time, emerges as the only real possibility.

After being rendered unconscious, Polly was laid down on her back. Dr. Llewellyn felt the abdominal injuries were inflicted first, but that idea was not popular then, nor is it now, and it was probably the throat stabs that were inflicted first. We know that the Ripper stabbed her neck twice, driving the knife blade in deep enough to cut bone, and then pulled the knife back towards himself, creating two jagged rips. To facilitate this he would have knelt at her right side and used his left hand to push down on her face and hold her head steady. He then would have lifted and spread her legs, raised her skirts, and inserted his knife into her, probably thrusting it back and forth, generating the two stabs detailed in Inspector Spratling's reports as well as the pool of blood under the legs reported by PC Thain. He then would have inflicted the various injuries to her abdomen, including the large incision from pubes to breast and the intersecting jagged cut that would have created an opening over the lower abdomen and would have provided the killer access to the victim's uterus. We know that when this injury was first observed, her intestines were protruding, but we cannot be certain whether this was the result of the killer's pilfering hands or from the transport of her body by police. The only opportunity we had to learn this was when the doctor examined her *in situ* in Buck's Row, but he failed to make the observation.

What happened next remains a matter of conjecture: If Harriett Lilley's timings were accurate, then Polly Nichols was murdered a full ten minutes prior to the arrival of Charles Cross and it would therefore be likely that the Ripper was already minutes out of the area, having succeeded in whatever his mission was. If Lilley's timings or account are incorrect, then it remains possible that the Ripper had been disturbed by the approaching footsteps of Cross and fled ahead of schedule. His escape route from Buck's Row remains a matter for debate but I feel it's most likely he would have simply slipped back into the anonymity of Whitechapel Road.

The research and consideration of the evidence presented here does not point us to any particular person as having been Jack the Ripper, but the wealth of new information and the fresh interpretation of the data might give us a firmer grasp of the facts that might one day lead to further breakthroughs and, possibly, a solution to history's most enduring murder mystery.

SECTION TWO

The Berner Street Mystery

JACK AND THE GRAPE STALK

The Berner Street Mystery Part 1

I N THE GREAT canon of Ripper victims, Mary Kelly undoubtedly attracts the most attention – or, in some cases, obsession – of the modern Ripper student. Next up we have Annie Chapman and Catherine Eddowes, who, along with Kelly, have books devoted to them, and seemingly endless threads of discussion on internet message boards. Even Polly Nichols finds unanimous acceptance as a Ripper victim. So what is it about Elizabeth Stride that keeps the Ripper writers at bay? Why is it she is not afforded the same studious analysis that is given to the other victims? The likely answer is the grey area that surrounds her candidacy as a Ripper victim.

Stride was the only victim of the so-called canonical five who was not mutilated, which leaves a great big question mark next to her name on Jack's death list. Perhaps this is why most modern books on the case simply rehash the witness evidence, lay out the basic facts relating to Stride's murder, drop the big question mark, and then move on to safer ground in Mitre Square, with little or no new interpretation added to the study. The end result of this is a generation of Ripperphiles less familiar with the Stride murder than any of the others, and a willingness to accept the foregone conclusions without understanding why they are foregone.

Perhaps these conclusions are correct,

and perhaps they're not. Until we spend some quality time in Berner Street, how are we to know? So let's do just that.

What you are about to read is the first installment in a series of articles examining different areas of the Berner Street Mystery. I felt a good place to start would be disposing of certain red herrings corrupting the investigation. This is, of course, crucial to getting at the truth. Along the way we'll meet many interesting individuals, learn a few things we didn't know before, and indulge in fresh interpretations of familiar evidence that may just make a little sense. So, without further preamble, let's set aside our preferred suspects and preconceived notions and take the first of many walks together along Berner Street. We'll answer some old questions, ask some new ones, and simply have fun enjoying a good mystery. You needn't bring anything but an open mind – the grapes are on me.

The Grapes of Myth

There are few people around these days who still see any truth in the statements offered up by Matthew Packer, who claimed to have seen Stride on the night of her death. All versions of his statement differed in varying but significant degrees, and all involved the selling of grapes to Stride and a mysterious man who may have been her killer. However, the suggestion that grapes were found at the Berner Street crime scene did not originate days later with Packer, but instead with Louis Diemshitz and other Berner Street residents within 24 hours of the murder. This inconvenient little fact has assured the grapes a place in Ripper lore to this very day; they're the lifeblood of various conspiracy and Freemasonic theories and central plot points of fictional treatments across all mediums, such as the graphic novel and film *From Hell*. Was Louis lying, misquoted, or mistaken? Time to borrow a candle from Mrs. Diemshitz and see if we can shed some light on the matter.

It all started when a press conference of sorts was held in which Diemshitz along with fellow club members Isaac Kozebrodski and Morris Eagle, nosy neighbor Mrs. Mortimer, and Berner Street youth Abraham Ashbrigh, among others, told reporters what they had seen – or thought they had seen – in the moments or hours following the discovery of Stride's murder. The oft-repeated notion that words had been wrongly attributed to Diemshitz can be fully dismissed as his statement was recorded simultaneously by journalists from different papers, a comparison study of which reveals little variance in detail. All reports from Oct. 1st (the day after the murder) mentions grapes. The *Evening News* of Oct. 1st offers more detail than most[65], indicating their version of the statements taken may be the closest to what the interviewees actually said. According to their report, Diemshitz stated that 'her hands were tightly clenched, and when they were opened by the doctor I saw immediately that one had been holding sweet-meats and the other grapes.'

Isaac Kozebrodski[66], a recently transplanted native of Warsaw and resident of the club, was present when Diemshitz first rushed in to notify members that a woman – either drunk or dead – was lying in the passageway. He was among the first to join Diemshitz in investigating the body and stood by (some sources place him on the steps) while Diemshitz leaned in close with a candle[67] and pointed out to him the stream of blood running from Stride's neck. Though Kozebrodski's English was poor, the reporter persevered and recorded the following statement:

I immediately went for a policeman, and ran in the direction of Grove-street, but could not find one. Then I went into the Commercial-road, where I found two policemen. I brought them back with me, and they sent for a doctor. The doctor arrived shortly afterwards, and with him came an inspector. While the doctor examined the body I saw that there were some grapes in her right hand and some sweets in her left hand.

The details given here are important in that they describe the specific circumstances under which Diemshitz and Kozebrodski made their observation of what they believed to be grapes.

We will now analyze these statements in context with other relevant information in order to reach a satisfying conclusion to not one but two mysteries that continue to linger over the murder of Liz Stride: the grapes reported seen in her right hand and the blood later found on the same hand.

Through Kozebrodski we know that a doctor arrived accompanied by an inspector and proceeded to examine the body, and it was during this brief amount of time that he and Diemshitz made their observations. As one doctor's assistant (Edward Johnston) and two doctors – Frederick Blackwell and George Bagster Phillips – were to arrive at the yard in the hour following the discovery of the body, each examining the body in turn, we must first discover which person was attending the corpse when the two clubmen witnessed the grapes. We can eliminate Dr. Phillips from the enquiry as Kozebrodski tells us the doctor arrived 'shortly after' a doctor was called for, and Phillips wouldn't arrive for a good 20-30 minutes following the other doctors. This leaves Edward Johnston and his employer, Dr. Blackwell, each arriving only 3-4 minutes apart, with Johnston, who was Blackwell's assistant, being the first on the scene.

We turn first to the inquest testimony of PC Henry Lamb, who remained alone at the scene after sending his colleague to fetch a doctor. He testified that "Dr. Blackwell was the first doctor to arrive…Inspector Pinhorn arrived directly after Dr. Blackwell. When I blew my whistle other constables came, and I had the entrance of the yard closed. This was while Dr. Blackwell was looking at the body. Before that the doors were wide open."

PC Lamb's evidence puts the inspector arriving 'directly after' Dr. Blackwell, which means he had to have been the doctor witnessed by the two clubmen, right? Not exactly. Following PC Lamb to the witness box, Dr. Blackwell stated the following: "The double doors of the yard were closed when I arrived, so that the previous witness must have made a mistake on that point." Fortunately, Johnston cleared up the matter once and for all when he informed the coroner that "the other gates were closed shortly after I came." PC Lamb can be forgiven for his confusion as his attention would have been given to the inspector to whom he would be obliged to brief. Following this, Lamb immediately took up investigation of the yard and club interior. He likely didn't get a good look at Johnston and by the time he returned to the yard would have found Dr. Blackwell in attendance of the body. In any event, we can safely conclude that it was Johnston's brief examination which Diemshitz and Kozebrodski witnessed. Further testimony given by Diemshitz and Johnston at the inquest, which will be looked at later, leaves little doubt about this.

Although Johnston was not a doctor himself, he might be perceived as the first medical man on the scene, though he was not the first person to get close to the body. He was, in fact, at least the third person to make physical contact with it. Let's examine the rarely considered evidence of one Abraham Ashbrigh, who was described by the *Evening News* as 'a young fellow, living at 28 Berner Street[68] and was an early arrival at the scene:

> Yes, I was one of those who first saw the murdered woman. It was about a quarter to one o'clock [sic], I should think, when I heard a policeman's whistle blown, and come down to see what was the matter. In the gateway two or three people had collected, and when I got there I saw a short, dark young woman lying on the ground with a gash between four and five inches long in her throat. I should say she was from 25 to 28 years of age. Her head was towards the north wall, against which she was lying. She had a black dress on, with a bunch of flowers penned on the breast. In her hand there was a little piece of paper containing five or six cachous. The body was found by a man whose name I do not know – a man who goes out with a pony and barrow, and lives up the archway, where he was going. I believe, to put up his barrow on coming home from market. He thought it was his wife at first, but when he found her safe at home he got a candle and found this woman. He never touched it till the doctors had been sent for. The little gate is always open, or, at all events, always unfastened. There are some stables up there – Messrs. Duncan, Woollatt, and Co.'s I believe and there is a place to which a lot of girls take home sacks which they have been engaged in making. None of them would be there, though, after about one on Saturday afternoon. None of us recognised the woman, and I do not think she belonged to this neighbourhood. There seemed to be no wounds on the body.

The statement of 17 year-old Ashbrigh is very compelling in that it not only displays a good knowledge of the neighborhood, but Ashbrigh is, I believe, the first to describe the "sweet meats" properly as cachous and to offer the detail that they were wrapped in "a little piece of paper."[69] He is also the only source on record to offer the number of cachous present: five or six. Unfortunately, this particular point cannot be corroborated, and there are some internal problems with his statement that need to be dealt with before we can evaluate his evidence.

The first police whistle blown was by PC Lamb, who stated there were about 30 people in the yard upon his arrival and more that followed him in. Unless a civilian, such as a member of the vigilance committee, was first to blow a whistle, it would have been Lamb's whistle that caught Ashbrigh's attention, in which case he was not among the first people at the scene. Being young, he may have pushed his way to the front. Even though his boasting of being one of the first at the scene might have been exaggerated, there is no reason to doubt the veracity of his statement. After all, think of how many policemen were 'first at the scene' in Miller's Court. Indeed, his statement was more accurate than many of the ones given at the inquest.

So, what can Ashbrigh's statement tell us? What stands out here is that he did not report having seen any grapes or bloodstains in or on Stride's right hand. Given the details he was able to provide about the flowers and cachous, he certainly would have noticed grapes or blood had there been any.

This takes us next to Edward Spooner, the first person known to have touched the body. Neither in his statement to the press (to whom he gave 'Joseph Koster' as his name, presumably to protect his privacy) nor during his testimony at the inquest did he mention having seen any grapes. He stated that he had lifted the chin of the deceased and noticed the wound to the throat and the blood running from it. He claimed he never touched the wound and in response to a direct question from Coroner Wynne Baxter answered that he did not get any blood on his hands. He noticed a "piece of paper doubled up" in one hand and "some red and white flowers pinned on her breast". Stride's right hand would have laid close to the flowers and closer to him than the left hand containing the cachous, leaving the right hand constantly in his line of sight. He apparently saw neither blood nor grapes about the right hand.

The next person to arrive in Dutfield's Yard and examine Stride was PC Henry Lamb of H Division, whom we've already met. He stated that when he arrived none of the people present was closer than a yard to the body. Edward Spooner had stood guard over the body until his arrival and no one had touched it during that time. PC Lamb testified at the inquest that he touched the victim's face and felt for a pulse on the wrist. This would have been the right wrist because he did not notice the cachous and said he did not move the body, which he would had to have done to effectively reach the left wrist. Coroner Baxter asked if he had noticed anything in the right hand, and he replied in the negative. There was no blood on Stride's face, so none could have gotten onto PC Lamb's hands.

The fact that Ashbrigh, Spooner and Lamb never noticed either grapes or blood on, in, or around Stride's right hand, is a strong indicator that neither was there at the time.

So how did the blood get on her hand, and what about the grapes Diemshitz and Kozebrodski saw?

Dr. Blackwell arrived about three or four minutes following Edward Johnston. He checked his watch upon arrival and recorded the time as being 1:16am. He proceeded immediately to the body and began his examination. The following are excerpts from his inquest testimony as reported by the *Daily Telegraph*: 'Her dress was unfastened at the neck... the right hand was open and on the chest, and was smeared with blood. The left hand, lying on the ground, was partially closed, and contained a small packet of cachous wrapped in tissue paper.'

Dr. Blackwell's observations are significant in that he is the first person to observe blood on her right hand and also that her dress had been unfastened at the neck. Dr. Blackwell told a *Daily News* reporter within hours of the murder that "one of her hands, too, was smeared with blood, so she may have used this in her rapid struggle." As for how the blood ended up on Stride's right hand, Dr. Phillips told Coroner Baxter, "It is a mystery. There were small oblong clots on the back of the hand. I may say that I am taking it as a fact that after death the hand always remained in the position in which I found it – across the body." If Phillips sounds unsure of the facts here, it is for good reason, and the only mystery is why there was such a communication breakdown between Phillips, Blackwell, and Johnston.

Now would be the perfect time to join the much overlooked Edward Johnston as he convenes to examine the body of Elizabeth Stride by the light of a lone lantern, while a small crowd gathers to watch, among them

Louis Diemshitz and Isaac Kozebrodski. Those few moments are crucial in solving the mystery.

Johnston, who shared a residence and practice at 100 Commercial Road with Drs. Kay[70] and Blackwell, was the first medical man of sorts to arrive on the scene, preceding Dr. Blackwell by three or four minutes and Dr. Phillips by the better part of half an hour. When Johnston arrived in the yard he bent over the body and undid the buttons at the neck to allow for examination of the throat wound. His only source of light was a constable's lantern, which he said provided "very little" light. Johnston then reached in and felt her chest for warmth. The constable holding the lantern was asked to do the same, and they agreed the chest was warm. He then felt the hands and found them cold. He testified that he did all this without moving the head or body of the victim at all. If so, that means he was reaching around the body, still lying on its side, and operating by touch, explaining in his statement that he "did not notice at the time that one of the hands was smeared with blood."

It is therefore no surprise that he never realized (though he likely later suspected) that it was he, himself, who had transplanted blood from the victim's neck onto her hand and wrist during his examination.

Dr. Phillips described these blood marks as "small oblong clots on the back of the hand" in addition to blood on the wrist. This description is consistent with finger impressions, and among those who examined the body that night, Edward Johnston was the only one prior to Dr. Blackwell who touched the area of the wounds and thus came into contact with blood. No one before Johnston noticed blood on her hand, but everyone after him (Drs. Blackwell and Phillips) did. We can therefore reasonably conclude that Dr. Johnston was responsible, though probably unwittingly, for the bloody smears on Stride's hands. Given these severe doubts about that blood being there at the time of the murder, we must exclude it as being a genuine piece of crime scene evidence.

But what of the grapes Diemshitz and Kozebrodski reported having seen?

Let us consider a statement made by Diemshitz at the inquest that was heavily condensed in the *Times* and *Daily Telegraph* coverage but presented in greater detail in other papers, such as the *Morning Advertiser* of Oct. 2nd. The coroner asked "How was she lying?" to which Diemshitz replied:

> She was lying on her side, with her face towards the wall of the club. I could not say whether the body was on its side, but her face was. As soon as the police came I ceased to take any interest in the matter. I did not notice in what position her hands were. I only noticed when the doctor came up he undid the first buttons of her dress next to the neck, and put his hand in. He then told the constable that she was quite warm yet. He told the constable to put his hand in and feel the body, and he did so.

His understandable lack of interest in studying a corpse aside, this leaves little doubt but that the only time Diemshitz took a close look was after Edward Johnston began his unwarranted examination. He states quite clearly that he "ceased to take any interest in the matter" once the police came, which would have been just a few minutes after he returned with Edward Spooner. He had not even taken notice as to what position her hands were in prior to Johnston's examination. Referring back to his earliest statement, published in numerous sources on Oct. 1st, Diemshitz describes seeing her hands open for the first time: "Her hands were tightly clenched, and when they were opened by the doctor I saw immediately that one had been holding sweetmeats and the other grapes." Although Johnston swore at the inquest that he did not at all move the deceased, this suggests he may have done so, unless he was able to open both hands in view of witnesses without moving the head or body, which would have been difficult, although not impossible. In any event, this might explain why Dr. Blackwell found her hands "open" or "slightly open" upon his arrival, as opposed to "tightly clenched".

Isaac Kozebrodski corroborates this by stating that "the doctor arrived...and with him came an inspector. While the doctor examined the body I saw that there were some grapes in her right hand and some sweets in her left hand." Either Diemshitz and/or Kozebrodski stuck around for Dr. Blackwell's examination and merged the two men in their minds (as we saw PC Lamb do) or Johnston's examination was more thorough than he let on at the inquest and may, in fact, have involved moving the body to get at the left hand.

In any event, what is important to us here is what the two members saw – or did not see – in Stride's hands when they were opened. Given the wealth of testimony we have from those who were much closer to the body than either Diemshitz or Kozebrodski and who afforded it much closer attention, we can accept as fact that Stride was not holding grapes at the time she was murdered. Nor did the two clubmen knowingly tell a mistruth. What they saw from the distance of a yard or more and in scant light was the red bloodstains left on Stride's right hand by Edward Johnston. Given that her hands were "tightly clenched" and when opened revealed dark, liquid stains, it's understandable how either Diemshitz or Kozebrodski mistook this for grape juice, or even the "oblong clots" as actual grapes. The presence of the cachous in the other hand would even have suggested such a possibility.

These imaginary grapes were likely the conclusion of one man who suggested it to the other. Soon this was spread around to others observing at the crime scene[71] and then to the press, and a myth was born.

We'll now construct a timeline of each person to examine the body in Dutfield's Yard:

1:00am: Louis Diemshitz discovers the body and runs into the club. Within seconds, he, Isaac Kozebrodski, Morris Eagle (who was too weak in stomach to take notice of the corpse), and others are in the yard and on their way to find the police. No one is known to have touched the body.

1:05am (approx.): Edward Spooner arrives and lifts chin of deceased, noting wound to throat. He testified at the inquest that he saw a "piece of paper double up in her right hand [sic – left], and some red and white flowers pinned on her breast." In response to questions from Coroner Baxter, Spooner testified that there was no blood on Stride's chin and that he did not get any on his hands. He did not attempt to feel for a pulse and made no mention of having seen blood on either hand. He remained near the body until the arrival of PC Lamb and stated he saw no one touch it during that time.

1:10am (approx.): PC Henry Lamb arrives on scene. A crowd gathered around him and attracts his attention from the body. His examination was brief but he felt the deceased's face and right wrist. He did not come into contact with blood.

1:12am (approx.): Edward Johnston arrives and by the light of a constable's lantern, proceeds to examine the body. This was witnessed by Abraham Ashbrigh, Louis Diemshitz and Isaac Kozebrodski, among others. He unfastened Stride's dress at the neck and felt around the body, almost certainly getting blood on his hands, and then tried to find a pulse, placing the blood evidence on her hand that no one before saw but that was clearly evident after. This blood also very likely explains away the problem of the sighting of grapes that were, in fact, never there.

1:16am: Dr. Frederick Blackwell arrives and confirms the time by his watch. He takes charge of the body and commences his examination. The following are excerpts from his inquest testimony as reported by the *Daily Telegraph*: "Her dress was unfastened at the neck…The right hand was open and on the chest, and was smeared with blood. The left hand, lying on the ground, was partially closed, and contained a small packet of cachous wrapped in tissue paper…I could not ascertain whether the bloody hand had been moved." Upon being recalled following Dr. Phillips's testimony, Blackwell would be compelled to mention that he had removed the cachous from the victim's left hand, spilled some, and apparently replacement the packet, anticipating Dr. Phillips's arrival.

1:36-1:46am (approx.): Dr. George Bagster Phillips arrives. As divisional surgeon (H Division) he would now have been in charge of the body. The following are excerpts from his inquest testimony, as reported by the *Daily Telegraph*: "The left arm was extended from the elbow, and a packet of cachous was in the hand. Similar ones were in the gutter. I took them from the hand and gave them to Dr. Blackwell. The right arm was lying over the body, and the back of the hand and wrist had on them clotted blood…there were small oblong clots on the back of the hand… neither on the hands nor about the body of the deceased did I find grapes, or connection with them. I am convinced that the deceased had not swallowed either the skin or seed of a grape within many hours of her death.[72]

This timeline should hopefully clear up any confusion about who said what and when and demonstrate how all the misconceptions regarding the mythical grapes in Stride's hand came about. It's important to address and dispel once and for all the idea of a police conspiracy occurring over the alleged grapes. After the two private detectives (Le Grand & Batchelor) hired by the Whitechapel Vigilance Committee brought forth Matthew Packer and their bloody grape stalk, the *Evening News* published its sensational story, taking bows for having discovered a clue the police missed and erroneously informing its readers – in the boldest manner possible – that the police never bothered to question Packer. The police rightly responded by issuing statements dismissing Packer's utterings as unreliable and flat out denying the presence of any grapes in or around Stride's person. Naysayers point to Diemshitz's earlier press statements and his alleged conflicting inquest testimony where he stated "I did not notice what position her hands were in" and see this as evidence that the police were saving face by downplaying the supposed clue and that Diemshitz was compelled to play along.

Of course, this was not the case. Diemshitz was not denying having seen what was in the hands after they were opened, he simply could not say what position they were in before Johnston's arrival. In any event, Dr. Blackwell's Oct. 1st statement to the press effectively blows any idea of a police cover-up out of the water: "I should say that as the woman had held sweets in her left hand that her head was dragged back by means of a silk handkerchief she wore round her neck, and her throat was then cut. One of her hands, too, was smeared with blood, so she may have used this in her rapid struggle." Not only do these words from Dr. Blackwell, spoken within 24 hours of the murder, prove that no grapes were in her hand, but they also illustrate how crucial and often times difficult it is to separate genuine evidence from red herrings in an historical investigation.

It is remarkable to think that the entire grape debacle, which is still a popular topic of discussion almost 120 years later, likely started because Edward Johnston carelessly transferred blood from Stride's neck to her hand.

In any case, I would submit, based on the foregoing, that: a) no grapes or grape stalks were found on Stride's person; b) Diemshitz did not lie about seeing grapes but was merely mistaken; c) The blood on Stride's hands was a result of transference during Edward Johnston's examination, and c) the police in this instance at least should be absolved of any attempted cover-up.

AUTHOR'S NOTE: This piece originally appeared in the 25th issue (Jan. 2006) of *Ripper Notes* magazine, under the editorship of Dan Norder. It came about because Dan found an image of grapes he was quite fond of and wanted to include on the journal's glossy cover. He asked me to come up with something relating to the grapes in Berner Street. He had no idea what he was in for. As it happened, I was somewhat obsessed with researching the murder of Liz Stride at the time and was happy to take him up on his offer. The plan was to write a brief piece about Matthew Packer, but upon my reconsideration of the role of private investigator Charles Le Grand must have played, as well as the problems inherent in the witness testimony regarding the grapes, the brief article soon turned into a lengthy essay consuming one-fourth of the issue's 100 pages. And there was enough material left over for me to confidently assert that an ongoing series was in order. For our purposes here, the essay has been dramatically shortened and much of the material relating to Charles Le Grand has been taken out. So much new information has come forth since (and largely because of) the original publication of this piece that my next Ripper book will be devoted almost entirely to studying the mystifying facts and lore surrounding Charles Le Grand, and so the repetition of incomplete and in some instances incorrect information from a decade ago seems pointless. What remains, however, is the core of the original essay, and what I consider to be the truth surrounding the Grapes of Myth.

The Berner Street Mystery Part 2

BERNER STREET FIRST appeared on Horwood's map of 1807. At that time it was little more than a cul-de-sac extending south from Church Street and ending at the junction that later became Fairclough Street. The house at 40 Berner Street – where the socialists of the International Working Men's Education Society (IWMES) would later meet and where Elizabeth Stride would be murdered in 1888 – was then the last structure on the street. A large, rectangular garden occupied the space where the Nelson beer house would one day stand. Likely named after Charles Berner, a trustee on the vestry of St. George's-in-the-East, Berner Street would have been a wonderful place to live in the earliest years of the 19th century, surrounded by lush gardens and open fields and quite close (though not yet attached) to the main thoroughfare of Commercial Road.

But this was not to last. The development of the nearby docks demanded quick expansion and renovation. By 1830, Berner Street and the surrounding environs had fully expanded and the future beats of PC Smith & co. had firmly been laid. Sugar was a big import at the time, so bakeries and housing for the workers sprang up everywhere to process the sugar arriving at the docks. By 1860, no less than 23 such bakeries were reported in the parish of St. George's alone. The working conditions in these establishments were quite difficult, so it wasn't long before German immigrants arrived in droves, willing to subject themselves to whatever was asked of them so that they could live in the greatest city in the world. However, even these opportunities were short-lived, as by the 1870s the growth of the French sugar industry pushed London out of competition. The bakeries, one by one, closed their doors, so that by 1888 only a few remained in the East End.[73]

The Board School that served as an important physical landmark in witness statements for the Stride murder was also notable at the time of its construction in 1871. It was the first school built in London after the Forster's Education Act of 1870 established public schooling, in which the government pays for the elementary education of children. The building replaced approximately 20 dwellings on the eastern side of the street, reaching to where Fairclough Street intersected at Berner Street's mid-point, its opposite side occupying the western side of neighboring Berner Street.

Lower Berner Street

Let's examine this area in greater detail, starting in Commercial Road and proceeding in an easterly direction. At 82 Commercial Road we find ourselves standing in front of a sign reading 'Berner Street.' Turing the corner and keeping to the pavement on the western side of the road we first pass a cozy little greengrocer shop at #2 run by an Edward Sumner, who no doubt lost a good deal of business in the months following the murder when the curious crowds flocked to Matthew Packer's store further down the road. Moving on past Sumner's shop we find a small row of five or so bland, brick terraced houses, the entrance into each resembling the famous archway into Miller's Court. Identical houses make up most of the dwellings on this side of the street and almost the entirety of the eastern side of Berner Street leading up to the school.

Passing this short row of houses we arrive at a small lane named Sander Street that cuts off from Berner Street and runs west in a straight line, leading into neighboring Backchurch Lane. The houses here are kept in good condition, the pride of the street being the St. John's Working Men's Club, which seems to have enjoyed a much quieter reputation than another club we'll soon visit. In fact, upon performing his own walk-through of Berner Street and surrounding environs in 1898, Charles Booth (or his representative) noted that Sander Street was 'cleaner than the other streets' and that the St. John's Club sported 'clean windows and doorsteps,' no doubt made possible by the 2d per week subscription required of its members.

Backtracking on Sander Street, walking past St. John's on the south side and re-emerging onto Berner Street, we find ourselves almost at the door of #14, where the Rosenfields lived. Mrs. Rosenfield and her sister, Eva Harstein (whose family resided in Dutfield's Yard at the time[74] became part of the Stride murder investigation by claiming that they saw a grape stalk and rose petals at the crime scene after the body was removed. These statements were obtained – probably by illicit means – by Charles Le Grand, acting as a private investigator in his attempt to add credence to Matthew Packer's tale of having sold grapes to Stride and an unknown man.

Moving on past a few more houses, our noses curl at a pungent odor arising immediately from the east. We pause and look to our left to see a large stable yard across the street. We stand downwind from it only long enough to wonder why Louis Diemshitz rode all the way to George Yard, Cable Street[75] each night to stable his pony when adequate facilities were such a short distance from his home. Perhaps the stable yard proprietor chose not to accept Diemshitz's custom? In any event, we must keep moving along, not only to distance ourselves from the stench of the stables, but because we're about to visit the homes of some familiar figures.

At #28 we find the residence of Nathan and Ester Ashbrigh and their five children. Their eldest son, Abraham, is the young man referred to in the press at the time as 'Hoshberg', 'Heshburg', and 'Heahbury'.[76] The young assertive and seemingly bright Abraham was 17 at the time of Stride's death.

Living next door to the Ashbrighs at #30 were the Letchfords. Charles Letchford walked through Berner Street approximately 30 minutes before Stride's body was discovered and later remarked to the press that his sister was standing out front at 12:50am and had seen and heard nothing. It's often been speculated, even asserted, that his sister was Fanny Mortimer, who lived a few doors down at nearby 36 and had made her own statements to the press. However, we can safely dispose of this notion as Charles was only 22 years of age in 1888, making Fanny 26 years his senior and only 2 years younger than Charles's father, Edward. Most likely, the sister Charles observed standing in front of their home at #30 that evening was either Elizabeth (20) or Ada (15).[77]

Although it appears that Ms. Letchford was standing in front of her door for some time prior to 12:50am, it is a true shame that we don't know the exact time, as she was in a perfect position to witness a man fleeing via all but one of Berner Street's potential escape routes. Directly next to her door would have been the arched entryway into Batty's Gardens, a dark, narrow alleyway that meandered through a row of small cottages and exited into Backchurch Lane, the next street over to the west. Had she been standing at the door and looking straight ahead across the street, she would have been staring at the entrance to another alleyway. Hampshire Court, as it was named, led out into Batty Street, exiting between numbers 22 and 24. Immediately to the left at #22 was the home and office of a certain German laundress who claimed to have been left some shirts by a suspicious foreign man who just may have been a lodger of hers. It has been suggested that this lodger was none other than Francis Tumblety.[78]

Whoever the lodger may have been, it's likely he stepped in front of the Hampshire Court archway to visit the Red Lion pub next door at #24, where some amiable chap was sure to have informed him that not more than three doors down from his lodgings, at 16 Batty Street, a famous murder had taken place the year before. A man living in the attic of that residence was convicted of the murder of a pregnant woman to whom he'd somehow contrived to administer a fatal dose of nitric and sulfuric acid. The young man, Israel Lipski, would eventually confess the crime to his rabbi before being executed.[79]

Having seen enough of Batty Street for the time being, let us slip back through Hampshire Court, returning once again to Berner Street. Emerging onto the pavement, we find the back of the board school just to our left, occupying the rest of the eastern side of the street until it terminates at the Fairclough Street intersection. Immediately to our right are a few small homes and the stable yard we passed earlier. Stepping back across the cobbles, we find ourselves once again at the door of Charles Letchford. But we must not linger as we have much more to see.

Continuing our walk south along the street we pass by #36, the home of 48 year-old Fanny Mortimer, her husband, William (a carman and a year her senior), and their four children. One door past them at #38 lives Mr. and Mrs. Barnett Kentorrich, whose lives were occasionally made intolerable by the goings-on at the socialist club next door.

The club is an old (even for 1888) three-story brick building plastered with flyers, some in English, and some in Yiddish. A large sign in front informs us that this is the home of the International Working Men's Educational Society. The flyers argue that socialism is a necessity for London's Jews, even at the expense of their religious traditions. A fellow by the name of Morris Eagle will be leading a talk on that subject tonight. Adjoining the club is a passageway into the yard. It's far too dark to see anything past the two wooden gates, which are tall and open inward to the passage. It was here, just a couple of yards in front of us, that Liz Stride met her death. The area will require closer scrutiny, so we will return to the yard for a closer examination after our tour of Berner Street is complete.

Pulling ourselves away from the site and moving on, we find ourselves standing at the door of Matthew Packer's greengrocer shop. Just to our right is a window from which he and his wife, Rose Ann, conduct a good portion of their business. Right now the shutters are closed, but when open, a healthy selection of fresh fruit is to be seen on display at prices that, while generally out of reach of homeless unfortunates, were quite affordable to the average employed East Ender. Packer's residence at #44 was a larger building with multiple dwellings. No less than four families (including Matthew and Rose Ann) lived there in 1891.

Turning around to face the board school once again, we might expect to find children tumbling out at the end of the school day, most of them Jewish and surprisingly clean and well dressed in hats and boots and certainly not wanting for food. At least that's the scene Charles Booth encountered upon his trek through Berner Street.

Business at the Nelson beer house would be picking up around this time. At the inquest into Stride's death, a juryman noted that the Nelson generally closed at 9pm. Matthew Packer, in various statements, mentioned that the 'pub' closed at midnight. While the Nelson was only licensed to sell beer and not hard liquor, and thus was not exactly a pub, it could have been referred to as such by neighbors. However, Packer may have been referring to the George IV pub further down the street. In either case, the Nelson was certainly closed for business well before Stride was murdered. If we were to go inside the Nelson, we'd likely find the proprietor, Louis Hagens, hard at work behind the counter. One wonders if he was working late on the night of Strides death...and if he smoked a pipe.

Standing at the main doors of the Nelson and looking out at the intersection, we find the ever-present Board School to the east and, in the southeast, a private residence with a gas lamp attached to its wall. It's previously been stated that this was the closest lamp to the murder site. A photograph recently discovered by researcher Rob Clack, however, shows a lamp over the entryway to Batty's Gardens. The photo was taken in about 1909, but an 1873 map of the area confirms that the lamp was present at that time as well. It was therefore the closest one to the entrance of Dutfield's Yard, but it was still too far away to have helped illuminate the murder scene.

Upper Berner Street

Turning our attention to the southwest, we walk across the cobbles of Fairclough Street and end up standing at the door of Henry Norris's chandler shop, witness James Brown's favorite spot when he fancied a late night supper. Norris's shop at #48 marked the start of what had, in years past, been known as Upper Berner Street, stretching from the Fairclough Street intersection and running about 110 yards in a straight line until Berner Street meets its end at Ellen Street.

Moving on past the chandler shop we come to a row of ten houses, identical to all others on the street. The next to last in this particular row, #64, belonged to witness William Marshall. Standing right outside his door on the night of the murder, 47 year-old Marshall had watched a woman he later believed to be Liz Stride walk with a man down the street in front of him. Marshall heard the man tell the woman, "You would say anything but your prayers," to which she laughed. This occurred around 11:45pm and Marshall remained outside until about midnight. The couple did not enter the George IV pub, only two doors down from Marshall at #68, but instead passed it and headed towards Ellen Street.

The George IV pub, owned and operated by Edmund Farrows, stands on the corner of Berner Street and Boyd Street, another lane like Sander Street that detours west towards Backchurch Lane. Although there appears to have been no one who witnessed Stride inside the George IV, the fact that we have reports of her cuddling with a man only five doors down from it might be an indication that she was soliciting men as they left the pub. Stepping across Boyd Street to the adjacent corner, we find ourselves at the door of #70, a bakery owned by Louis Friedman. In the 1891 census this address is listed as the residence of Maurice Kosminski (the 1895 office directly has the name as 'Morris Kozminski'[80]), a baker, who either managed the shop for Friedman or had purchased it from him outright. If the former, then it is possible Kosminski was a resident here in 1888. Of course, even if this were shown to be so it would likely be inconsequential, as there appears to be no reason to think this man was anything but one of many people who shared a surname with a known suspect.

Moving on now past the baker we pass another row of five houses before coming to Everard Street – a short lane identical in proportions to Boyd Street that also fed into Backchurch Lane. Stepping across the Everard intersection, we are only a few yards away from where Berner Street disappears into Ellen Street. As we reach Berner Street's last corner, we find ourselves outside a small chemist shop. This nondescript little store at #82 belonged to an elderly chemist named John Simkin.

On Saturday, Sept. 8th, Simkin and his daughter had gone downstairs to man the shop. No doubt during the course of the day they learned of the gruesome murder of Annie Chapman. They were probably still discussing this tragedy when a man named William Seaman walked in, asking for some ointment and alum. As Simkin turned to retrieve the items, Seaman brandished a hammer and repeatedly beat the man upside the head. Simkin's daughter, thinking on her feet, ran outside and gained the attention of a passerby who apprehended Seaman and held him until the arrival of police. Simkin almost died from his injuries, but after a slow recovery, he was able to return home. Seaman admitted never having seen Simkin before and offered no motive for his crime.

That concludes our tour of Berner Street, but we are far from finished. It is now time for us to return to where Liz Stride met her end and see if we can't make a little sense of an otherwise senseless crime.

Inside Dutfield's Yard

Stepping up to the gates leading into Dutfield's Yard, we find them to be quite large. They reach as high as the club sign on the front of the building and are approximately 9'2" across, each gate door 4'6" individually. Stenciled in white along the top of the gates are the names of Walter H. Hindley & Co., sack manufacturers, and Arthur Dutfield, van and cart builder. Built into the right gate[81] is a door made of wicker to allow foot traffic into and out of the yard when the gates are closed. But the gates are often left open.

Walking between them we step into a passageway about 10ft. wide and 57 ft. long, paved in irregular stones. To our left is the windowless, two-story northern wall of #42, and to our right is the three-story southern wall of the club, which is plastered with posters – many of them in Yiddish – advertising the club and its events. About six feet in on the right, on the wall near the ground, is an iron grate opening from the cellar of the club. From behind the swing of the gate and running 18-20ft. along the wall is a crude gutter walled with rough and jagged rocks. The gutter terminates at a short set of steps leading up to the side door of the club.

Standing on the steps and turning around we see the back of #42 on the other side of the passage. Where #42 ends, the passage widens out a bit, and tucked into the shadows are two lavatories. Following these is an old house converted into a row of three white-washed cottages. Above the side door of the club is a fanlight – a half-circle of decorative glass that would pass light from indoors but which is barely sufficient to light the steps in front of the door. The fanlight may have extended down along each side of the door frame. Contrary to many modern sources and a couple of contemporary claims, there may have been no ground floor window at the side of the club that would allow for a view down the passage to the murder site.[82] Just past the steps, on the first floor (second floor to Americans), there was a window looking out from the lecture room onto the cottages opposite. This, and the light filtering from the cottages themselves, would have been the only significant light source facing the passage. It would have been useless in illuminating the area where the murder was committed.

Moving on past the door and the cottages, the yard opens up widely on the right. On the left side the cottages give way to the workshop of Hindley & Co. that stretches along the back of the yard, facing the wooden gates. It is likely that a recess existed between the last cottage and Hindley's shop and that dust bins rested here. Next to these shops are some unused stables.

The existence of these stables once again prompts one to wonder why Diemshitz stabled his pony in George Yard. One possible explanation is that, being in the overcrowded and impoverished East End, people might have used the stables as residences. Another possibility is suggested in the book *Beyond the Horizon*, the 1944 memoirs of IWMES member Thomas Eyges. Eyges describes attending small meetings in "an upper story over a barn, the entrance to which was up a ladder through a trap door." Eyges, writing more than 50 years after the fact, may have confused meetings he attended in the stable with others in the club building itself. Otherwise, it seems peculiar that he would refer to a three-story brick club house as "an old wooden two-story building." Unfortunately, Eyge's erroneous description of the club still appears on web sites and occasionally in books on the murders. The loft being used as a secret meeting place might also explain why police investigating the Stride murder found it to be locked on the inside, suggesting a second route of escape in case of police raid.

The entire right side of the yard was occupied by the club itself as well as two small separate buildings that comprised the offices of *Der Arbeter Fraint* (the Worker's Friend). This small, weekly anarchist paper was printed in Yiddish and edited by Philip Krantz, who was in this office at the time of the murder. The club and all outlying structures surrounded an open courtyard. Three windows from the first floor lecture room, where most of the members were, faced this back courtyard.

The Scene of the Crime

Now that we've seen the murder site as clearly as time will allow, let us consider how Stride and her killer would have known it at approximately 12:55am on the morning of Sept. 30th, 1888.

One of the most problematic aspects of the murder for modern researchers is its proximity to so much activity. Antonio Sironi, in an essay published in the October 2004 edition of *Ripper Notes*[83] argues not only that Dutfield's Yard was the most daring of the canonical five murder sites but that its very precariousness indicates that all did not go as Stride's killer had planned. Sironi suggests that her killer (whom he believed to be Jack the Ripper) had chosen either a location further into the yard or in another dark corner elsewhere on Berner Street. He argued that Stride must have resisted, forcing the killer to take care of matters on the spot and flee without performing his typical mutilations.

Other commentators prefer the idea that the victims lured themselves to the slaughter. Some use this to conclude that Stride could not have been a Ripper victim, arguing that a prostitute would not have chosen a spot where foot traffic was so frequent and the prospect of discovery was almost assured. This, some suggest, is a strong point in favor of the domestic crime theory that places Stride's estranged (and certainly strange) beau, Michael Kidney, at the forefront of suspicion.

In truth, the spot where Stride was murdered was the safest spot in the entire yard for a killer on the move and, it can be said, the Stride murder site was less precarious than those of Annie Chapman or Mary Kelly. No doubt many will consider that a bold statement, and perhaps it is, but when the scene is considered in detail – and in contrast with Kelly's and Chapman's – the evidence itself supports this conclusion.

First, it should be said that all the murder sites in the series, 'canonical' or otherwise, were quite precarious. The killer (or killers) showed a remarkable amount of daring. Whether or not you believe that the Ripper scouted and selected his murder sites in advance, he would surely have known that a great amount of luck would be required for him to get away without capture and, if possible, without even being seen.

In the case of Annie Chapman's murder at the back of 29 Hanbury Street, the Ripper was working in front of a high wall of windows, and behind each of these were individuals who at any moment could peer out and see him in action. If Chapman's commonly accepted time of death is correct[84] the location was especially dangerous. There were 17 people about to start their day while the Ripper crouched with bloodied hands between them and their water closets. To the killer's immediate right and just on the other side of a fence, Albert Cadosch was tending to his personal business, going back and forth between his house and loo. Assuming that the conversation Cadosch overheard was between Chapman and her killer, there can be little doubt but that the Ripper heard the noise Cadosch made going in and out of doors – and yet he persevered. If we dispose of the unlikely proposition that Jack - like his mythical spring-heeled predecessor - made good his getaway by hopping fences and running through yards, we're left with only one exit from the scene of the crime: the passageway through which he and Chapman had entered.

One point in the Ripper's favor was that he (or Chapman) had been very wise in selecting the murder spot. It was the one location in the yard that would have worked to his advantage if he had been interrupted. To enter the yard one would have had to open a door that swung outward and towards the left. Almost the entirety of the yard would be immediately visible, with one exception: the area where the open door and steps created a recess between themselves and the wooden fence that separated #29 from Cadosch's yard. Chapman was murdered and mutilated in this location. From this vantage point the Ripper would have been aware of anyone entering the yard before he could be spotted by them. Three steps led from the doorway to the pavement of the yard, and someone coming upon the scene would have probably reached the third step – or even the ground if he were moving quickly – before the door closed and the gruesome sight came fully into view. At the opening of the door or the sound of approaching footsteps, the Ripper would have been poised to strike and run.

Even with that point in his favor, the Ripper left himself open to risk. If more than one individual had entered the yard at the same time they could have more easily captured him, and a witness coming upon the scene might have seen him well enough to identify him later.

The situation that the Ripper faced at 13 Miller's Court was in some ways more private but in other ways even more risky. The locked room prevented entry from casual passersby and Mary Kelly had likely assured him there was no chance of interruption – an assurance the evidence of his aftermath tells us he took for granted. On the other hand, he was inside a locked room. If acquaintances had come to call on Kelly they would first knock on the door. This would alert the Ripper to their presence, but he would be standing there covered in blood. His only chance for escape would be if they satisfied themselves that Kelly was not at home and went away. But if an acquaintance knew of the broken window panes and peered inside, as Thomas Bowyer later did, the Ripper's proverbial goose would have been cooked. An alarm would have been raised and a crowd might have blocked the Ripper's only escape route. Even if he managed to flee through the door while the visitor was at the side of the house peering in the window, a blood-covered (and possibly naked) man would not get very far in Dorset Street at the height of the Ripper hysteria.

Let's now reconsider the murder of Elizabeth Stride in Dutfield's Yard with these considerations in mind.

Imagine you're standing in the passageway next to the club, a couple of yards in from the gate, and leaning up against the right wall. The spot where you are standing is almost pitch black, but further up the yard there's light coming from the window on the middle floor and from the cottages across from it. The side door of the club is slightly open, but this may not even be visible to you, as any light coming through is pointing away from you. If someone were to step out of one of the cottages, or exit from the club's side door, he or she would be in silhouette from the light streaming from inside and would be quite visible. In the darkness you would be hidden. A quick sprint to your left (or right, if facing the wall) is the pavement and then the street. If someone were to come out of the club or cottages, you'd be through the gateway and out of the neighborhood before the body was found and an alarm raised. At most, you'd be remembered as the sound of hurried steps or a dark blur as you disappeared around the corner.

On the other hand, if you had gone further into the yard and behind the club, you'd be a great distance from your exit. You'd also have to contend with the light coming from three large windows in back of the building and the club members who could look out through them. There are also the people living in the cottages just to your left who might be in position to block your getaway should they become aware of your presence. And what of the light coming through the window of one of the small buildings just to your right? Someone must be about in there (Philip Krantz, burning the midnight oil on the next edition of his propaganda rag).

As we can see, the Ripper (or Stride) was quite smart in selecting a private location.

We'll now turn to the inquest coverage in various newspapers to determine, with as much accuracy as history will allow, the precise spot within the passage that Stride's body occupied.

Taking the various witnesses into consideration, I decided that the most reliable would be those who viewed the body prior to Dr. Blackwell, whose assistant, Edward Johnston, almost certainly perjured himself when he said he didn't move the body at all. Compare Dr. Blackwell's evidence in any of the papers to that of the other witnesses and you'd think he was describing a different crime scene altogether. This leaves us with Louis Diemshitz, Isaac Kozebrodski, PC Henry Lamb, and Mr. Johnston. Diemshitz and Kozebrodski, by their own admission, paid little attention to the corpse after noting the river of blood running from its neck. Johnston's evidence was something I decided I did not want to rely on, but then all he had offered relating to the matter at hand was that "the knees were nearer to the wall than the head." This leaves us with PC Lamb as the most reliable source for information on the position and location of Stride's body.

Not only was Lamb a policeman, but he spent a considerable amount of time in the presence of the body. Indeed, a study of his inquest statement as reported by the various newspapers leads to a very enlightening conclusion. The *Daily News* reporter chose not to include any mention of the discussion between PC Lamb and Coroner Baxter regarding the precise location of Stride's body. The *Daily Telegraph* touches upon it by quoting that "the feet of the deceased extended just to the swing of the gate, so that the barrier could be closed without disturbing the body." The *Times*, in what might be considered an exception to the rule, actually provides the fullest account in the form of the actual exchange on this point between coroner and witness:

Baxter: Did anyone say whether the body had been touched?

Lamb: No. Dr. Blackwell examined the body, and afterwards the surrounding ground. Dr. Phillips arrived about 20 minutes afterwards; but at that time I was at another part of the ground. Inspector Pinhorn arrived directly after the doctor arrived. When I got there I had the gates shut.

Baxter: But did not the feet of the deceased touch the gate?

Lamb: No. They went just behind it, and I was able to close the gates without disturbing the body.

Lamb's testimony offers a revealing clue. In fact, it is probably the single most significant clue we have in determining exactly where Stride and her killer were standing at the moment of her death. As there was absolutely no sign of struggle, and Stride's knees were buckled and near to the wall, we can say with confidence that she fell where she was killed. Lamb's testimony that her feet were behind the gate (*Times*), or just to the swing of the gate (*Daily Telegraph*), seems on the outset a little vague – were her feet literally tucked between the gate and the wall or did Lamb simply mean that when he closed the gate it breezed past the foot, almost, but not quite, touching it? Given that her knees were described as buckled and pointing towards the wall, the soles of her feet would then be pointing the other direction and could not have been hidden behind the gate.

The proximity of Stride's head and knees to the wall tells us she was standing face first against the wall when she collapsed. In doing so, her knees would bow out and against the wall, forcing her feet to slip out of position beneath her as she fell. This would move her feet from their original standing position, but would nevertheless provide a solid indicator of where she was standing prior to the fatal attack. If we were to straighten her buckled knees and stand her up into the position she had been in when attacked, we'd likely find her face first against the wall standing behind the right door of the gate.

This hypothesis, arrived at by the best available evidence, strongly conflicts with the post-modernist view that Stride was not a Ripper victim. For one, it disposes of the notion that Stride and her killer stood for all to view in the open passageway. It instead places them behind the relative privacy of a large gate door. The *Star* of Oct. 1st tells us that the wicker walkthrough door was affixed to this very gate. This would allow anyone hiding behind it to see out, but because of the sheer darkness in the recess, no one on the other side could see in with a casual glance. Images of the gate at the time tell us that they were flat against the walls of numbers 40 and 42 when fully opened. It is probable that Diemshitz upon entering with his cart would have noticed that the gate was not all the way to the wall had anyone been trying to hide behind it. Because he did not mention such a thing, we might presume that no one was behind the gate when he entered. It's worth noting, however, that Diemshitz himself was of the opinion that he had interrupted the killer and that he could have still been in the yard at the time. If the Ripper were still with the body when Diemshitz arrived he could have moved close up against the wall, making his presence far less obvious. When Diemshitz left, the wicker door in the gate would have enabled an easy escape.

With Stride behind the gate at the time of attack the actual murder spot was quite in keeping with the Ripper's method of operation up to that point. The murder site greatly resembles that of 29 Hanbury Street where the Ripper and his victim stood in a recess next to the only available exit, partially obscured by a door. The gates of Dutfield's Yard also bore a striking resemblance to those of the stable yard on Buck's Row in front of which Polly Nichols was murdered. In contrast, the Hanbury Street location was more dangerous to the killer, as he was a further distance from the street and anyone stepping into the yard would quickly be aware of him. In the case of Stride, someone could walk through the passage and be completely unaware of his presence.

It must also be said that the evidence from PC Lamb greatly challenges the notion of a domestic crime of opportunity in which Michael Kidney stumbled upon the woman who had recently abandoned him and murdered her in a blind rage. The location of the murder certainly indicates the attempt for privacy, and the notion that Kidney himself would have thought of such a spot is almost as absurd as the suggestion that Stride would have lured him there herself to be brutalized. However, even if we accept the likelihood that Stride was killed by a prospective client, or at least someone other than Michael Kidney, this alone does not prove that the man was the Ripper and not a copycat.

Is it possible after all this time to determine whether Stride was a Ripper victim? Perhaps not with absolute certainty or to the satisfaction of everyone, but I do believe that a thorough reconsideration of the evidence would help. An answer to the question of whether or not Stride met Jack the Ripper may just lie…

In the Palm of her Hand

You will not learn the name of Stride's killer in this section. I will leave that for someone more qualified than myself to unveil. Instead, our quest is to let the evidence reveal the most likely way in which Jack the Ripper approached his victims and assured their silence. First, we'll consider a short list of evidence agreed upon as reliable by most Ripper scholars:

- There were no visible signs of struggle between Stride and her killer.
- Between the thumb and forefinger of her left hand she held many pieces of cachous wrapped lightly in a thin piece of tissue paper. None are thought to have been spilled in the course of her murder.
- Not one of the many people nearby heard any noise from the passage. That is not to say that no sound was made but simply that none was heard.
- On Stride's front side below each shoulder blade there were 'pressure marks' that progressively became more visible in the hours and days following the murder.
- The scarf she wore around her neck was pulled quite tightly to her right.
- Apart from the wound to her throat, Stride was not interfered with in any way by her killer, and there was no attempt at further mutilation.
- The blood evidence indicates that Stride was not standing when her throat was cut.

There are two ways to view these pieces of evidence. The first is to see them as mysteries, problems, or hurdles to be overcome in seeking a solution – a common view over the years, resulting in an unfortunate state of confusion. The second option – the one which we'll adopt for our purposes here – is to view this evidence as a series of helpful clues that in and of themselves reveal the truth of what happened that night.

It was unanimous among those who witnessed Stride's body *in situ* that her clothes had not been disturbed and that there were no signs of a struggle. The medical evidence tells us that no signs of strangulation, smothering, head trauma, drugs, or any other detectable means were discovered to explain Stride's subjugation.

There was equal unanimity among those present in the club and living nearby that no sounds of a struggle or screaming were heard. While it is just possible that Stride did cry out but was not heard, the weight of the evidence indicates that Stride was caught unawares and made no attempt to defend herself or call for help. The problem inherent in this for investigators, then and now, is how the Ripper maneuvered her so peacefully onto the ground before slicing her throat. The lack of blood to the front of her clothes, or any arterial spray on the walls, eliminate the possibility that her fatal wound was inflicted while she stood upright. Yet she was not strangled, was not drugged, and was not hit over the head.

To answer this we'll first consider what Dr. Blackwell told the inquest jury about Stride's scarf. In comparing Blackwell's testimony on this point I found all the papers to be in agreement on the details. The *Daily Telegraph* reported that 'the deceased had round her neck a check silk scarf, the bow of which was turned to the left and pulled very tight. In the neck there was a long incision which exactly corresponded the lower border of the scarf. The border was slightly frayed, as if by a sharp knife.'

It is important to pause here and consider Blackwell's words. He is not saying, as has sometimes been reported, that the scarf was pulled from the left, but instead that the bow or knot was turned to Stride's left side and was pulled in tightly to her flesh. For this to happen the killer had to pull with force inward to himself while Stride's weight shifted the opposite direction. In short, as Stride lay on her left side, her killer stood to her right and above her as he pulled the scarf tight.

Following this piece of evidence, Blackwell was asked by a juryman if he could say whether Stride's throat was cut before or after she had fallen to the ground. This time, not all the papers agreed on the answer. The *Times* reported that Blackwell said, "I formed the opinion that the murderer first took hold of the silk scarf, at the back of it, and then pulled the deceased backwards, but I cannot say whether the throat was cut while the woman was standing or after she was pulled backwards." Thanks to other news reports we can rest assured that in this instance the *Times* had it wrong and that Dr. Blackwell was nowhere near this ignorant of the blood evidence. For example, the Oct 3rd edition of the *Daily Telegraph* quoted Dr. Blackwell as noting that "…the blood would have spurted about if the act had been committed while she was standing up." The *St. James Gazette* of the same day reported his answer to this question in the greatest detail:

> In reply to a juryman, who asked whether he could give any information as to whether the throat was cut while the woman was lying down or standing up, the doctor said: I formed the opinion that probably the murderer took hold of the silk scarf, which was tightly knotted, and pulled the woman backwards, and cut her throat in that way. The position of the blood would indicate that her throat was cut when she was lying down or as she fell. It is, perhaps, most probable that she was on the ground first before her throat was cut.

Dr. Blackwell is correct in observing that had Stride been standing erect when her throat was cut, the wall in front of her would have been stained, yet no such stains were found. He leaves us with two possibilities: that her killer pulled back on the scarf and cut her throat as she fell, or that he waited until she was prostrate on the ground before cutting. Understandably, Blackwell favors the latter.

Yet, despite the inherent logic in supposing that Stride was already on the ground before her throat was cut, some believe there is good reason to consider the alternative.

Blackwell describes the scarf as pulled "very tightly" against Stride's throat. It must have been so for the knife blade to follow its course, fraying it in the process. This rules out the possibility that she was cut while standing erect or that she was lying prostrate on her back. Therefore, some researchers argue, the wound must have been inflicted as Stride was falling to the ground. This is possible, but would have been physically difficult and improbable, considering it requires a good amount of physical force and stability to slice a knife deep into human flesh. But if we're to consider this possibility, we have to consider why it might have been that Stride was falling in the first place. One possibility is that she was overcome with fear and disoriented by the darkness and simply fainted. Another possibility is that when her killer pulled on her scarf she lost her balance and fell, and her killer took advantage of the situation and silenced her quickly, already having hold of the scarf in his left hand. That her sense of balance might have been compromised is supported by Dr. Phillips's observation of "a deformity in the lower fifth of the bones of the right leg, which are not straight, but bow forward."[85] He also noted that on the left leg there was a thickening in the bones above the ankle. With both legs affected in such a way, walking may have been difficult for Liz. Indeed, her well-known nickname of 'Long Liz' – a play on the surname Stride – might have been informed by a long gate brought about by her compromised legs.

However, if Liz fell but was otherwise conscious and felt her life was in danger, we might expect that investigators would have seen clear signs of a struggle. But she still held delicate cachous in her hand, wrapped in thin tissue paper, and only her left side was caked in mud, showing she did not roll, crawl, or try to kick herself free. In fact, she came to rest with her head over one of the jagged stones that comprised the make-shift gutter, a particularly large stone, and yet there was no impact injury to her head. The collected evidence forces the conclusion that she was unconscious at the time she was laid down on her left side and her throat was cut. She was not strangled, nor drugged, nor knocked upon the head, and the idea (occasionally suggested) that her breathing had been sufficiently restricted merely by the tightening of her scarf is simply untenable. The scarf would not have been of the thick woolen variety we wear today during the coldest of nights, but a more decorative scarf of much thinner material. This leaves us with one viable option, aside from the convenient fainting of his victim, to consider as the killer's method of subduing Liz Stride, and that is 'garroting' by arm, or 'carotid chokehold' (described in detail in Chapter 7 of The Buck's Row Murder). As this mysterious method of quietly subduing a victim without leaving the tell-tale marks of strangulation is present not only in the Berner Street murder but in the earlier murder of Polly Nichols, it's yet one more forensic link tying the Stride murder to the murders unanimously attributed to Jack the Ripper.

Following publication of my first book, where I discussed 'garroting' in depth, I've since done more research and learned that today it's commonly called the 'carotid choke hold' by medical examiners. Viewers of the TV show 24 will be quite familiar with this method, regularly employed by character Jack Bauer, to render someone unconscious. The choke hold often leaves no visible bruising or damage in the way that manual strangulation will, but will sometimes leave its mark in the form of a bruise on the back of the neck, one over each shoulder.

We will now consider the 'pressure marks' found on Stride. Dr. Phillips described them as a 'bluish discolouration.' Dr. Blackwell made a point of saying that pressure marks are not the same as bruises which are the result of blunt force. What he means here is that for pressure marks to appear there must be constant applied pressure for an appropriate amount of time. Depending on the individual this would need only be a few seconds for others it may take as long as a minute. Dr. Phillips, as recorded by the *Times*, tells us: "Over both shoulders, especially the right, and under the collar-bone and in front of the chest there was a bluish discolouration…" It's not clear if 'under the collar bone' and 'in front of the chest' describes the same bruise or not, but we'll not concern ourselves with this just yet. What is of interest is the bruising he describes appearing over both shoulders. Dr. Blackwell, when questioned by a juryman, speculated that the shoulder bruising might have been caused by 'two hands pressing on the shoulders'; this is possible, but such bruising also lends itself to a chokehold, whereas two hands pushing down does not render a person unconscious and would presumably have dirtied her dress at the knees (she was not so soiled). It's also worth noting that Blackwell contradicted Phillips about the extent of the marks to Stride's right shoulder, informing the jury that 'each shoulder was about equally marked.'

The overriding question is, of course, whether or not these marks had anything to do with her murder. Just such a thought occurred to the jury. They put forth to Dr. Blackwell the question of how recently the marks might have been caused. He offered the non-committal response of "That is rather difficult to say." Fortunately, elsewhere in his testimony he affords us a clue, remarking that "at first they were very obscure, but subsequently they became very evident." Dr. Phillips had likewise become intrigued by the marks, informing the coroner that from Oct. 1st through the 3rd he'd seen the marks appear and followed their progress, observing them subsequently on two occasions, though offering no information beyond this.

Today this would be recognized as ante-mortem bruising, or bruises caused around the time of death that don't become apparent until afterwards. The web site of the University of Dundee's Department of Forensic Medicine[86] offers the following information:

> Gravitational shifting of deep bruises may result in their appearance at the skin surface being delayed. The more superficial the source of bleeding, the sooner the discolouration will be apparent on the skin surface. Deep bruises may require as long as 12 or 24 hours to become apparent and some may never do so. In a living victim, a second examination after an interval of one or two days may disclose bruising where previously there had been only swelling or tenderness on pressure. Similarly, in the dead, a further examination one or two days after the original autopsy may disclose bruises which were not previously evident as well as revealing more distinctly bruises which previously appeared faint. This may be particularly the case with 'fingerpad bruises' produced by handgrips.

The paper goes on to caution:

> It is not possible to distinguish a bruise sustained at the time of death from one which occurred some minutes earlier: such bruises are best described as having occurred at or about the time of death.

This being the case, Dr. Blackwell was perfectly correct in stating that he couldn't be certain as to when the bruises were left, and even now the best we can say is that they were inflicted some time on the evening of her death. The chest bruise may have been caused by the jagged stones of the yard's pathway, or perhaps she bruised it earlier in the day while cleaning the lodging house; or perhaps it was caused by the butt of her killer's knife. There might even be an alternate explanation for the shoulder bruising, such as an overzealous client, but the best evidence suggests she was rendered unconscious by a chokehold and the bruises were inflicted during this process.

We now come to the most enigmatic of clues - the cachous (sweet-meats) found wrapped in tissue paper and clenched between the thumb and forefinger in the palm of Liz's left hand. Many suggestions have been put forth to explain their presence: the killer gave them to her to put her at ease; she was freshening her breath in between clients (though the doctors make no mention of her having recently consumed any); or they were placed in her hand by her killer after death. Though mostly plausible, these explanations remain less than satisfying.

I wouldn't dare try to guess at the number of brain cells I burned trying to figure out just how these cachous got into Stride's hand. Yet, like so many things, the closer you look at it the harder it is to see, and so it was when my mind was preoccupied with something totally mundane and unrelated to the Ripper murders that it hit me. I was standing in the line at a grocery store and reached into the pocket of my loose-fitting slacks to obtain some change. When I pulled my hand out and began to sift the coins, I noticed a few bills that were folded together had lodged themselves between my thumb and forefinger; a perfectly natural occurrence that anyone accustomed to carrying money in his or her pockets can relate to. After all, change is flat and heavy and falls to the bottom of the pocket while anything larger will rest above it. Unless you take the time to sift through the pocket, other items will come out with the change.

With this in mind, imagine yourself a Victorian woman with deep, loose pockets. The only money you possess is a few pence. Earlier that evening you purchased or were given a packet of cachous (the fact that the thin tissue paper wrapping the cachous was intact suggests the cachous only recently made it in her possession) and put it in your front pocket. Now, imagine that a man approaches and draws a knife, stating he will kill you where you stand unless you give him your money. If you're like any sane person, you hurriedly grab your money and hold your hand out to him. He takes the money and you drop your hand down to your side, fists clenched, poised for whatever might happen.

This explanation may seem too simple to some and not in keeping with how Jack is most commonly perceived. I believe, however, that the evidence itself compels us to consider that Jack used a ruse of robbery to both assure the silence of his victims while maneuvering them into position and to revel in their fear and his power over them before finally taking their lives. I am not by any means suggesting robbery as a motive for the killings, but simply as a means to an end. After all, robbery was common to denizens of the East End streets and was something they could understand, if not condone. Introducing himself as a mugger and possibly also a rapist, the Ripper could assure his victims' silence as he moved into position with his knife and the women would feel relatively secure that they could escape with their lives by complying.

This is a common psychological ploy used by murderers throughout history, perhaps most notably by Charles Manson in his preparation for the murders of Leno and Rosemary LaBianca. Manson, noting that the massacre at the Polanski house had been chaotic, suggested that this was because the victims knew they were going to die, and with nothing to lose, made every effort to escape. Only because the house was isolated did the brutal goings-on not attract attention. At the LaBianca house, tucked snuggly inside a populated suburban neighborhood, Manson himself went in first and obtained the compliance of the LaBiancas by promising them that if they did only as told, they would escape unscathed. A killer utilizing this maneuver gives his victim the illusion of control. Feeling as though they have control over their own fate provides the victim with a sense of comfort and hope and virtually assures the would-be killer of their compliance. Indeed, many victims of violent crime are compliant to the point of not reporting the incident for fear of their attacker making good on his threat. A robbery/rape approach such as this, if utilized by the Ripper, would explain the relative silence of his murders. It also makes more sense than the perfect stealth with which he is usually attributed.

This hypothesis is lent considerable support by evidence in the other cases attributed to the Ripper. When the body of Catherine Eddowes was discovered shortly following Stride's, a thimble was lying quite out of place next to her right hand, as though she had been gripping it at the time of her murder. In the case of Annie Chapman there are a number of details that suggest a robbery had taken place.

Chapman had been wearing two rings on her left hand, understood by most writers to have been taken by her killer. It is popularly assumed the purloining took place after her death, but certain evidence suggests this is not the case. Dr. Phillips testified at the inquest that he found Chapman's left side to be stiffer than the right, 'particularly the fingers, which were partly closed.' Added to this we have the testimony of James Kent, who was at work only three doors down from 29 Hanbury Street when the man who discovered the body, John Davis, notified him of his find and escorted both he and another man back to view the body. Kent informed the coroner that 'her hands were raised and bent, with the palms towards the upper portion of her body, as though she had fought for her throat.' These descriptions do not indicate that her hand was interfered with after death. Moreover, Dr. Phillips noted that her ring or rings had been removed by force and pointed to an abrasion over the first phalanx of the ring finger – or between her fingernail and first knuckle. Had the Ripper attempted to remove the rings after her death we would expect to find such an abrasion over the second (larger) knuckle, as once over this hurdle the rings would have slid easily past the first phalanx, leaving it unscathed. However, forcefully pulling rings from a frightened, living woman is a different matter altogether, and it should be remembered that Dr. Phillips never suggested the rings had been removed after her death.

It is also generally supposed that Chapman's killer emptied her pockets and arranged the items by her body, but here's another scenario: The killer holds her at knife point and demands money. Chapman resists, possibly proclaiming that she has no money, so the killer demands she empty her pockets. She does this and brings out one or two handfuls of items from her pockets. In her right hand Chapman likely held the portion of envelope containing pills; in her left she have held the muslin and the comb. The Ripper would have taken what he wanted (if there was anything) and knocked the other items out of her hand, or picked them up and dropped them himself.

Dr. Phillips testified that the muslin and comb were 'lying at the feet of the woman near the paling' of the fence. This means that Chapman was either standing with her back to the fence or (more likely) standing upright at about the same spot her feet ended up resting on in the yard, with her left side towards the fence. Items dropped from her left hand while standing in either position would result in them landing in precisely the spot Dr. Phillips indicated. As any two objects dropped will land in a straight line (or on top of each other), it's difficult to understand how Phillips concluded the muslin and comb had been "arranged" there. As for the torn envelope found near Chapman's head, this likely fell into place as or after she was placed on the ground, much like the thimble with Eddowes.

Moving backwards in time to the murder of Mary Ann Nichols, we find reports that there were marks on her fingers where rings had been, but that they were removed without struggle. This is perfectly consistent with the robbery scenario and is in fact the first of four successive murders in which items were either missing from the victim, found next to the hand, or both.

In short, Stride's cachous, Eddowes' thimble, the items surrounding Chapman, and Nichols's missing rings are direct crime scene evidence that, while superfluous to the murders themselves, suggest some activity prior to each murder, almost certainly robbery. This not only offers the most likely explanation for how silence was encouraged with the victims but also argues against the theory that one or more of the four victims were felled by the hand of a copycat.

AUTHOR'S NOTE: 'A Murder in the Neighborhood' originally appeared in the 27th issue of *Ripper Notes* (2007) and was the promised follow-up to the first installment from the year before. I was pleased and humbled when author Philip Hutchinson referenced the geographical information in this piece for talks given about his historically significant and well-received volume *The Jack the Ripper Location Photographs: Dutfield's Yard and the Whitby Collection* (2010), which for the first time presented a photograph inside Dutfield's Yard. New information and interpretation has allowed me to update the article extensively and I believe its true value is in the compelling explanations it provides for the manner in which Stride was rendered unconscious, how the packet of cachous ended up in her hand, and how these and other factors figure into our understanding of the Whitechapel murders.

EXONERATING MICHAEL KIDNEY
A Fresh Look at Some Old Myths

'While there is not a shred of evidence to support the belief that Elizabeth Stride was murdered by the Ripper this murder is included, for, like that of Martha Tabram, no account of the East End murders would be complete without it.

The murder of Stride was a coincidence and, merely because her body was found in a yard, both Press and public jumped to the conclusion that both this murder and that of Eddows [sic] which took place an hour later, was the work of the Ripper…'

— *William Stewart, Jack the Ripper: A New Theory, 1939*

AND SUCH IS the genesis of a perspective that not only continues to this day but thrives and multiplies along with the number of publications that appear each year dissecting the Ripper's crimes: that the murder of Elizabeth Stride was not one of them. But what reason did William Stewart give for so confidently striking her from 'the list'? He had only one reason, but he clearly felt it was good enough – 'In each of the Ripper murders the victim was killed by the throat being cut from left to right. This characteristic alone marked the murder of Elizabeth Stride as not being the work of Jack the Ripper.' What he assumes to be the truth here is that Stride's killer was left-handed, whereas the Ripper was right-handed. Even the most ardent 'non-canonical' adherent today will concede that Stewart was wrong and that all the canonical victims had their throats cut from left to right, which indicated a right-handed killer in each case, not the left-handed murderer that Stewart incorrectly arrived at; it was a mistake that stood uncorrected for almost 40 years until Stephen Knight put the lie to it in his 1976 book *Jack the Ripper: The Final Solution*. But 37 years is a long time and far more than enough for the idea of 'Stride out' to assume a place in the collective consciousness of researchers coming to the case in the interim.

Once an idea takes hold in our minds, it is not always an easy thing to let go of, even if we come to discover that the reason we adopted the idea in the first place was founded in error. We might simply invent other reasons to support our flawed conclusion. Now, it is not my intention to empirically state that the same hand that slew Catherine Eddowes killed Stride, but simply argue that most of the reasons given for concluding otherwise are founded in myth, exaggeration, or a confused understanding of the source material.

Anyone who has followed or even occasionally perused the numerous Stride threads that have appeared at *Casebook.org* since 1996 will be quite familiar with the following reasons given by those who feel Stride could not have been, or was most likely not, the work of the Ripper:

She was killed with a different knife: This argument usually includes the qualifications that the knife used on Stride was dull or blunted at the tip, or that the doctors said she was killed with a much shorter knife than that used on Eddowes. None of this is true. The confusion arises over a knife found a street away and a full day following the murder that subsequently was given much attention at the inquest. The knife was found by Thomas Coram shortly after it was dropped on the street by some unknown passer-by and could not have been deposited by her killer in the minutes following the murder. The tip had been ruined, and this is likely why it had been discarded. The doctors did not think Stride's killer would have used such a knife, although they conceded the possibility. There was only one wound, that being the cut on her neck, and from this the only possible conclusion the medical men could draw regarding the weapon was that it was sharp. There is not one iota of testimony that suggests Stride was killed with a dull or blunted knife.

The notion that the blade used on her was 'short' came from Drs Blackwell and Phillips questioning the ease at which her killer would have been able to maneuver a long blade under her neck, given the condition in which her body was discovered – her neck lying over the jagged stones that comprised the make-shift gutter of 40 Berner Street. However, they provided the solution to their own mystery when they discussed the matter of Stride's scarf, which had been pulled very tight on the left side, undoubtedly by her killer.

As there was no sign of struggle it is extremely unlikely that the killer utilized the scarf in order to take control over a conscious Stride. She must have been unconscious and lying down when the scarf was tightened, and the fact that the wound followed the line of the scarf proves that it was being held tight in her killer's left hand at the time her wound was inflicted. If Stride was already lying in the position in which she was found when the scarf was tightened it can only mean that her killer used the scarf to pull her head and neck up from the jagged stones so that he could maneuver his knife into position. This is the only practical solution to the scarf mystery and suggests the use of a long-bladed knife, in keeping with the Mitre Square murder, and at the very least puts to rest the supposition that her murder in any way indicated the use of a short-bladed knife.

The wound to her neck was less severe than in any of the other cases: This is certainly true, but it should be remembered that Jack the Ripper was a human being and not some pre-programmed robot. We should expect to see variance in his crimes, and indeed we do with each sequential slaying. It should also be remembered that the single wound to Stride's throat was sufficient to kill her, which was his primary objective. He went for the carotid artery and fulfilled his mission with a single swipe of the blade, something very rarely witnessed in knife murders. The darkness of the pathway, the jagged stones, the fact that her head was not as well-supported as the other victims, and the obstacle of her scarf are all very good reasons why we might expect not to see the same severity in the wound.

She was killed at an earlier time than the other victims: This is also true, but if we strike Stride from the list the same argument would have to be applied to Catherine Eddowes, who was murdered at 1:45am, anywhere from 2 to 3 ½ hours earlier than the times Annie Chapman is variously described as having lost her life to the Ripper's blade. Conversely, if we are to accept as mere coincidence that Stride's murder occurred within an hour's time and ten minutes' walk from that of Catherine Eddowes, then we must also accept as coincidence that the Ripper decided to get 'on the game' early that night of all nights. Had three hours separated the two murders there'd be a much better case for supposing two unrelated assassins were at work.

The location (Berner Street/Dutfield's Yard) was not one Jack would have chosen: I am surprised at how often I see this particular nugget brought forth. There are two different arguments here, one being geography – that because Berner Street is off Commercial Road and not Whitechapel Road that it was out of Jack's wheelhouse, as though Jack wore a leash that tied him only to the one major thoroughfare. The fact that Berner Street was only a mile from Hanbury Street and only a ten minute walk from Mitre Square renders this argument moot. The other, more frequent, point made against Stride's candidacy as a Ripper victim is that the yard at 40 Berner Street was too busy and the house too noisy for Jack to have chosen it as a murder spot. Confusingly, when this same point is offered as the reason why the Ripper chose to abandon his prey pre-mutilation, the naysayers call foul and it becomes a circular argument.

Of course, one very significant point is often lost in the debate - that a murder did, in fact, take place in the gateway, and occurred without anybody seeing or hearing a thing. It is therefore rather futile to suggest it wouldn't make a good murder spot. The Ripper (or his victims) chose risky spots from the first to the last. The inquests into the murders of Polly Nichols and Annie Chapman left the Ripper in no doubt that the police were baffled and the doctors amazed at his skill and bravado, so when the Ripper left his home that evening in search of victims, he would have done so with a confidence he'd never had before. In fact, 29 Hanbury Street and 40 Berner Street are more similar than any two Whitechapel murder locations: both Annie Chapman and Liz Stride were murdered in the yard of a house fully occupied; both women were murdered next to the only exit in order to assure a quick escape for the killer; in both locations, the killer would have known if someone was coming before they would be aware of him. If anything, the Hanbury Street locale was more precarious for the killer because he would have had to push past anyone coming out of the door in order to make his escape, and he must have been aware of Albert Cadosch going to and from the water closet as each could have seen the other through the breaks in the fence.

By contrast, Louis Diemshitz himself stated that the killer could have remained in the gateway and exited behind his cart without his knowing. Whether this actually occurred or not isn't important, only that someone intimately familiar with the yard as it was that night felt he wouldn't have been aware if someone had been standing only a few feet from him. This is what made it as good a murder spot as others and better than some.

The man Israel Schwartz saw did not behave as the Ripper would have behaved: This is a very presumptuous argument, because it presupposes that a) Schwartz was an honest/accurate witness, and b) that the man he saw was Stride's killer. Many modern commentators will tell you that it's beyond the realm of coincidence for the same woman to be attacked twice within 15 minutes, yet they're perfectly willing to accept two stealthy knife murderers killing prostitutes at the same time and in the same area. Being one who doesn't put too much stock in coincidence, I perfectly agree that if Schwartz really did see what he said when he said he saw it, then either or both the broad-shouldered man or the pipe-smoking man (from here on referred to as BS Man and Pipeman, respectively) was the killer(s).

This brings us to presupposition c) that we are in a position to decide how Jack would or would not have behaved. When we consider what Schwartz saw, we have a man and a woman quietly talking before the man takes her and throws her to the ground, whereupon she softly pleads 'no'. Returning briefly to Hanbury Street and the firmly canonical murder of Annie Chapman, we have 'ear witness' Albert Cadosch describing soft conversation followed by a 'thump' against the fence and a voice saying 'no'. Either the Ripper was completely oblivious of Cadosch's movements only feet away, which would strongly suggest he was a confident and somewhat careless risk-taker, or he was perfectly aware of Cadosch's presence but continued on, which would also suggest he was a confident and somewhat careless risk-taker. What Cadosch heard and what Schwartz saw are so similar that what is often regarded as non-Jack-like behavior perhaps should be considered as perfectly Jack-like.

Regarding the unlikelihood of the same woman being 'attacked' by two different men in short of time, let's examine the later murder of Frances Coles, who on the evening of her murder was walking with a 'colleague' whom a man attempted to solicit. Coles's friend refused the custom and the man pulled her along before punching her and running away. Had Coles been alone as Stride was, might she not have attracted the same attention to the same end as her friend, leaving us proclaiming that this oversexed brute must be her killer? And what of the man accused of Coles's murder, James Sadler? He himself was mugged and beaten up twice that same night.

Stride was not mutilated like the other victims: This is really the only true piece of evidence that can be put forth to suggest someone other than the Ripper as Stride's killer. Once all the nonsense is stripped away, this is all that remains, and there's no question but that all the myths, misunderstandings, and mistakes that have been passed down over the years came into being for no other reason than to explain why Elizabeth Stride's body was not mutilated below the neck. The very simple explanation, put forth by Louis Diemshitz himself and the contemporary investigators – that the Ripper was interrupted – is now scoffed at. But isn't that a far simpler explanation that stays in keeping with the evidence? And isn't it just possible that the Ripper planned on killing two women that evening? If that's the case, it explains why he 'got to work' so early, and he certainly couldn't risk having blood on his person if he was to seek out another woman and get away clean, so his plan would have been to not mutilate the first victim. Maybe he just didn't feel comfortable in the Dutfield's Yard pathway and decided to follow his instincts to leave. These are all far simpler explanations for why Stride was not further mutilated.

The final and perhaps most convincing reason offered up for supposing that Stride was not a Ripper victim is that a ready-made murderer was already at hand in the person of Michael Kidney - her abusive, alcoholic, slave-driving, jealous boyfriend, from whom she'd permanently separated herself only a few days prior to her murder. At least, that is the picture usually painted of him.

Michael Kidney – The Man

Michael Kidney is reported as having been age 36 at the time of Stride's murder, though he may have been as old as 39.[87] Either way, he was much younger than the 45 year old Elizabeth, who lied to both Kidney and lodging house mate, Charles Preston, about her age, saying she was 36 or 38 years old. In fact, Elizabeth Stride lied to everyone in her life from her friends to her lovers to the courts of law: she had epilepsy; the roof of her mouth was deformed; her husband died on the famous and tragic Princess Alice disaster, the list goes on. All of these lies and certainly more we don't know about were created to camouflage Stride's perceived flaws and insecurities. It is crucial to keep this trait in mind when considering evidence relating to things she might have said.

In June of 1889, Kidney was still living at 36 Devonshire Street, the last address he shared with Liz. On the 11th of this month he was admitted to the Whitechapel Workhouse Infirmary for syphilis. He returned on August 17th with lumbago[88] and on October 11th with dyspepsia[89] For his last two visits, Kidney gave his address as 12 Thrawl Street; a significant downgrade from his rooms in Devonshire Street. Some researchers see this move as evidence that Kidney was Stride's pimp and that his circumstances worsened as a result of losing her income. While it is quite possible that Kidney turned a blind eye while Liz turned the odd trick, the fact that he remained in Devonshire Street for at least 10 months following Stride's death indicates that he wasn't reliant on her for his upkeep, and most likely his lowered circumstances were a result of his worsening health, which must have affected his work.

His declining health and financial situation could be viewed as the fruit of a guilty conscience, but could also be seen as signs of someone very much effected by the loss of a loved one. The same could be said for his drunken behavior at the Leman Street police station on Monday, Oct. 1st, the day following the discovery of Stride's body.

Kidney's Theory of the Murder

Michael Kidney arrived at the police station in a cab[90] and requested the inspector on duty. He asked the inspector to provide him with a 'strange, young detective', believing that the assistance of such a man could aid him in solving the murder of his common law wife. When the inspector refused, an angry Kidney called him 'uncivil'. Neither the police nor the coroner was able to get from Kidney just what his information was, but there are a few clues left for us to speculate upon.

Some writers, such as Dave Yost[91], have taken Kidney's request for a 'strange' young detective to be a misprint, suggesting that it should read 'strong'; however, this is not the case. Although often missed by researchers, Kidney explained to the coroner why he specifically needed a 'strange' – meaning locally unknown – detective: "I thought that if I had one, privately, he could get more information than I could myself. The parties I obtained my information from knew me, and I thought someone else would be able to derive more from them."

So at some point in the hours between Kidney identifying Stride at the mortuary and his arrival at the police station, Kidney received information from a source he apparently considered reliable but one who curiously did not want to reveal all they thought they knew. A clue to this source is to be found in how Kidney arrived at the police station.

It goes without saying that a hansom cab is beyond the means and wants of a broke, drunken waterside laborer. However, one was certainly in the possession of Charles Le Grand and his colleague, J.H. Batchelor. Le Grand, a career criminal employed as a 'private detective' with the Whitechapel Vigilance Committee, had been in Berner Street since just after the discovery of the murder and was also present at the mortuary on Oct. 1st. He was responsible for the 'breaking' of Matthew Packer's famous story in the *Evening News* edition of Oct. 4th that caused much consternation within all ranks of the police. With Inspector Abberline being out at the time, Inspector Henry Moore ordered Police Sergeant Stephen White to find Packer and get his statement.

White must have felt rather put out by this time as it was he who spoke with Matthew Packer only eight hours following Stride's murder and was told by the 52 year old fruiterer that he had seen and heard nothing out of the ordinary. Now that Packer was being hailed by the press and public as the man who saw the Whitechapel murderer, White had to protect not only his own reputation, but that of his entire force. He detailed the saga in a report dated October 4th.[92]

When White arrived at 44 Berner Street, Mrs. Packer informed him that two detectives had taken her husband to the mortuary. While on his way to the mortuary, White ran into Packer with one of the 'detectives'. As they were speaking, the other detective joined them. Only when pressed to prove their authority as detectives did the men show a card and admit they were really 'private' detectives. White noticed a letter in one of the men's hands addressed to 'Le Grand & Co., Strand.' They would not allow White to speak to Packer and induced him to go away with them. Later that day, at 4pm, White found himself back at 44 Berner Street, and as he was speaking with Packer, the two private detectives arrived in a hansom cab and once again induced Packer to go with them, stating that they were taking him to see Commissioner Charles Warren.

It's worth noting that the first time White ran into the men they were on foot, but when they were preparing a trip to the police station, they did so in a cab. As there doesn't appear to have been anyone else whisking away witnesses in hansom cabs, we can indulge in some speculation by considering that Michael Kidney's chauffer was none other than Charles Le Grand, and if so, it was probably he who Kidney wanted the 'strange, young detective' to elicit further information from.

It seems that the vigilance committee, by whom Le Grand and Batchelor were employed, had its own theory of the murders, and it was likely a version of this theory that was conveyed to Kidney.

The *Daily Telegraph* of Oct. 3rd, reported, 'A member of the Vigilance Committee informed our representative last night that a great deal of information about the state of the streets, and suspicious men who frequent them, had been collected by them, and they believed that at least some of it might turn out of value. Although many people think differently, he and some of his colleagues consider that the murders were not the work of one man, or, at all events, that he had associates. Their belief is that at least four or five men were engaged in the murderous plot, and it was in the hope of inducing one of them to turn informer that the committee were so anxious that the Home Secretary should offer a reward. This opinion, however, was formed when what is now known as the "medical requirement" hypothesis gained credence. Several members of the committee even thought they were on the track of the gang, but investigations have neither substantiated the theory nor led to the unravelling of the mystery. Nevertheless, the Vigilance Committee, under the presidency of Mr. George Lusk, continues to meet daily, and focus, as it were, the sentiments of the inhabitants.'

Le Grand and Batchelor would have had no trouble in locating Michael Kidney. All had been to the mortuary on the same day and may have met there, or it might have been through the police contacts of the 'private detectives', or even in Berner Street, where Kidney was sure to have gone, and where it is known that Le Grand and Batchelor spent a good deal of time in the days following the murder. A reporter for the *Echo* newspaper spent the morning of Oct. 1ˢᵗ in Berner Street and describes with irritated bemusement a couple of men who had managed to gather a crowd with their tale of intrigue.

Very little additional information was to be obtained (writes an Echo reporter shortly after noon) concerning the murder of the woman Stride up till noon to-day. Except for a couple of hundred or so of men, women, and children, whose morbid curiosity had attracted them to the scene of the crime, there was nothing to indicate that another of these mysterious murders had taken place. Among the loungers were, of course, many who professed to be in possession of all the details connected with the unfortunate woman's death, but on being questioned, it transpired that the stories which they were obligingly disposed to relate were nothing more than conjecture. Several men who were surrounded by respective groups of eager listeners went so far as to say that the woman Stride had been seen in the neighbourhood of Berner-street about twelve o'clock on Saturday night in company with a middle-aged man of dark complexion, but here the description of the supposed murderer of the woman stopped. In answer to questions, however, neither of the men would father the story, preferring to escape any direct, or to them inconvenient, inquiries on the subject by saying "They had heard so."

It is possible these men were Le Grand and Batchelor, offering up an early version of what would become the Packer story.

As regards the vigilance committee theory, the source described a gang of four to five men who met the 'medical requirement' imposed on the Ripper following Dr. Phillips' testimony at the inquest into the death of Annie Chapman, where he described, in a state approaching awe, how Chapman's killer executed in record time operations that would have taken him much longer. Le Grand and Batchelor must have imparted no more information than this to Michael Kidney, and perhaps under a sworn oath of secrecy, and refused to divulge any further details. It is with this false hope that a drunken, frustrated Kidney entered the Leman Street station and requested a 'strange, young detective', in hope that such a man might glean more information from the two private detectives. These seem like the actions of a man in agony trying to find answers and not that of a murderer perpetrating a ruse.

Michael Kidney – The Suspect

While the notion that Stride was killed by someone other than Jack the Ripper goes back as far as the murder itself, the idea of Michael Kidney as the perpetrator did not start in earnest until 1993 and the publication of *Jack the Myth: A New Look at the Ripper*, by A.P. Wolf. While A.P. Wolf is certainly one of the most talented authors to write about the Ripper, he's also one of the most imaginative; most myths about the Stride murder in general, and Michael Kidney in particular, are to be found within the pages of his book, and as the text of the book has been available to peruse for free at *Casebook.org* for years now, it continues to have an influence on new students coming on to the case.[93] There is no question but that Wolf's theories about the Stride murder influenced a great many books to follow, some of which we will also consider in this section. But to understand the genesis of the Kidney theory, we must start with the blundering error that first convinced A.P. Wolf that Kidney had murdered Stride.

The following excerpts are from chapter two of his book as it once appeared at *Casebook.org*:

> The final evidence for Michael Kidney's guilt is so surprisingly obvious that it is difficult to believe that it has lain around for so many years without anyone realizing its importance.
>
> One day after the murder of Long Liz - Elizabeth Stride - Michael Kidney arrived in a drunken condition at Leman Street Police Station, Whitechapel. He demanded to speak to a detective, ranting and raving that if he had been the constable in the area where the murder took place he would have killed himself. This is a vital point because Kidney did this before the inquest opened on Long Liz and her body had still not be[sic]identified, in other words nobody knew who the victim was, and even later, after the inquest had opened, she was still being wrongly identified as Elizabeth Stokes. So how then did Kidney know that the latest murder victim was his ex-girlfriend Long Liz before she had even been identified?
>
> There is no doubt now that Kidney did murder Long Liz… going to the police to complain about the circumstances of her death before anyone knew she was dead clinches it.
>
> It is astonishing that the inquest jury were so quickly satisfied with his testimony, particularly after he admitted lying to them. Equally, one can only wonder at the total incompetence of the police in failing to realize that Kidney could not have known that it was Long Liz who was murdered before her body had even been identified, unless of course he had committed the crime himself. Again, as in other inquests on the so called Ripper murders, the attitude of the police is quite unbelievable. The failure of the police in Long Liz's case of not calling the single eyewitness to her murder, Israel Schwartz, to give vital evidence at the inquest is absolute criminal neglect.

Wolf is correct in only one point in his write-up of Kidney: it would indeed have been unprecedented incompetence on the part of the police if a man had walked into their station and berated them over a murder that had yet to be discovered and then was allowed to walk about scot-free without serious investigation. It would also be quite the anomaly if this person were to then stand at the inquest and deliver the same tale without anyone catching on. Then to consider that 105 years of solid research should follow in the most studied murder series in history with no one being any the wiser about Kidney and what essentially amounts to his loud and public confession.

The truth is that Stride had been identified at the mortuary by many people, including Kidney, prior to his drunken trip to the police station. Nevertheless, Wolf's error in reading had convinced him of Kidney's guilt and he supported his erroneous conclusion with a host of equally poor miscalculations – that Kidney padlocked Stride in their rooms, that he habitually abused her, that he had lied to the inquest jury. These and many more fallacies continue to plague the research of writers on the case.

Wolf's writing teaches us more about his lack of faith in the police and his fellow researchers than it does about the Ripper murders, but the impact of his work is everlasting and continues to influence researchers to this day

Although Stewart Evans was too wise to be convinced by Wolf's 'final proof' and years ago pointed out the errors apparent in Wolf's narrative, he did follow along in his thinking that Kidney was Stride's killer, and along with co-author Paul Gainey, summed up his thoughts in a single paragraph in his 1995 opus, *Jack the Ripper: The First American Serial Killer* (U.K. title 'The Lodger'):

The evidence surrounding the Stride murder is very problematical, and extremely confusing when read in full. The lasting impression is of a domestic dispute-related murder. On the Tuesday before her death, Stride walked out of the home she shared with Michael Kidney, a brutal, heavy-drinking labourer, who was known to have frequently assaulted her. The case does not bear the distinctive stamp of a Ripper killing.

Here again we are told without evidence that Kidney was 'brutal' and 'frequently assaulted' Stride. We are also told that Stride's murder resembles a domestic homicide, although I can't think of one domestic murder that even remotely resembles the Berner Street case. If nothing else, Evans and Gainey could not be accused of playing with the evidence to support their suspect, Francis Tumblety. Quite the opposite, in fact, as they believed Francis Tumblety to have been the fabled 'Batty Street Lodger', living at 22 Batty Street; so close to the scene of Stride's murder that one could have probably heard the singing from the club from an open window at the Batty Street address. Also, as far as witnessed suspects go, the Berner Street murder offers about the only candidate for the tall, fair-haired Tumblety, in the way of Pipeman. Nevertheless, Evans and Gainey did not feel that Tumblety would kill so close to home, so Michael Kidney is brought in as the murderous BS Man, with Pipeman being nothing more than an innocent passerby.

James Tully, in his impressive and woefully overlooked work on the case, 1997's *Prisoner 1167, The Madman Who Was Jack the Ripper*, makes equally short work of condemning Kidney, believing him to have been a heartless pimp wanting to punish Stride for leaving him and killing his golden goose:

> All the circumstances point to the fact that Liz had had enough of Kidney and was intent upon leaving him for good. That she was frightened of him is beyond doubt, as is the fact that Kidney would not have been at all pleased to discover that his steady source of income had taken flight...Let us then convict Michael Kidney, in absentia, for the murder of Elizabeth Stride and hasten to Mitre Square.

Here we are told that Liz Stride was leaving Kidney for good and never coming back; that it is 'beyond doubt' that Stride was frightened of Kidney; and that only he could have been her murderer. Tully was indeed in such a hurry to get to Mitre Square that he forgot to give us the evidence for his conclusions.

The next year, 1998, brought us Bob Hinton's *From Hell: The Jack the Ripper Mystery*, which served indictments on both George Hutchinson and

Michael Kidney. Unlike many authors on the case, Hinton spends a good deal of time on Berner Street, discussing the evidence and offering his insights. As he served as a magistrate and has a very strong knowledge of the case materials, many of his insights are delightfully fresh and deserve serious consideration. However, as with many authors, he seemed to have blinders on when it came to the murder of Liz Stride and the history of Michael Kidney. Indeed, the influence of the authors already discussed, A.P. Wolf in particular, is very apparent in the following paragraphs:

> If we were to look at the Stride killings in isolation, discounting the other killings entirely, what path would the police follow. Liz Stride is living with a man, who when drunk becomes violent and beats her up. She has twice had him in court for this offence, once she failed to turn up and the charges were dropped, the second time she gave evidence and he was gaoled. A few days before her murder she apparently had another violent quarrel with Michael Kidney (he denied this) and moved out to lodgings of her own... We know that Kidney was violently jealous of Liz Stride, before when he thought she had another man he beat her and padlocked her in their lodgings...Given all these indicators I believe that we are justified in saying that if we were to examine Liz Stride's murder in isolation, the police would have wanted to interview Mr. Kidney. Because the police wanted to keep Israel Schwartz and his testimony secret, he never gave evidence at the inquest, an inquest where we know Michael Kidney was present, it is interesting to know what would have happened if they had met.

Hinton is absolutely correct in that we should look at each murder in the series independently. However, his look at the Stride case seems to have told him that whenever Kidney got drunk he beat up Stride, and that she took him to court twice, providing evidence against him and putting him in jail the second time. He also tells us that Kidney, far from being Tully's heartless pimp, was an insanely jealous man who would padlock her in their rooms whenever he felt another man might be lingering about. We also learn that she left Kidney the last time as a result of 'another violent quarrel'. We are once again deprived of any evidence for these conclusions.

But by the time Hinton's book came out, five years following Wolf's, the myths had been so oft repeated that they had become accepted knowledge.

It is not my wish to disparage the authors whose work I've quoted here. In fact, it is my sincere hope that none of them become offended that I've put their work 'on the spot'. All of their books offer cases against viable suspects, and I consider Evans's and Gainey's tome to be the model example of how a 'suspect book' should be approached. However, we all share the common goal of getting to the truth, and in order to understand a popular and persistent mode of thought in the field – in this case, Kidney's culpability for Stride's murder – it is absolutely essential to study how that mode of thought came into being.

Michael Kidney – The Facts

All we know about Michael Kidney's character comes from his testimony at the Stride inquest, where he was described by an attending *Daily News* reporter as "morose", "rough-spoken" and occasionally "incoherent". Members of the press must have been clamoring for an interview with him, not only to discuss Liz but also the tantalizing theory mentioned by him in court; all the more tantalizing because Kidney wouldn't let the police have it. Yet to date no interview with Kidney has been discovered, suggesting he refused publicity. Had he known the speculation that would surround him more than a hundred years later, he might have been a little quicker to set the record straight, but since he did not, we must work with what we have. In this section we will look at each of the favored arguments used by writers to speculate upon Kidney's guilt in the Stride murder and see how they compare with the facts. We will also consider some important information that will be new to most readers.

That Kidney would padlock Stride into their rooms is one of the most commonly repeated myths, appearing in virtually every book that favors Kidney as the killer (Evans and Gainey being the exception); even Casebook.org, with its barebones, just-the-facts approach, has offered the following paragraph for many years now to anyone clicking Stride's picture and wanting to learn more about her: 'Their relationship is best described as stormy. He says that she was frequently absent when she was drinking and he even tried, unsuccessfully, to padlock her in (see list of possession at time of death)'. It is difficult to say with certainty just where this myth originated from, but it is almost certainly from the inquest reportage of the *Times*, which in the pre-internet days of Ripper research was the favored and most accessible newspaper available. Unfortunately, the *Times* coverage of the Stride murder left much to be desired, and many writers to this day fall victim to its errors or poorly constructed sentences. However, even the *Times* can't take all the blame for this particular error, as its coverage of Kidney on this point wasn't altogether ambiguous:

Inspector Reid: When you and deceased lived together I believe you had a padlock on the door?

Michael Kidney: Yes; there was only the one key, which I had, but she got in and out somehow.

From this sentence, countless researchers have concluded that Kidney kept Stride prisoner in her own home, overlooking the fact that he didn't say 'she got out somehow', but that 'she got in and out somehow'. This is a significant difference. In fact, other papers did a much better job of reporting what Kidney said; the *Scotsman* of Oct. 6th reported Kidney's reply to Inspector Reid as follows: "When deceased and I lived together, the door was padlocked when we were out. I had a key, and she borrowed one to get in or waited till I came. On the Wednesday before her death, I found she had gone into the room and taken some things, although it was locked."

This makes it clear that Kidney and Stride would leave together, him locking the door behind them. Sometimes she would let herself in, explaining that she borrowed a key, probably from the landlord. In reality, it seems she had applied to the landlord for a duplicate some time before and simply hadn't told Kidney, as indicated by the fact that the key remained in her possession after she moved away and was found amongst her belongings. Nevertheless, it is nowhere intimated that Kidney at any time kept Stride prisoner in her own home.

Other comments of Kidney's are often taken completely out of context and painted with the blackest possible motives. For instance, when he states that he was a great believer in 'discipline', he meant not that he had disciplined Stride, but was responding to questions from coroner Baxter about his career and pension as an army reservist. He was also still steaming about the police handling of her murder.

The *Times* reported Kidney as having said, "I have cautioned her the same as I would a wife," again misinterpreted by modern researchers to mean that he would punish or beat Stride. In fact, Kidney never said this, but instead said, "I treated her the same as I would a wife," meaning simply that they lived together as man and wife and he financially provided for her. A reading of his inquest testimony in other newspapers bears this out.

There is absolutely nothing in Kidney's inquest testimony to suggest an abusive relationship and it seems to go without comment that none of Stride's lodging house mates held any suspicions against Kidney, even though they were asked point-blank if Stride was frightened of anyone or felt anyone wanted to hurt her.

Regarding the confident assertions of many authors that Kidney 'frequently abused' Stride or, in one author's case, that Kidney indeed served jail time for abusing Stride, all we have in the way of official documentation is that on one occasion, on April 6th, 1887, Stride accused Kidney of assault but failed to turn up at the hearing, so the charges were dropped. While it is well-known that abused women often refuse to press charges, we have only this one accusation across a three-year long relationship, and when one considers that Stride was an habitual liar who herself was arrested a remarkable eight times between 1887 and 1888 alone, it might be charitable of us to extend Michael Kidney some benefit of the doubt. In July of 1888, a little over two months before the murder, Kidney served three days in jail for being drunk and disorderly and using obscene language, but this had nothing to do with Stride, although some authors have assumed it had and used the incident to bolster the idea that Kidney 'repeatedly abused' Stride.

In reality, Stride and Kidney were both alcoholics, with Stride seemingly the worse of the two, so there probably was an element of abuse on both sides, although the official records don't bear this out and previous writers had no cause to accuse Kidney in the manner that has been done. However, my own research has turned up an acquaintance of Stride's who did inform a reporter that Kidney beat and ill-used her. Her statement, which appeared in the *Daily News* of October 3rd, 1888, is important less for this than for other reasons that shall be seen, so is offered here in full.

New Information on Stride's Movements

A *Daily News* reporter interviewing a woman at a mission house where Stride was known was told the following:

The woman who looks after these mission rooms," continued the speaker, "was another of the same class, and who used to be an associate of the poor creature murdered in Berner-street. She saw her only last Thursday, and she - that is, the murdered woman - said then that she felt all was coming to some bad end.

The missionary made mention of another associate of the Berner-street victim. She also was believed to be trying to regain respectability, and it seemed worthwhile to go down into the depths of the neighbourhood that was formerly known as Tiger Bay to hear what this woman had to say about her former companion. She was found in a small back room at the inner end of a dark court not far from the scene of the murder, and proved to be a vivacious widow with three children, and one eye to look after them with. She first knew the dead woman three years ago, she said, and she was then certainly very pretty, always had a nice clean apron, and was always smart and tidy. She took up with a labourer, said the woman, and "lived indoors with him," but he beat her and so ill-used her that she was forced to turn out in the streets. She took to drink, and seemed to grow reckless and desperate. For two years she never saw anything of her, but recently the deceased called on her old acquaintance, who had got her own room and a few scraps of furniture about her. The desolate woman congratulated her old acquaintance on having a comfortable home (!) invited her to come and drink with her, and, this being refused, she took out two pence-all she had in the world-and insisted on sharing it for old acquaintance sake. "Oh dear, oh dear!" ejaculated the woman, "ain't it awful though!" "No doubt all these poor creatures are dreading to go into the streets," it was observed. "I should just think they was," was the reply. "Why, they're a'most afraid to sit indoors. I gets my living among 'em," continued the woman with frank communicativeness-"not them as lives at the lodging-houses like her," she explained; "there ain't much to be got out o' them, but the regular respectable ones. I does charing for 'em, and lor' bless you they just are scared. 'I shall turn it up,' they says. But then, as I says, what have they got to turn to?"

There is little doubt but that this woman knew Stride, who did indeed 'take up' with Michael Kidney about three years before, as was her recollection. She stated that she hadn't seen Stride for about two years prior to just recently, when Liz turned up again, and that when she had previously seen Stride she had moved out from Kidney's place on account of abuse. The woman clearly was not aware that Stride returned to Kidney and that her leaving him was somewhat frequent.

Regarding the abusive behavior of Kidney, the woman could be a bit off in her time and this could refer to the same incident in April of 1887 when Stride accused Kidney of assault, or it could be another incident that occurred before this, or it could just be Stride using sympathy to get money to drink. The crucial point about this woman's statement is that it is the first evidence we have that Stride had been in the Berner Street area not long before her murder was committed. Tiger Bay was in the same neighborhood as Berner Street, so close that many mistakenly thought Berner Street a part of Tiger Bay as well. The reporter even remarked that the one-eyed woman's back room lodgings were 'not far from the scene of the murder.' It is unfortunate that the journalist did not press the woman for more details, such as how recently Stride had paid her a visit. But we do have clues, such as that Stride had apparently told the woman she was staying in a lodging house. If this is true, it means that Stride may have visited her the very week of her murder.

Without wanting to digress from our primary topic too much more, I will quickly mention that it is interesting that the missionary woman should say that the lady in charge of the mission rooms had seen Stride just the Thursday before her death. The mission in question was probably

Dr. Thomas Barnardo's mission in Hanbury Street, as Barnardo claimed that Stride was present in the lodging house at 32 Flower and Dean Street when he visited only the day before. He stated that the women were frightened of the Whitechapel murderer, and one woman called out, "We're all up to no good, no one cares what becomes of us! Perhaps some of us will be next!" A few days later he identified Stride's body as one of the women present.

Prior to now I had never given Barnardo's tale much thought, but as we find corroborating evidence from a mission worker that Stride visited the mission on the following day and told the mistress of the house a similarly bleak prediction (that she was herself coming to 'some bad end'), this indicates that Barnardo was correct in his identification, and allows us with some degree of accuracy to identify the mission Stride visited on Thursday with that of Dr. Barnardo's. Stride may even have spent Wednesday night at the mission, leaving on Thursday morning. This would explain why Catherine Lane and Elizabeth Tanner, the deputy of 32 Flower and Dean Street, did not see Stride until Thursday, but the watchman, Thomas Bates, recalled seeing her on Tuesday (the day she left Kidney). Although it may mean absolutely nothing in connection with her murder, I am suggesting that Stride had recently visited the Berner Street area, and was thus not a stranger to it, and was in nearby Hanbury Street only the day before her murder.

I would not, however, go so far as to suggest that Stride's comments to Dr. Barnardo or the mission worker reveal any knowledge of her killer or impending murder. Indeed, Barnardo never stated it was Stride herself who made the comment. Stride was an unhappy woman and her outlook appears to have been bleak regardless, and considering our sources are missionaries, it's certain that Stride would have played upon their sympathies in any way she felt might benefit her.

Moving forward, the next myth we will look at is the oft-repeated suggestion that Stride had left Kidney for the last and final time, with no intention to return, and that knowing this, an angry and/or jealous Kidney went in search for her. That these events took place is absolutely crucial to the argument that Kidney killed Stride. If she hadn't left for good or if Kidney hadn't gone in search of her, then the theory suffers a devastating blow.

Elizabeth Tanner, deputy of 32 Flower and Dean Street, who enjoyed a drink with Liz at the Queen's Head public house on the last day of Liz's life, gave the following testimony at the inquest[94]:

Coroner: Do you know any of her male acquaintances?

Tanner: Only of one.

Coroner: Who is he?

Tanner: She was living with him. She left him on Thursday to come and stay at our house, so she told me.

Coroner: Have you seen this man?

Tanner: I saw him last Sunday. (Oct. 1st)

Coroner: Did she ever tell you she was afraid of any one?

Tanner: No.

Coroner: Or that any one had ever threatened to injure her?

Tanner: No.

Coroner: The fact of her not coming back on Saturday did not surprise you, I suppose?

Tanner: We took no notice of it...Before last Thursday she had been away from my house about three months.

Coroner: Did you see her during that three months?

Tanner: Yes, frequently; sometimes once a week, and at other times almost every other day.

Coroner: Did you understand what she was doing?

Tanner: She told me that she was at work among the Jews, and was living with a man in Fashion Street.

This exchange is very revealing, and is also quite important as it is coming from a woman who had known Stride for six or more years and had recently been spending much time with her. She seems to have been aware of Stride's penchant for lying, as when she told the coroner that Stride had left Kidney on Thursday to live at their house, she chose to qualify the information with "so she told me", which meant the same then as it does now - that Tanner was relaying what she was told, for what it was worth, which might not be much. It's not clear whether both Tanner and Catherine Lane merely assumed Stride had left Kidney on Thursday because that's when they had first seen her, or if Stride chose to tell them she had left Kidney only that day. For this reason, many commentators assume that Kidney saw Stride on Thursday, two days after she left him, but this is clearly not so. There's no question that Stride left Kidney on Tuesday and no reason to suppose he saw her after that. Tanner's evidence conclusively shows that Stride had said she left Kidney after they had 'had words', and Tanner merely assumed (or was told by Stride) that this occurred on Thursday.

Coroner Baxter, ever quick on his game, tried to slip Kidney up by stating (in the form of a question) out of the blue, "You had a quarrel with her on Thursday?" to which Kidney immediately replied, "I did not see her on Thursday."

A point of significance here is that although Stride was seeing Tanner socially on a regular basis, she never at any time suggested she was frightened of Kidney or being abused by him, a point strongly enforced by the medical evidence, which reported no signs of abuse (other than some minor bruising left only that evening, presumably by her murderer or a recent client). Frequent abuse over a three-year period will leave its mark, particularly on the body of a middle-aged woman, yet Stride was free of any such indicators.

Another important point is that Kidney, allegedly on the hunt for Stride, never once showed up looking for her at the one place she was most likely to be found: 32 Flower and Dean Street.

From the evidence we've collected, the worst we can say with any certainty about Kidney is that he abused Stride early on in their relationship, but even on this there must remain some doubt considering our only source is Stride herself: an intelligent woman who knew how to play on people's sympathies and was flexible with the truth as and when it benefited her.

It is curious that she would choose to lie to her friend about where she and Kidney were living, telling her it was on Fashion Street. Compounding this curiosity is that, of all the streets in London, Catherine Eddowes should have chosen to give to the police a false address of '6 Fashion Street' in the hours before her murder. This may just be one of the many little coincidences that plague the case (and make it so compelling), or there may be something to it we don't yet see.

It's clear that Kidney was telling the truth when he said he had no reason to assume Stride wouldn't be returning to him. After all, she had gone off like this before and had always come back. But he had another reason to assume she'd come back, and that is the fact that when she left on Tuesday, she took nothing with her. She returned the next day when he was gone and took her Swedish hymn book and (presumably at this time) her long piece of green velvet. No doubt she took the velvet because of its financial value and the hymn book because of its sentimental value. She chose to leave the hymn book with their neighbor, Mrs. Smith, saying she would be back for it. No doubt she was worried that Kidney might do something with her more prized possessions once he realized she wasn't returning right away. Apparently, Liz did not trust Mrs. Smith enough to leave the velvet with her. But if she was not planning to come back at all, why leave belongings temporarily with a neighbor? It simply doesn't add up if one is to believe that Stride and Kidney had taken their final bow together.

Moving forward to the murder itself, virtually every writer who feels that Kidney murdered Stride has implied or stated outright their belief that Schwartz's BS Man was Kidney. This is a circular argument because they steadfastly believe that BS Man's behavior was not fitting with their perception of Jack the Ripper (as discussed earlier) and therefore wasn't the Ripper, but had to be Stride's killer, and Stride's killer was most likely her abusive boyfriend Michael Kidney, thus Kidney and BS Man must be one and the same. This all sounds well and good, but like the other persistent myths about Kidney and the Stride case, it doesn't stand up to scrutiny.

Schwartz got a good look at his man before and after BS Man's assault on Stride, so we would expect the more pertinent points of his description to be accurate. According to Swanson's summary of the police report, BS Man was 30 years old, 5' 5" in height, fair complexioned, with dark hair, small dark moustache, full face, broad shoulders, and wearing a dark jacket and trousers and a black cap with a peak. This description is in keeping with what Schwartz told the *Star* newspaper, adding the detail that he was 'respectably dressed'. Kidney was between 36 and 39 at the time of the murder, and probably appeared older than his age, so it is doubtful he'd register in anyone's mind as being 'about 30', but on this point we will give Schwartz the benefit of the doubt. We do not know Kidney's height, and even if we did, height along with age are where witnesses can often be mistaken, so unless Kidney should turn out to be a dwarf or outlandishly tall, we couldn't in good conscience use this as an identifying characteristic. However, Kidney was a waterside laborer and probably deeply tanned, so it is difficult to reconcile this with a 'fair complexion', and as Kidney was very poor and would have had no cause to own good clothes, it would require a healthy imagination to describe him as 'respectably dressed'.

A press artist at the inquest did a good job in capturing the likenesses of those giving testimony, and Kidney was no exception, so we have in our possession an extremely good idea of what Kidney looked like; he was not stout, nor full-faced, nor apparently broad-shouldered. More damning is the fact that he sported a very full and obvious moustache, whereas BS Man had a small moustache. This is not a point at which Schwartz would have been in error. If you would have difficulty imagining yourself looking upon Francis Tumblety, even for half the amount of time Schwartz had to witness BS Man, and coming away describing him as having a 'small moustache', then you must conclude that when Schwartz described BS Man, he was describing someone very different from Michael Kidney.

Supporting this conclusion is Kidney's behavior after the murder. He went willingly to the police, identified the body, volunteered a statement, drew additional attention to himself by going back drunk and raving, then appeared not once but twice at the inquest. And if he were BS Man, then he did all this knowing that at least two people, and possibly more, had seen him attacking Stride and would quite likely be at the inquest as well. And it should be noted that his behavior is more in keeping with a bereaved loved-one and quite in contrast to Catherine Eddowes's steady beau, John Kelly - generally held up as the sympathetic antithesis to Kidney – who while identifying his mate's body had the presence of mind to sift through her bonnet looking for money she may have stashed away. And there is no record of Kelly pressing the police for justice in the way Kidney had done.

When we consider the evidence of the Stride murder, we see none of the signs of a domestic murder. Stride was not in any way abused, no one heard any yelling or screaming, there were no signs of any struggle, and her killer efficiently dispatched her with a single swipe of his blade. There was absolutely no passion or anger in the murder at all, and Michael Kidney was, if nothing else, a passionate person when unhappy, as his behavior at the police station and his overall demeanor at the inquest attests to.

The final and perhaps most remarkable argument proposed for Kidney's guilt is the notion that the investigating police never considered, or were close-minded to the idea, that the killer could have been anyone other than Jack the Ripper. This, of course, couldn't be further from the truth. Another woman, Catherine Eddowes, had been murdered on the same night in City Police territory, which must have put considerable pressure on the already pressed Metropolitan Police to discover their killer. Even if they could have solved just this one murder, the press - which clearly favored the City Police due to their more open attitude about sharing information and offering a reward - would have shifted their light across the boundary. The investigation into Stride's murder was exhaustive by any standards, and like all such crimes, they started with her closest associates.

In Chief Inspector Donald Swanson's lengthy report of Oct. 19th, he states:

> The body was identified as that of Elizabeth Stride, a prostitute, & it may be shortly stated that the enquiry into her history did not disclose the slightest pretext for a motive on behalf of friends or associates or anybody who had known her.' A little later on, Swanson reports that, 'The numerous statements made to police were enquired into and the persons (of whom there were many) were required to account for their presence at the time of the murders & every care taken as far as possible to verify the statements.

We know that Kidney was one of the 'many' inquired into, and as a recently separated partner, he would have topped the list of priority inquiries, yet we are told here by the man overseeing the investigation that his statement was taken, his alibi investigated, and he was cleared of all suspicion.

Michael Kidney was cleared of the murder of Elizabeth Stride in 1888, and now in the 21st century, he must once again be found 'Innocent'.

SUMMATION

Although the relationship between Kidney and Stride appears to have been a stormy one, and quite likely physical at times, there is no evidence that Kidney was habitually abusive, and indeed there are some indicators (medical and otherwise) that he was not. The popular idea that Kidney locked Stride in their rooms is without a doubt untrue, as are the suggestions that his inquest testimony indicated a violent man, or that he had any reason to suspect that Stride had left him for good. He clearly did not go looking to find her, otherwise he would have first gone to the lodging house at 32 Flower and Dean Street where she had been staying when he met her and where she went to stay every time she left him. He certainly couldn't have expected to find her standing in a dark gateway in Berner Street.

Michael Kidney could not have been BS Man, assuming Schwartz got even half his details correct. Kidney provided a statement and an alibi and put himself up to the scrutiny of witnesses at two different inquest hearings, proving he had nothing to hide.

The circumstances surrounding the Stride murder indicate a quiet, efficient, passionless murder; if Kidney murdered Stride, then the crime is an anomaly in the annals of domestic homicide and not at all in keeping with their 'stormy' relationship.

Kidney's health and financial situation deteriorated rapidly in the year following Stride's death, and it's likely the one led to the other. I believe that Michael was truly in love with Liz, or at least emotionally dependent upon her.

Michael Kidney, along with all of Stride's close associates, was thoroughly investigated and his alibi confirmed. As desperate as the police were to catch her killer, they were able to clear Kidney of all suspicion.

All arguments given to eliminate Stride from the Ripper's tally, save that she wasn't mutilated, are shown to have little in the way of factual support; and it is only from a complete misinterpretation of the facts that Kidney was ever offered up as an alternate killer to begin with.

Michael Kidney did not murder Elizabeth Stride, but somebody did.

The case for discounting Elizabeth as a Ripper victim is not as weighty as it first appears. The differences between her injuries and those inflicted upon Polly Nichols and Annie Chapman do not oblige us to take the view that she was slain by another hand.'

—*Philip Sugden, The Complete History of Jack the Ripper*

AUTHOR'S NOTE: Had *Ripper Notes* survived (its final installment was #28), some version of the preceding would have been presented as a 'Berner Street Mystery Pt. 3'. However, by 2010 it was apparent that *Ripper Notes* was no more, and Donald Souden, a former editor of *Ripperologist* magazine, had teamed up with *Casebook.org* to launch the vibrant if short-lived *Casebook Examiner*, a pdf e-journal that in its short run presented many fine works from some of the best voices in the field today. I was honored and excited to be a part of the journal's first issue (April 2010), and was grateful to have the opportunity to set the record straight about the much-maligned beau of Liz Stride. As you will have noticed, I also took advantage of my allotted space to present new and overlooked findings, such as the fact that Stride was no stranger to the Berner Street area.

A BERNER STREET ROGUES GALLERY

If not Michael Kidney, or the Ripper, then who?

BELOW ARE PRESENTED the curious cases of some men who might have been fortunate to have avoided suspicion for murder.

James Johnson

Less than 48 hours before Elizabeth Stride would enter through the gates of Dutfield's Yard, another prostitute by the name of Alice Anderson was plying her trade near the Lamb public house in Kingsland Road. It was between one and two in the morning, she said, when a man approached her and asked, "Where are you going?"

"Towards home," was her reply.

"Shall I come with you?" he asked, to which she replied, "If you please." And off they went together.

As they approached a particularly darkened spot, the man surprised Anderson by attempting to throw her to the ground. His attempt was unsuccessful and she was able to get away. At a run, she made it to the nearest door where she knocked loudly, screaming 'Murder!' When she turned to look for her assailant she saw that he was fleeing.

A short time later and very nearby, another 'unfortunate' by the name of Elizabeth Hudson was standing at the corner of Richmond Road, Dalston, when a man came up to her and threw her to the ground in the open street while producing a large knife from his outside coat pocket. She described the knife as 'something like a carving knife', 8 to 10 inches long, with a sharp point. He attempted to stab her, but was not so quick that she didn't have time to scream out 'Murder!' Frightened, the man ran away.

PC Nue 460J was on duty in De Beauvoir Square when he heard cries of 'Police!' and 'Stop him!' He then saw a man running and gave chase, soon capturing his quarry.

The man's name was James Johnson.

Mr. Johnson told PC Nue that two women had stopped him and asked him to go with them down the mews in Richmond Road. When he declined to do so they screamed and chased him.

At the same time that PC Nue heard the screams, Alice Anderson had heard them as well, and headed in that direction. She stumbled upon Ms. Hudson who was standing between the Lamb and Swan public houses, having just pulled herself from the ground. Hudson was motioning in the direction of the fleeing man.

PC 183J, who was on duty in nearby Englefield Road, also heard the screams and ran in their direction. When he arrived he found Ms. Hudson 'holloaing' and saying that a man had attacked and tried to stab her. He made no mention of finding Ms. Anderson present, so it's possible they arrived at about the same time.

PC Nue, with Mr. Johnson in tow, headed back towards Kingsland Road where they found the other PC with the two women. Ms. Hudson identified Johnson as her assailant and said she wanted to press charges. Johnson was promptly taken to the police station and searched but no knife was found on him. PC 183J seems to have found it odd - or at least worth remarking on - that Johnson asked no questions to any of the constables.

The next morning, all parties appeared before the Honorable R. R. Bros at the Dalston police court where Mr. Johnson was charged with assaulting Elizabeth Hudson. James Johnson was described as a pale-looking, well-set, clean-shaven man of 35, with a decided American accent. He stated that he worked as a waiter for Spiers and Pond's and resided with his wife at 18 Birdhurst Road, St. John's Hill, Wandsworth.

The story Mr. Johnson had to tell was, not surprisingly, far different from that of the two women. He stated that he had been out that night to see a friend, but finding his friend not at home, he decided to play some billiards. He found the two women together, not separated as they stated, and said that as they passed him, they asked if he'd like to go down the mews with them. When he declined, they asked him for money (one paper reported, probably erroneously, that they also asked for eggs), which he also refused. One of the women then tried putting her hand in his pocket. He pushed her away, and because of her drunkenness, she fell down. The women then shouted at him in 'dirty, insulting language' and he ran away. He stated that he owned no such knife and never carried one upon him. Indeed, the police seem to have failed in finding a knife anywhere near the scene.

Mr. Johnson had asked the police not to make any inquiries because his wife was 'delicate'. His request was ignored and later that afternoon his landlady appeared as a character witness. She gave a favorable account of him and since no knife was found the magistrate let him go with a slight admonishment, telling him that 'he'd got into an awkward scrape due to his own silliness.'

While the magistrate was obviously not convinced by the story the women told, he apparently felt that Mr. Johnson's intentions weren't as innocent as he made them out to be.

It transpired that the two women lived together and were known to the police as 'disorderly' and had previously been reprimanded for accosting men.

As no knife was recovered, I'm inclined to believe that Mr. Johnson was innocent of the charges brought against him. But this story is remarkable for other reasons. First of all, it occurred only two days before the 'double event', and we have a story of a man pushing a woman down in the open street, quite similar to the scenario described by Berner Street witness, Israel Schwartz. It will also be observed that the women were allegedly taking their clients to a mews, harking back to the possible Ripper assault in front of the mews in Brady Street on the night of the Nichols murder. The 'Dear Boss' letter had already been written and received, but had not been made public, and yet we have a suspect with a 'decided American accent.' And most curious of all is what the two constables had found near the scene of the crime: 'The police state, as an extraordinary circumstance, that when they went on duty, about half-past ten last night, they saw the word "Look' written in chalk on the pavement, on both sides of a lamp-post. Under the lamp-post was also written, "I am Leather Apron." Under this was drawn two figures- one of a woman and the other of man holding a knife in his hand. Again under this were the words, "Five more, and I will give myself up." The matter was treated as a joke at the time, but the officers say it is very strange that such a singular case should come to light so soon after.'

Other papers give the additional details that the graffiti was found in Kingsland Road and that a long line had been drawn to the word 'Look' on one side of the lamppost.

This story had been widely circulated in the various papers and even distributed by the Central News Agency. The graffiti echoes the apocryphal Hanbury Street graffiti reported following the murder of Annie Chapman. But two days later, two very real murders occurred, and a torn portion of one of the victims' apron was found under a piece of writing far more obscure in its meaning, and therefore more ominous, and possibly written by the Ripper himself. Was the Ripper's work influenced by the press he himself had generated?[95]

Mr. Harris

On October 2nd, 1888, Edward Spooner stood at the inquest into the murder of Elizabeth Stride to discuss his minor role in the mystery. The young horsekeeper for Messrs. Meredith, biscuit makers, who exhibited such a capacity for leadership in the first hour following the discovery of the crime, proceeded to tell coroner Baxter and the inquest jury about the course of events that led him to Dutfield's Yard and into the history books.

In the course of reading and rereading the case materials, there was one part of Spooner's testimony that nagged at me, and I wasn't sure why. It had to do with a man he met on his way along Fairclough Street while following the two club members who had alerted him to the murder. This was the only person whom Spooner would see on his trek, and he knew him by name – Mr. Harris.

The *Daily Telegraph* reporter covering the inquest, who otherwise did a fine job, chose not to record Spooner's mention of Mr. Harris, so his name does not appear in the inquest testimony provided on the Casebook. org proper, arguably the most referenced coverage of the inquest today. However, the *Times* reporter in the room did see fit to provide readers with this bit of information. The relevant portion was published as such: 'As I was going to Berner-street I did not meet any one except Mr. Harris, who came out of his house in Tiger Bay (Brunswick-street). Mr. Harris told me he had heard the policeman's whistle blowing.'

Of the major papers covering the Stride inquest, I've found the *Times* to be the most error-riddled and incomplete, so it was a rare thing to find a complete piece of information present in this journal but missing from the *DT*. Checking every other available newspaper, I found that they too offered this bit about Mr. Harris, and in almost the same language. Following are a couple of examples:

Morning Advertiser: By a Juryman. - I did not meet anyone as I was hastening to Berner-street, except Mr. Harris, who was coming out of his house in Tiger Bay when he heard the policeman's whistle. He came running after me.

Daily News: I did not meet any one as I was hastening to Berner-street except Mr. Harris, who was coming out of his house in Tiger Bay, having heard the police whistle.

From these sources there can be no doubt but that one other man was to be seen in the street near the crime scene shortly after the murder was committed. Tiger Bay was a colloquial term applied to some of the less desirable streets in the area. A few pieces in the papers even put Berner Street in Tiger Bay, although this is a mistake. The *Times* was alone in assigning a particular street to our Mr. Harris (Brunswick Street), and we can't be certain if this was a guess on the reporter's part or if he took the initiative to follow up with Spooner following that day's inquest hearing. It is possible that Spooner provided this extra detail in his testimony and only the *Times* saw fit to report it.

The curious thing about Mr. Harris isn't that he was in the street - a man has a right to be in his own street at any hour – but the reason *why* he told Spooner he was there.

Spooner states that as he was hurrying along, he saw Mr. Harris coming out of his house. Spotted by Spooner, and probably addressed by him, Mr. Harris stated that he had heard the police whistle and was coming out to check what the matter was. He then followed Spooner to Dutfield's Yard.

The problem with this statement is that no one had whistled.

Edward Spooner reached the yard a 'good five minutes' before PC Henry Lamb, the first policeman to blow his whistle. In fact, PC Lamb was the first person the neighbors had heard blow a whistle of any kind. Therefore, Mr. Harris could not have heard a police whistle and it seems unlikely he alone would have heard Diemshitz and company as they ran along Fairclough Street. Unlikely, but not impossible. Had Spooner misheard or misremembered Mr. Harris' words? Did Harris, in fact, tell Spooner he had heard the two men hollering 'Police!' and 'Murder!'? Or had Mr. Harris been caught by Spooner like a deer in the headlights going back into his house following his gruesome act, and when pressed to answer for himself, told the first lie that came into his mind? On a balance of probabilities, we must conclude that the former is the likeliest answer, and that Mr. Harris had been misheard by Spooner. Another explanation is that someone other than a policeman had blown a whistle. Neighborhood teen, Abraham Ashbrigh, claimed to have been one of the first on the scene and stated he had first heard a whistle blown.

But who was our Mr. Harris?

Researcher extraordinaire, Debra Arif, was kind enough to go on a hunt through the census records, and as one can imagine, there were numerous Harris families living about. There weren't any in Brunswick Street in the years 1881 or 1891, but that doesn't mean there weren't in the intervening years. And we shouldn't take the *Times* reporters word that Harris lived in Brunswick Street. The following are the nearest matches:

Henary Harris
Age in 1888: 35
Address: 8 Fairclough Street
Occupation: Commercial Traveler
Henry Harris
Age in 1888: 27
Address 1 Sander Street
Occupation: Fruiter's Assistant
William Harris
Age in 1888: 37
Address: 41
Christian Street
Occupation: Horsekeeper

One of the above may be the mysterious Mr. Harris, or perhaps some researcher out there will find a 'Harris of Brunswick Street' while trawling through the press and we'll have our man. But was he Stride's killer? Probably not, but in the world of Whitechapel 1888, no rock should be left unturned. It might be of interest to note that a Mr. B. Harris and a Mr. H. A. Harris were members of the Whitechapel Vigilance Committee. If Spooner's 'Mr. Harris' should prove to be one of them, it might make sense of why Mr. Harris – and Mr. Harris alone – came out of his house to investigate the cries of 'Murder'.

Berner Street Club Member/Attendee

Keeping with the theme that we are looking in Berner Street for a killer other than Jack the Ripper and Michael Kidney, the most logical place to start would be inside of the house occupying the very yard in which the murder was committed. Although this might seem obvious to an outsider of the case, it is a remarkable fact that the clubman theory has never been seriously pursued in Ripper literature. This oversight may be attributed to the general perception of the club as a gathering place for middle-aged, politically minded Jews, where talks are delivered, songs are sung, and everyone goes quietly home at the end of the night.

None of this was the case. Of all the club members who figure in the Ripper investigation, it is *Der Arbeter Fraint* editor, Philip Krantz, who stands as the club elder at the ripe old age of 29 in 1888. All of the members appear to have been under thirty, with many in their teens (such as Isaac Kozebrodski) and early twenties. In short, the club was a collection of young, angry men, who had turned their backs on religion, and wanted to bring down the establishment by any means necessary. Add to this the fact that beer was served at the club and it's rather remarkable that a murder had not occurred on the premises before this time.

The club and its members were not appreciated by their neighbors. Barnett Kentorrich, who lived next door to the club, felt that the yard had a "'low character" at night; his wife described the premises as "a nasty place." Both of these statements stand in opposition to those of the ranking club members, who stated no prostitution was carried out in the yard.

The socialists were notorious for their loud, late nights, their frequent rows within their own ranks as well as with the police, and most especially for their very public demonstrations against the Jewish religion.

Of the over 100 individuals who attended the event at the club on the evening of September 30th, 1888, only a small percentage were due-paying, card carrying members. Recruitment of new members and the soliciting of financial support was a constant process for the club and was the sole purpose for having these large, weekly gatherings. Therefore, many of the people on the premises that evening would have been strangers to the club leaders, and it is no secret that anarchy often can attract some very unstable and dangerous people. The possibility that Stride's murderer came from within their midst, albeit unknowingly, is not one to be dismissed lightly.

It may be that the last two sightings of her alive were with members or attendees of the club. First there was PC Smith, who witnessed Stride standing just opposite the club with a well-dressed young man of about 28, carrying a 'newspaper parcel' that measured about 18" in length and 6" or 8" in width. Philip Krantz edited the club's weekly newspaper, *Der Arbeter Fraint* (The Worker's Friend), from a small printing press in back of the club. New editions would be passed out at the club's weekly gatherings. The latest edition was printed earlier that day. Unlike traditional newspapers, *Der Arbeter Fraint* was not folded in the middle. A stack of such papers, if not properly bound by string or twine, would become rather unruly, so it's reasonable to expect such a stack would be loosely bound in some way. I personally measured a copy of a *Der Arbeter Fraint* edition and found it to be 18" in length and 6" in width.

It is quite possible that the young man PC Smith saw talking with Stride was not carrying a parcel wrapped in newspaper, but a quantity of actual newspapers that, due to their dimensions, would register with a passing constable as a package. As the man Smith saw was standing idle opposite the club and was of the appropriate age to be among their brethren, he may have been associated with the club. His duty would have been to meet people in the street, offer a complimentary copy of the paper, and invite them in. Someone that evening would have had this duty; if not this young man, then who?

As for the identity of the man, it could have been Philip Krantz himself, or perhaps Joseph Lave, a Russian from America, recently arrived, and staying at the club until he could find a permanent residence. Lave stated at the time that he had left the club for some fresh air and walked "as far as the street" some twenty minutes before the body was discovered. We know from other testimony that he had returned to the club before Morris Eagle, who arrived at approximately 12:40am, so this puts Lave out in the street around the same time that PC Smith noticed the couple.

Regarding Morris Eagle and Joseph Lave, we will now consider what Israel Schwartz said he saw. According to the Swanson summary, Schwartz turned on to Berner Street from Commercial Road at approximately 12:45am and saw a man walking some length in front of him. The man stopped at the gates of Dutfield's Yard and spoke to a woman later identified by Schwartz as Stride. Schwartz drew closer as the man and Stride spoke to each other. He must have been right on top of the couple when the man suddenly took hold of Stride and started pulling her towards the street before turning her around and throwing her down. At this point, Schwartz crossed to the other side of the road to get away from the man. Upon reaching the other side of the road he turned around and the man yelled 'Lipski'. At precisely this moment, a taller man emerged either from the doorway of the Nelson Beer shop across the street from Schwartz, or from around the corner of Fairclough Street. The man was lighting a pipe, but upon hearing the first man's cry, he took off in a run towards Schwartz. Wasting no time, Schwartz ran along Fairclough Street to escape the man with the pipe. Schwartz could not be certain if the two men were known to each other.

One persistent question raised by this story is why the first man would pull Stride towards the street. Where was he taking her? If we stick to what Schwartz tells us, the man pulled her out of the gateway and threw her down on the pavement, so it doesn't seem he was taking her anywhere but out of the gateway. Stride must have spoken to him as he passed the gateway, as he would never have seen her in the darkness of the passage. But if Stride was soliciting, why not stand where men can see you? The answer might simply be that the man turned to enter Dutfield's Yard and found himself face to face with Stride. After ascertaining what she was doing there, he physically removed her from the yard. If this were the case, then the man may or may not have been Stride's killer.

The last man to arrive at the club prior to Louis Diemshitz was Morris Eagle at approximately 12:40am. Mrs. Sarah Diemshitz and the club servant girl, Mila, were in the kitchen whereupon opens the only entrance into the house from the pathway; both women confirmed that Eagle was the last person to enter the club and that it was about 20 minutes prior to Diemshitz's arrival. If we allow for a discrepancy of five minutes in timing, Schwartz may have seen Eagle returning to the club and rudely removing a middle-aged, gentile prostitute from out of his way. Eagle's behavior upon seeing the body in the yard must have been out of character for him, because he felt the need to explain that he is squeamish and had to look away from the bleeding corpse. It may have been not a weak stomach but instead recognition of the woman that caused him to react in such a manner. I don't for a minute suggest that Morris Eagle killed Stride, but only that he behaved in a manner not altogether uncommon for East End men at the time, and roughly moved her from his way. This might explain some of the confusion brought about by the timing of various witnesses. If what Schwartz saw occurred at 12:40, then James Brown could have seen Stride five minutes later and 20 yards away at the corner of Berner Street and Fairclough Street, talking with a man who was likely Pipeman, who returned to check on Stride after chasing Schwartz away and seeing the other man enter into the club. This would mean that either Pipeman, or some unseen man who came by following his departure, was Stride's killer.

Another suspect for Schwartz's first man could be Joseph Lave. He admits to having left the house for a time but "only going as far as the street". He didn't say how far up the street he went. It's interesting that Schwartz did not see his man turn onto Berner Street from Commercial Road. Either he wasn't paying attention or the man had been on Berner Street all along. Lave likely exited from the front door of the club, as did Eagle after him, although he would have had to reenter through the side because the front door is always kept locked. Had Lave exited the club through the front and taken a quiet walk down Berner Street almost but not quite to Commercial Road, then turned around and discovered Stride in the yard upon his return, he may have reacted in shock or repulsion. Lave had only recently arrived from America and would have been an unknown entity to most or all of the club members, so we have no record as to his character. Lave may have been no more than a bully, or he may have been Stride's killer.

Of course, another possibility is that Schwartz's man chose not to enter the club after being witnessed by one and possibly two men. If he were Stride's killer, then he certainly would not have remained where a witness, returning with the police, could have identified him. So it's possible the killer was a clubman but escaped police questioning by fleeing the scene.

Another possibility that I'm surprised to have never seen mentioned is that Stride may have been solicited by or came to visit a person living in one of the cottages in the yard of the club. If this were the case, no one who was in the club would have had call to see her. More than likely, Stride was in the yard that night waiting to solicit men exiting the club. The beer shop had closed, and by 1am, the George IV may have been dead, but the sound of men singing through open, lighted windows, would have been a beacon to an idle prostitute.

I have done quite a bit of research to date on the club and its various members and have not found any reason to suspect anyone in particular, although there's much more research to be done. Nevertheless, the police were probably more thorough in their investigation of the club and its members than the surviving files and press reports make apparent. As late as December, 1888, and probably well in 1889, plain clothes detectives were employed to keep watch on Berner Street and, presumably, the club.[96]

Israel Schwartz

Why not? He's been branded one of the most significant witnesses in the whole of the mystery, or he's been called a bald-faced liar. What if the truth lies somewhere in between? What if Schwartz described a true scenario, but changed his role in it?

I'm going to assume that all readers are familiar with the testimony of Schwartz both as given by Swanson in his October, 19th summary and the 'alternative version' as published by the *Star* newspaper. If not, both sources can be found in the essay on Schwartz elsewhere in this book. I'd like to use our time here considering the Schwartz tale from a different perspective and to consider another published account discovered by Chris Scott and identified by myself for what it was. Truly, enough cannot be said about the Casebook Press Project and its volunteers. But I digress...

Israel Schwartz is the last identifiable person to have seen Liz Stride alive, but unlike his counterparts in Buck's Row (Charles Cross, the discoverer), Hanbury Street, (John Richardson), and Miller's Court (George Hutchinson), he has to date never seriously been written about as a suspect. The reason may simply be that we are all so busy discussing the many other questions surrounding him (Was he telling the truth? Why wasn't he at the inquest? Why did his account differ so much in the *Star*? Were Pipeman and Broad-shouldered Man known to each other? ad infinitum), that we've simply never gotten around to it. But let us rectify that now.

Schwartz stated that as he turned on to Berner Street from Commercial Road he found himself walking a short distance behind another man who stopped at the gates leading into Dutfield's Yard. Schwartz continued walking along until he was on top of the couple. The reason for this, as I've argued elsewhere, may have been because he had been staying at the club until his move to Ellen Street that day, and therefore he wanted past the couple to see if his wife or any belongings were to be found there before heading to his new home. Whatever the reason, he got close enough to get a good look at them both. As the man became forceful with Stride, Schwartz crossed the street. Almost simultaneously, another man emerged from the shadows lighting a pipe while the first man yelled 'Lipski!' The man with the pipe then moved towards Schwartz, who took off into the night.

Now, let us imagine that Schwartz was Stride's killer. Having just committed the deed, he exits onto Berner Street from Dutfield's Yard and heads in the direction of Fairclough Street. Meanwhile, another man fitting the description of his Man #1 (Often referred to by Ripperphiles as Broad-shouldered Man, or BS Man, for short) is walking along from Commercial Road and finds Stride. He calls out 'Lipski!' to Schwartz, in effect accusing him of the murder. The man with the pipe (Pipeman) hears the cry, knows there's a murderer about in Whitechapel, sees the wide-eyed Schwartz, and takes after him, believing he's chasing Leather Apron.

This scenario would explain the discrepancies in the *Star* report. By putting a knife in Pipeman's hands, Schwartz made both he and BS Man menacing characters. If they came forward, it would be their word against Schwartz, who already had the ear of the police.

This may sound far-fetched, and it probably is, but the idea occurred to me while researching the suspect, Charles Le Grand, and learning that he would abuse prostitutes in the street and then seek out a constable as quickly as possible to turn them in for a trumped up charge, so he could get the jump on them turning him over.

There is also one contemporary source that suggests at least the possibility of Schwartz being pursued as the murderer. An ambitious reporter for the *Echo* newspaper hit Berner Street shortly after the murder and talked to everyone he could. Ironically, he may have spoken to Charles Le Grand and J.H. Batchelor themselves. He was allowed into the Berner Street Club where he sat in on an executive meeting discussing how much to charge the gawkers outside their gates for a glimpse at the murder scene. Afterwards, he had a private chat with club secretary and inquest witness, William Wess, who provided the following information:

A MAN PURSUED. - SAID TO BE THE MURDERER.

In the course of conversation (says the journalist) the secretary mentioned the fact that the murderer had no doubt been disturbed in his work, as about a quarter to one o'clock on Sunday morning he was seen- or, at least, a man whom the public prefer to regard as the murderer- being chased by another man along Fairclough-street, which runs across Berner-street close to the Club, and which is intersected on the right by Providence-street, Brunswick-street, and Christian-st., and on the left by Batty-street and Grove-street, the two latter running up into Commercial-road. The man pursued escaped, however, and the secretary of the Club cannot remember the name of the man who gave chase, but he is not a member of their body. Complaint is also made about the difficulty there was experienced in obtaining a policeman, and it is alleged that from the time the body was discovered fifteen minutes had elapsed before a constable could be called from Commercial-road. This charge against the police, however, requires confirmation. There is, notwithstanding the number who have visited the scene, a complete absence of excitement, although naturally this fresh addition to the already formidable list of mysterious murders forms the general subject of conversation.

Prima facie, this statement is a bombshell. It tells us that either BS Man or some unknown witness watched Pipeman chase Schwartz and concluded that Schwartz was the murderer. The identity of this witness was apparently made known to Wess, though he conveniently forgot the man's name while being interviewed.

Could there really be a mysterious fourth person on Berner Street at 12:45a.m. that night? How is it that Wess knew about this and the police didn't? Could BS Man have been Morris Eagle who preferred that his evidence go no further than the club? Wess' comment that "the public" regarded the chased man as the murderer suggests that many others were aware of the incident by this time.

It is just possible that this is all true and that upon reading the story supplied to the *Star* by Schwartz, Wess and company decided the matter was resolved and that the man chased was not the murderer. Or, for fear of the world thinking one of their own was the Whitechapel murderer, they chose to keep their mouths shut.

But before we get too excited about this new avenue of thought, let's temper it with a bit of logic. Why would Wess tell information to a reporter that he didn't want to get out? It seems from the report that the journalist was trying to 'blend in' with the crowd and therefore wouldn't have been taking notes. Could the story have been reported wrong? Of course it could have been. More than likely, Wess knew Israel Schwartz and that's how he heard the story. He may even have been Schwartz's interpreter to the police. After all, he acted as interpreter on behalf of Leon Goldstein at the Leman Street police station, the same station Schwartz and his unnamed interpreter attended. We know from the *Star* report that Schwartz chose not to give his name to the press, or was otherwise forbidden to by the police. This explains why Wess would say he 'forgot' the man's name. William Wess probably told the reporter something closer to the truth – that the murderer chased another man – and the reporter simply misremembered and reversed the characters.

There's probably a lot more about this article that should be discussed, but for our purposes here, we can only conclude that there is no solid reason to suspect Schwartz of the murder.

Liz's Secret Lover

Some commentators on the Ripper mystery feel there's reason to believe that Liz Stride had a lover other than Michael Kidney whom she kept secret. I say 'kept secret' because it's clear that she told none of her closest friends of any man in her life other than Kidney. This theory finds its footing more in romance than in scholarship, but it's worth considering. Proponents of the 'secret lover' theory invariably point to warehouse worker and inquest witness, William Marshall, whom it is largely believed saw a kissing couple.

Hollywood tells us that prostitutes will not kiss their clients. While this may or may not be the case with a $300 an hour call girl today, can we honestly say if it was so with an 1888 'unfortunate' trying to get her next drink and, if she's lucky, a bed for the night? Nevertheless, some believe that because Stride and her man were 'making out' they must have been more intimate than mere pro and punter. But a reevaluation of what Marshall testified to actually having seen might prove enlightening.

Following is William Marshall's inquest testimony as reported by the *Daily Telegraph* on Oct. 6th. I've selected this paper's coverage because it is the most extensive. Additional details appearing in other papers will be noted.

William Marshall, examined by the Coroner, said: I reside at No. 64, Berner-street, and am a labourer at an indigo warehouse. I have seen the body at the mortuary. I saw the deceased on Saturday night last.[97]

[Coroner] Where? - In our street, three doors from my house, about a quarter to twelve o'clock. She was on the pavement, opposite No. 58, between Fairclough-street and Boyd-street.[98]

[Coroner] What was she doing? - She was standing talking to a man.

[Coroner] How do you know this was the same woman? - I recognise her both by her face and dress. She did not then have a flower in her breast.

[Coroner] Were the man and woman whom you saw talking quietly? - They were talking together.

[Coroner] Can you describe the man at all? - There was no gas-lamp near. The nearest was at the corner, about twenty feet off. I did not see the face of the man distinctly.

[Coroner] Did you notice how he was dressed? - In a black cut-away coat and dark trousers.

[Coroner] Was he young or old? - Middle-aged he seemed to be.

[Coroner] Was he wearing a hat? - No, a cap.

[Coroner] What sort of a cap? - A round cap, with a small peak. It was something like what a sailor would wear.

[Coroner] What height was he? - About 5ft. 6in.

[Coroner] Was he thin or stout? - Rather stout.

[Coroner] Did he look well dressed? - Decently dressed.

[Coroner] What class of man did he appear to be? - I should say he was in business, and did nothing like hard work.

[Coroner] Not like a dock labourer? - No.

[Coroner] Nor a sailor? - No.

[Coroner] Nor a butcher? - No.

[Coroner] A clerk? - He had more the appearance of a clerk.

[Coroner] Is that the best suggestion you can make? - It is.

[Coroner] You did not see his face. Had he any whiskers? - I cannot say. I do not think he had.

[Coroner] Was he wearing gloves? - No.

[Coroner] Was he carrying a stick or umbrella in his hands? - He had nothing in his hands that I am aware of.

[Coroner] You are quite sure that the deceased is the woman you saw? - Quite. I did not take much notice whether she was carrying anything in her hands.

[Coroner] What first attracted your attention to the couple? - By their standing there for some time, and he was kissing her.

[Coroner] Did you overhear anything they said? - I heard him say, "You would say anything but your prayers."

[Coroner] Different people talk in a different tone and in a different way. Did his voice give you the idea of a clerk? - Yes, he was mild speaking.

[Coroner] Did he speak like an educated man? - I thought so. I did not hear them say anything more. They went away after that. I did not hear the woman say anything, but after the man made that observation she laughed. They went away down the street, towards Ellen-street. They would not then pass No. 40 (the club).

[Coroner] How was the woman dressed? - In a black jacket and skirt.

[Coroner] Was either the worse for drink? - No, I thought not.

[Coroner] When did you go indoors? - About twelve o'clock.

[Coroner] Did you hear anything more that night? - Not till I heard that the murder had taken place, just after one o'clock. While I was standing at my door, from half-past eleven to twelve, there was no rain at all. The deceased had on a small black bonnet. The couple were standing between my house and the club for about ten minutes.

Detective-Inspector Reid: Then they passed you? - Yes.

A Juror: Did you not see the man's face as he passed? - No; he was looking towards the woman, and had his arm round her neck. There is a gas lamp at the corner of Boyd-street.[99] It was not closing time when they passed me. [100]

The Jack the Ripper A-Z[101] have the couple walking towards the IWMES as they leave Marshall, but this is an error apparently carried over from the *Times*, who completely garbled Marshall's testimony. Every other paper consulted makes clear that the couple moved in the opposite direction, towards Ellen Street, after having spent approximately 10 minutes together in front of the door of 58 Berner Street. It would be nice to know who resided at this address in 1888, although since Marshall didn't recognize the man, and would presumably be familiar with his neighbors, at least by sight, the information would only hold an academic value.

One important element of Marshall's testimony is that at no time does he describe the couple as kissing *each other*. When first asked what the woman was doing, he replied to the coroner by saying she was "standing talking to a man." He later observed that "they were standing talking to each other." When asked by the coroner what drew his attention to the couple, he remarked that it was because they had been standing there for some time and because "he was kissing her." This is quite different from the common conception that the two were kissing each other for ten minutes. Apparently, he was kissing her early on in the interaction, but then the better part of the couple's time was spent talking. And the fact that the man was kissing on Stride (assuming that's who Marshall saw) does not mean that she was kissing him back or that he was kissing her on the lips.

The man put his arm around Stride as they made their way past Marshall. Along with the kissing, this does appear as evidence of intimacy, but it could just as well be the evidence of a rather 'amorous' man looking to have a quick turn. The brief exchange Marshall overheard seems to suggest the latter rather than the former. "You would say anything but your prayers" is not exactly courting language and would not then or now be an appropriate remark in most circumstances. A situation where such an observation would not be taken offense to is one where the relationship is strictly sexual in nature, such as with a prostitute and her client. Stride laughed at the man's words.

The time of Marshall's sighting was about 11:45pm. Since he estimated he watched them for about 10 minutes, which means they headed off towards Ellen Street at about 11:55pm. Stride would next be seen about 30-35 minutes later by 26 year old PC 452 William Smith of H Division, standing outside the IWMES speaking with a man holding what Smith took to be a 'newspaper parcel' or a package wrapped in newspaper. A comparison of the man seen by Marshall with the man seen by the constable would now be useful:

Marshall: Middle-aged, about 5'6", rather stout, wearing a black cutaway coat, dark trousers, and a round cap with a small peak, like what a sailor would be. Appearance of a man in business (clerkly) with an educated voice, presumably an English accent. Could not be sure but didn't think the man had facial hair.

PC Smith: aged 28, height 5ft 8in, complexion dark, small dark moustache; dress, black diagonal coat, hard felt hat, collar and tie; respectable appearance; carried a parcel wrapped up in a newspaper.[102]

At the inquest, Smith added the detail that the hat the man was wearing was a 'deerstalker'. While the two descriptions tally in some respects, it seems reasonably clear that they cannot be the same man. PC Smith was 26 years old, and felt that the man he saw was around the same age as himself, whereas Marshall, who was in his 50s, described a middle-aged man. The hats each man describes are completely different, and Marshall was certain that the man he saw held nothing in his hands (though one could argue he picked up his mysterious parcel sometime in the 30 minutes when the couple was out of sight).

The inescapable conclusion is that Stride was with more than one man that night…more than two if you count the broad-shouldered man Schwartz saw speak to and attack her. Given her long history as a prostitute and the fact that she no longer had Michael Kidney to support her, it's reasonable to expect her to be out making money the quickest way she knew how. Liz was a heavy drinker, so she had her habit, as well as her doss, to support.

Other information that some feel are indicators that Liz had a secret man in her life are the fact that she asked fellow lodger Charles Preston for a lint brush and that she had in her possession a length of green velvet. Of course, all this proves is that Liz owned a piece of green velvet and cared about her appearance. Although she and Kidney were poor, they were not destitute by East End standards. Until three days before her murder, Liz enjoyed a regular bed and even an allowance from Kidney. Mary Kelly, who likewise enjoyed an existence somewhat above that of many other women in the area, also kept a very clean appearance and possessed some personal belongings. There's nothing here to indicate Liz had a new regular lover.

The last piece of evidence we'll consider is that of J. Best and John Gardner, two men who had decided to pop in for a late drink at the Bricklayer's Arms, a pub two streets down and across Commercial Road from Berner Street. They told the press they came in at just before 11pm, and as they were entering the pub, they noticed a couple preparing to exit. Due to the rain outside, the man and woman hung back near the door, cuddling and kissing. What first drew their attention to the couple was the fact that the man was dressed respectably whereas his partner was 'poorly dressed'.

Best and Gardner no doubt concluded quickly that the man was with a prostitute and decided to have a little fun at his expense, urging him to "bring the woman in and treat her." The man completely ignored the taunts, which bothered Best, who told an *Evening News* reporter that "if he'd been a straight fellow he would have told us to mind our own business, or he would have gone away." Speaking from hindsight, he then boasted that he was so sure something was wrong with the situation that he would have charged the man had there been a constable handy. The taunting of the couple continued and the woman, like the man, refused to acknowledge Best and his friends. Speaking to Stride, one of the men jested, "That's Leather Apron getting 'round you." Stride continued to ignore the men, and the couple took off "like a shot" shortly after 11pm when they noticed the rain had stopped.[103]

The Best and Gardner encounter is easy for writers to overlook or ignore. I confess I have made a habit of doing so myself. This is because it occurred two hours prior to the murder and with Stride being seen by so many people after this time, and presumably in the company of different men, the story just lacked any evidentiary value in determining who her killer might have been. There's also the fact that Best and Gardner are nowhere to be found in the official records, were not called to appear at the inquest, and even disappeared from the newspapers almost as soon as they appeared. Perhaps this is because upon investigation, the police either found out their story was fabricated, or determined that the men were mistaken in thinking it was Stride they had witnessed. After all, there were many other people in the Bricklayer's Arm that night, including the bartender and serving girls, any one of whom might have known the woman personally and could have given the police her name, proving she wasn't Stride.

But if Marshall is one pillar upon which rests the 'secret lover' theory, then Best and Gardner certainly comprise the other pillar, so I decided this portion of my essay would offer me the perfect opportunity (or excuse) to put these two pub-crawlers under the microscope.

On the face of it, their statement seems truthful and not fabricated. They paint themselves somewhat negatively as barroom bullies, resist imbuing their story with sensational details in order to make it more attractive, and the movements they ascribe to the couple make perfect sense when you consider that it had indeed been raining that evening, with the rain stopping right around 11pm, precisely the time Best and Gardner place their couple by the door awaiting a break in the rain and then taking off 'like a shot' once the skies had cleared.

Even if the two men were telling the truth as they knew it, that doesn't mean they had seen Liz Stride, only that they thought they had. In fact, Best seems to have had his reservations after viewing the body in the mortuary:

"I had been to the mortuary, and am almost certain the woman there is the one we saw at the Bricklayer's Arms. She is the same slight woman, and seems the same height. The face looks the same, but a little paler, and the bridge of the nose does not look so prominent."

As with James Brown and his Fairclough Street couple, Best's lack of certainty is a double-edged sword; it supports the idea that what he's telling us is the truth as he knew it, but it forbids the researcher from being any more certain than the witness as to what and who he saw. John Gardner, who had accompanied his friend Best to view the body at the mortuary, was far more confident in his recollections:

"Before I got to the mortuary today I told you the woman had a flower in her jacket, and that she had a short jacket. Well, I have been to the mortuary, and there she was with the dahlias on the right side of her jacket. I could swear she is the same woman I saw at the Bricklayer's Arms, and she has the same smile on her face now that she had then."

While evaluating the witness information, it is important to remember that Best and Gardner, like William Marshall, were taken to the mortuary on Sunday - the day following the murder - to view the body. This means that what they claim to have seen was very fresh in their minds, perhaps no more than 12 hours old, and certainly less than 24 hours.

Gardner, a man of few words, clearly feels confident in his evidence, and perhaps a bit annoyed at his friend's caution. The fact that he had remarked about the flower to the reporter prior to seeing the body lends significant weight to his veracity when he says Stride was the woman he saw. Fresh flowers were not a common garnishment for East End 'unfortunates' and would be sure to catch attention.

Although it's rarely mentioned in modern literature, Best and Gardner were accompanied to the mortuary by a third friend who saw the couple in the pub that evening and who identified Stride as the woman. He seems to have refused commenting to the reporter, and did not offer his name, but he acknowledged his agreement with Best's version of events.

Regarding the slight differences of appearance Best noted after seeing the body in the mortuary, one can hardly be surprised that Stride appeared 'paler', since she was, after all, dead, and had lost much of her blood. If this is all he meant, then we can hardly call it a discrepancy. However, if Best had taken death and blood loss into consideration, which might be expected of a grown man to do, then the fact that the woman in the mortuary seemed 'a little paler' to him might carry with it more significance than previously thought. For instance, if the woman in the pub had been tanned at all, this would have been evident on the corpse. Liz Stride, who had spent the summer in London and worked primarily indoors, would have had no tan. As far as the difference Best noted in the 'bridge of the nose', this once again could be explained by the fact that Stride was now a corpse lying prostate on a table. Not only was Best now looking at her from a different angle than before, but her dead facial muscles were now relaxed and pulled back. What is perhaps more significant are the men's observations about her face. If we agree that Best and Gardner did not fabricate their story, then we have two men who had a prolonged look at a couple in a well-lighted room. No other witness that evening enjoyed such conditions. Stride's most easily identifiable feature would certainly have been her mouth with its large bottom lip, having earned her amongst her associates the nickname of 'Hippy Lip Annie'. Gardner's poignant comment that 'she has the same smile on her face now that she had then' and Best's rather offhand remark that 'the face looks the same' prove that nothing about Stride's face, and in particular her mouth, was different from the woman they saw in the pub.

To borrow Best's words, I would say it is 'almost certain' that Best and Gardner are solid witnesses who 'almost certainly' saw Elizabeth Stride in company with a man at the Bricklayer's Arms public house around 11pm on the night of her death. That they were not called to appear at the inquest and were not mentioned in Swanson's lengthy report is simply because Stride had been seen at later times in the company of a different man and therefore the evidence of the two men would have been considered useless in determining her killer, her time of death, and her method of dispatch.

To support this conclusion we need look no further than 36 Berner Street and the home of Fanny Mortimer. Mortimer had stood in her doorway for approximately 10 minutes, going back inside and shutting her door just a few minutes before Louis Diemshitz arrived home and discovered the murder. During that time, she witnessed a young man carrying a black bag walk quickly down Berner Street. He glanced toward the club (only two doors down from Mortimer) and kept walking, turning left at the Board School and heading along Fairclough Street. Leon Goldstein, a member of the IWMES, recognized his description in the paper and went, along with interpreter and club secretary, William Wess, to the Leman Street police station to clear up the matter and free himself of any suspicion. Had he not done so, Mrs. Mortimer most certainly would have been called as a witness at the inquest and her description of Goldstein would be listed in every modern book on the case, right after that of Schwartz's men. As it happens, Fanny Mortimer was not called as a witness to the inquest, presumably because it was determined the man she had seen was not the killer of Stride – even though Goldstein had corroborated her story, making her a pivotal witness in determining the time as to when Stride could have been killed. If such an important and qualified witness as Mortimer was not deemed significant enough to appear the inquest, then there is little reason we should expect Best and Gardner to have been.

If Best and Gardner gave true evidence, which seems probable, and were correct in their identification of Stride as the woman they saw, which seems likely, then we must consider what we know about this man. They described the man they saw as about 5'5" tall, with a black moustache, no beard, weak, sore eyes, either sandy eyelashes or none at all, respectably dressed, wearing a black morning suit with a black morning coat [cutaway coat], with a rather tall billycock hat [wide-awake hat], with a collar, and a tie, although they didn't notice the color, and he was definitely English.

It is both remarkable and unfortunate that the *Evening News* reporter did not ask them about the man's build and approximate age. Dave Yost, in his book *Elizabeth Stride and Jack the Ripper: The Life and Death of the Reputed Third Victim*, repeatedly refers to their man as a 'young man', although I've found no evidentiary support for this. In fact, if the man had been appreciably younger than the woman, Best almost assuredly would have commented on it, since the difference in the couple's class of dress immediately struck him.[104] The clothes the man were wearing, his height, and the fact that he was English, all jibe with the couple William Marshall would see approximately 40 minutes later, but there are two differences, and they're not insignificant ones.

First of all, both Best and Gardner recalled seeing a flower on the woman's chest, as would PC Smith 90 minutes later, and it would still be there when her body was discovered at 1am. However, Marshall stated that there was no flower on the jacket of the woman he saw. This could be accounted for by a number of factors: there was not a lot of light where Marshall was standing and the couple was a few yards from him. When they walked in front of him the man was closest to him with his arm around Stride and would have been obstructing Marshall's view of her right side. The way coroner Baxter had to probe him for details might also suggest that Marshall wasn't a man to notice such details. However, he didn't merely say that he didn't notice a flower, he specifically said she didn't have one on her, so it's also possible she had temporarily removed it after leaving the Bricklayer's Arms. Flowers were also cheap and easily purchased from girls on the street, so Stride may have worn different flowers throughout the evening.

Forty minutes separated Best's couple leaving the pub in Settles Street and Marshall seeing his couple in front of 58 Berner Street. That spot was only about 250 yards from the pub, so it's possible they stopped somewhere in between to have sex, prompting Liz to remove her flower to protect it. After passing Marshall and saying good evening to the man, she may have put it back on to seek a new client. However, there's a far more serious discrepancy between Marshall's man and Best's man that would be harder to explain.

Best and Gardner described their man's headgear as a 'Billycock hat, rather tall,' whereas Marshall said his man wore a 'round cap with a small peak, like what a sailor would wear.' In 1888, hats were status symbols in the way cars are today. There is no way that either Marshall or Best could have confused one hat for the other; it would be like mistaking a 1978 Volkswagen for a 2011 Lexus.

PC Smith, who would see Stride talking to a man opposite the IWMES about 40 minutes after Marshall watched his couple disappear in the opposite direction, said that the man he saw wore a dark-colored hard felt deerstalker hat. This is much more in keeping with the hat Marshall described and just as contrary to that which Best and Gardner saw on their man. However, other aspects about the man described by Smith are not at all in keeping with Marshall's man.

What this means is that while Best and Gardner, Marshall, and Smith, in all probability saw Stride that night, each saw her with a different man. While the 'kissing and cuddling' and respectable dark clothing make it tempting to conclude that Marshall saw Stride with the same man as Best and Gardner, the difference in headwear makes such a conclusion improbable.

A curious factor is that Stride seems to have been witnessed with a different man every 40 minutes from 11pm to 12:35pm. She also seems to have set her sights a little higher than many of her colleagues as each man was described as 'respectably dressed'. This was almost certainly intentional on her part and she very well may have purchased her own flower and cachous to this end. Unlike most or all of the other victims, she had money when she left her doss that evening.

For the sake of comparison, we should also consider the man and woman James Brown saw standing on the Fairclough Street side of the board school at approximately 12:45am, only about 10 minutes following PC Smith's sighting of Liz with a man opposite the IWMES. It would only have taken seconds for Stride and her man to walk from where Smith saw them to where Brown saw his couple, so the timing presents no problem. Like John Best, Brown was 'almost certain' that Stride was the woman he saw, but unlike Best, it was only for a fleeting moment and not in the best of light. This leaves open the very real possibility that the woman Brown saw was not Stride. Brown did not see a flower on the woman's breast and did not notice what kind of cap the man was wearing. But he did notice that he wore a long coat that reached almost to his heels, which would rule out this being the same man that PC Smith saw with Stride a short time before.

If we assume Brown was correct in having seen Liz Stride, then we now have her placed with 4 different men inside of two hours. All of the sightings were within the vicinity of pubs, and the behavior of the men sound like descriptions of oversexed men looking to score as opposed to two middle-aged people romancing. When you also consider that Stride's closest companions were unaware of any men in her life besides Michael Kidney and stated that Stride did not say she was going to meet anyone in particular that evening, it seems rather safe to conclude that she was out prostituting on the night of her death and that there was no psychotic secret lover following her around in a jealous rage.

Studying the data, only two possibilities came to me as possible lovers of Stride, though neither is likely to have been the murderer. The first comes from Michael Kidney himself. Testifying at the inquest, the coroner asked Kidney 'Do you know whether she picked up with anyone?' to which he replied, 'I have seen the address of the brother of the gentleman with whom she lived as a servant, somewhere near Hyde Park, but I cannot find it now.'

It's fairly clear that upon finding this name and address Kidney questioned Stride about it, otherwise it's unlikely he would have known he was the brother of the man she had worked for so many years before he'd known her. The fact that he thought of it when asked if she might be seeing other men suggests that he did not put much faith in Stride's explanation of the strange address. Stride - a habitual liar - should be expected to lie if the address led somewhere she did not want Kidney to know about. But if not the brother of her former employer, who or what was located 'near Hyde Park'? The fact that Kidney could not rediscover the address means that Stride took it with her upon leaving. That the address was not found on her person suggests she disposed of it. The author would welcome any suggestions readers might have, but it would be remarkable if a man with a house in that area should take Stride on as a lover.

The second person I believe Stride may have shared feelings with at some point is Charles Preston, a barber who had resided at 32 Flower and Dean Street for about 18 months prior to her murder. Elizabeth Tanner, deputy of the lodging house, had known Stride for six years, but only knew her by the name Long Liz. Likewise for Stride's other lodging house friends, Thomas Bates, Catherine Lane, and Ann Mill. But Charles Preston and John Arundel identified her correctly as Elizabeth Stride. He may have been the first to do so. This might suggest that Stride enjoyed a more intimate friendship with Preston than she did her other friends. Curiously, on the day that was to be her last, she asked Preston to borrow his lint brush and he refused. While that doesn't sound like a very friendly thing to do, it makes perfect sense if Preston was jealous and did not approve of her prostituting herself. While it is interesting to think that Stride may have shared a bond with the apparently well-kempt barber, we should probably look elsewhere if we are to find her murderer.

In closing, while it is not impossible Stride had a secret lover, it is very unlikely, and all the evidence points to her having spent the last evening of her life in search of money. If Stride knew her killer, he was not among her love interests.

AUTHOR'S NOTE: 'A Berner Street Rogues Gallery', which appeared in the 7th edition of Don Souden's *Casebook Examiner* (April 2011), was essentially a follow-up to 'Exonerating Michael Kidney', and came about due to my frustration from posters to the Ripper message boards insisting that the Ripper didn't kill Stride, acknowledging that Kidney had not, but then refusing to offer up a viable alternative candidate. I decided to do their work for them and wrote this piece. While I've never shied from expressing my opinion that Stride was most likely killed by the Ripper, I concede that it's by no means a certainty that she was. The same applies to most other victims. The experience in writing this was a lot of fun and quite rewarding as it casts a light on some the darker corners of the Berner Street mystery. The evidence of witnesses Best & Gardner (along with their mysterious unnamed friend) discussed at length here along with some other ideas were at the time of publication were considered fresh and innovative (or completely barmy, depending on your perspective). Having said that, I don't personally endorse any of these men as the killer of Stride.

Did Albert Kill Long Liz?

I N A CAREFUL study of the Whitechapel murders, you cannot turn a corner in Whitechapel without running into Albert Bachert. It also seems that there is no end to the number of ways an English reporter could misspell Albert's simple surname.

It is hard not to smile when you see his name (in whatever form) pop up in a newly discovered press report. In some ways, he's like the unofficial mascot of Ripperology, but we all must admit that at one time or another, the thought has occurred to us that there's *something* about Bachert that's just not right.

It might surprise some to learn that Albert Bachert was perhaps as young as 20—and no older than 28—at the time of the Whitechapel murders, just as it's surprising when you first learn that every known member of the Berner Street club was under 30, with some (such as Isaac Kozebrodski) being only in their teens.

But youth is where the similarities end between Albert and the Anarchists, and we will be looking at some curious coincidences involving Bachert and the time and place of Liz Stride's murder. But first, let us take a trip just a little past Berner Street to Mile End Road and the Great Assembly Hall, where Mr. Bachert was to make his first known attempt at public speaking.

On November 11, 1886, the *Times* reported how young Albert stood up in front of Frederick

Charrington and attempted to move an unspecified amendment, but got in his own way by declaring that "Mr. Charrington, having made a rich harvest out of liquor, [has] now turned against it." Well offended by the remark, Charrington refused Albert a hearing.

Bachert was on hand a year later for 'Bloody Sunday' and subsequently appeared at Bow Street as a witness to the events at Trafalgar Square. He claimed to have borne witness to a police assault on a well-known anarchist named John Burns. He said the police were so anxious to be the first to take their truncheons to Burns that two bobbies managed to knock each other out in the fuss. Bachert did not say what he was doing near the square, but he was quick to point out that he stood in opposition to the protest. This makes sense, because he seems to have nursed a passionate hatred towards anarchists and socialists.

In August of 1887, Bachert appeared before magistrate Lushington at the Thames Police Court (and not for the first time as we shall see) and the *Eastern Post and City Chronicle* reported his appearance, reproduced by authors Stewart P Evans and Keith Skinner in their seminal work, *Jack the Ripper: Letters From Hell*.

SINGULAR CHARGE AGAINST THE POLICE

A Mr. Albert Bechart [sic], of Gordon House, Newnham Street, Whitechapel, made a complaint to Mr. Lushington respecting the conduct of two police constables. Last Thursday fortnight he saw two constables interfering with a respectable woman, who was talking with her brother-in-law in the Commercial Road. Applicant told the officers he knew the woman and asked them for their numbers. They struck him, and afterwards knocked him down. The officers took him into custody, and having dragged him along the road afterwards let him go, saying they had made a mistake. Although he had since seen a number of constables, and had been in communication with the inspector, he had been unable to identify the two men in question. Applicant had since heard that there was a conspiracy amongst the police to raise a trumpery charge against him and take him into custody. His object in coming to the magistrate was to make him acquainted with the facts of the affair in case a trumpery charge might be brought against him.

Mr. Lushington replied that if any case came before him he would remember applicant had been there.

Applicant thanked his worship and withdrew.[105]

Depending on how you estimate Bachert's credibility, it's either convenient or not that he was unable to identify the two constables who assaulted him. If he really thought the police would bother conspiring against him then he either suffered from an elevated sense of self-importance or a persecution complex, or perhaps a bit of both. More likely is that he had been up to no good and was covering his bases with the good magistrate in the event he should get 'pinched'.

Our real story begins in November of 1885, the year following the formation of the International Working Men's Educational Society and the very same year they took the premises at 40 Berner Street and turned it into their club. Something happened between Bachert and the young socialists of Berner Street, because on November 23, Bachert brought himself in front of Mr. Lushington at the Thames Police Court to complain about one of its members. He claimed that Lewis Lyons and a Mr. Frederick (also probably a member) were sending him letters threatening death and even making the threats to his face. He also accused them of smashing all the windows in his house and informed Mr. Lushington that he fully expected a 'riot would ensue' and that his premises would be 'smashed' by the socialists. Since the Berner Street club was the band of socialists that Lyons was associated with at the time, it is clear that Bachert feared an attack from the group itself. It's unclear what he might have done to earn their ire. Bachert asked for protection and was told to go tell an inspector about it.[106] Hopefully, more information on these incidences will soon come to light.

Skip forward to September 1888. The murders of Martha Tabram and Polly Nichols are still on everybody's lips. Editors of every London paper have their desks flooded with theories from amateur detectives and, for whatever reason, Albert Bachert chose the *Evening News* as the vehicle to air his personal theory of who was behind the dastardly deeds. The Sept. 6th edition carried the following:

'SIR –

Permit me, as an inhabitant of twenty years in Whitechapel, to express on behalf of a number of tradesmen and shopkeepers in Whitechapel our deepest regret and indignation at the shocking and revolting murders which have further diagnosed the unfortunate district of Whitechapel of late. The question that now arises is what is to be done, and what can be done to check and prevent the further spreading of such dastardly crimes. In the first place I would suggest that the police force should be strengthened in the East End, and secondly that there should be more gas lights in our back streets, courts, and alleys. There is no doubt but that these unfortunate women were butchered by their bullies (men who gain their livelihood from these unfortunates) and were the police to watch the haunts and dens of these villains and thieves, no doubt in a short time we should have a decrease of these crimes which have disgraced the capital of England. There are several supposed clubs in Whitechapel which these villains frequent, which are open all night for the sale of wines, spirits, and beer, and where any non-member can be admitted and served with as much drink as he or she can pay for. It is in these vile dens that the seed of immorality and crime is sown which brings forth the fruits we have just witnessed. The police must know of these places; if not, I am prepared, if required, to give the names of these places to any person in authority. The East End police are, with a few exceptions, a good and noble body of men who at all times have a hard and difficult duty to perform, and I feel sure that the heads of these police, such gentlemen as Arnold, Final, and West will do their uttermost to stop the breeding of further crimes by these ruffians. In the second place I suggest more gas lights in our bye-streets, courts, and alleys. We pay rates and taxes, and have a right to have our district properly lighted. Only a little while back a City manufacturer living opposite me was knocked down, beaten, and robbed of a valuable gold chain within a few yards of his own street door, the villains escaping because the spot is dark. My sister also a short time ago was knocked down by some cowards. They also got away, the place being dark. Now, Sir, I hope and trust that the Whitechapel Board of Works and the Commercial Gas Company will awake to their duty, and do their best to have this grievance removed. Apologising for trespassing upon your valuable space,

I am, &c.,

ALBERT BACHERT

Gordon House, Newnham-street, Whitechapel,

*September 5, '[107]_*

One question brought to mind by the reading of this letter is why would Bachert be writing 'on behalf of a number of tradesmen and shop-keepers in Whitechapel' if he were not a member of some vigilance committee? The well-known Whitechapel Vigilance Committee had yet to be formed and Bachert isn't known to have been a part of any group under that name until 1889. This may be evidence of a short-lived effort on Bachert's part to form his own vigilance committee.

The true significance of this letter is how he points the finger at 'bullies' (pimps) and the clubs they frequent. It's important to note that Bachert focuses his hostility towards clubs and not public houses, where more prostitution was certainly taking place. Perhaps this is because Bachert frequented pubs but was harboring very dark feelings towards a specific club. He seems to have made a study of such clubs and it is perhaps no coincidence that the Berner Street club allowed entry from members and non-members alike and offered beer. Given his past history with the members of the IWMES and his hatred for socialists in general, we can bet the Berner Street club made it on the 'hot list' he prepared for the police.

Annie Chapman would be murdered two days after this letter was printed. Barely more than three weeks later, Elizabeth Stride would be found dead in the yard of this club, and within hours, Albert Bachert would for the first time put himself forth as a Whitechapel murder witness. The *Evening News* of Oct. 2nd carried the well-known account:

BASKERT'S [sic] STATEMENT

On Saturday night, about seven minutes to 12, I entered the Three Nuns Hotel, Aldgate. While there an elderly woman, very shabbily dressed, came in and asked me to buy some matches. I refused and she went out. A man who had been standing by me remarked that these persons were a nuisance, to which I responded "Yes." He then asked me to have a glass with him, but I refused, as I had just called for one myself. He then asked me if I knew how old some of the women were who were in the habit of soliciting outside. I replied that I thought some of them who looked about 25 were over 35, the reason they looked younger being on account of the powder and paint. He asked if I could tell him where they usually went with men, and I replied that I had heard that some went to places in Oxford street, Whitechapel, others to some houses in Whitechapel road, and others to Bishopsgate street. He then asked whether I thought they would go with him down Northumberland alley — a dark, lonely court in Fenchurch street. I said that I did not know, but supposed they would. He then went outside and spoke to the woman who was selling matches, and gave her something I believe. He returned to me, and I bid him good night at about ten minutes past twelve. I believe the woman was waiting for him. I do not think I could identify the woman, as I did not take particular notice of her, but I should know the man again. He was a dark man, about 35 years of age, height about 5ft 6in or 7in. He wore a black felt hat, dark clothes (morning coat) and black tie, and carried a black shiny bag.

In spite of Bachert's outburst in front of Frederick Charrington and his condemnation of clubs that serve alcohol, he was certainly not a tee-totaler nor was he opposed to having a pint at his neighborhood pub. It seems only natural that Bachert would see himself as the man to educate an otherwise ignorant Ripper on the comings and goings of 'unfortunates', just as he would later try to teach the police and coroner how to attend to their respective duties.

Possibly the only advantage we modern-day researchers have over the investigating officers of 1888 is the luxury of hindsight. What the police and people of Whitechapel knew in the first 24 hours following the murder of Stride was that Fanny Mortimer, who lived only two doors down from the IWMES, saw a man carrying a 'black shiny bag' hurrying past the murder site only minutes before Louis Diemshitz would return home and discover the crime. What they couldn't have known in those early hours was that Leon Goldstein — a young, Jewish man carrying a black shiny bag — would read of Mortimer's account in the papers and present himself at Leman Street police station to clear his name. Until that moment, Mortimer's description was given the highest priority. When Bachert walked in with his story, they must have thought they had caught their biggest break yet.

Unless we suppose that Bachert really did encounter a suspicious man, the spitting image of Leon Goldstein, we have to conclude his story was concocted. This is not hard to imagine given his subsequent involvement in the mystery. But the question that hasn't been asked, but needs answering, is 'How did Bachert know how to describe his imaginary suspect?' Why make it a dark man carrying a black bag and not one of the bullies he had promoted in his letter a few weeks before? His account first appeared in the papers at the same time as Mortimer's, so he could not have learned of her mystery man from the press.

The answer is most likely that he was in Berner Street in the first hours following the murder and heard Mortimer's tale and decided to use her description to imbue his story with more credibility.

But why concoct the story in the first place? The most obvious answer is publicity — Bachert couldn't get enough of it; but a cynic might suggest that his story conveniently took him out of the locality of Berner Street and placed him firmly in the Three Nuns, where he most likely did drink that evening and could be accounted for, even if (as reported by the *Times* of Oct. 1st) he left around the same time as the man with the black bag, with more than enough time to reach Berner Street and murder Stride. He may have decided that investigators would not look at him too closely if he had them looking another direction.

On October 20th, when the latest murder news was George Lusk's receipt of a postcard purporting to have come from the Whitechapel murderer and a kidney presumed to have come from Catherine Eddowes, Bachert was back in the spotlight, claiming to have received a similar postcard, drawn in red ink like the 'Dear Boss' letter, smeared with ink in a fashion obviously patterned after the 'Saucy Jacky' postcard, and written in a fake accent (with the word 'you' spelled correctly only once) reminiscent of the 'From Hell' missive. Somebody was definitely hedging his bets!

Addressed to 'Mr. Toby Baskett of 13 Newman Street, Whitechapel,' the postcard read:

> Dear Old Baskett
>
> Yer only tried ter get yer name
>
> in the papers when yer thought you
>
> had me in the Three Tuns Hotel
>
> I'd like to punch yer bleeding nose
>
> Jack the Riper[108]

The letter was a stroke of genius on Bachert's part. By attempting to mimic the vernacular of the From Hell letter, Bachert hoped to fool people into thinking it was a legitimate communication from the Ripper, as many people at that time assumed the From Hell letter to be. Not only did this get his name back in the press, it would also restore his credibility. By this time, Goldstein had cleared his name and Mortimer's evidence was useless in offering a description of the murderer. The 'Baskett' letter is, in effect, Jack the Ripper himself saying that was not him in the Three Tuns (or Three Nuns), but that Bachert is every bit as important as the Vigilance Committee to receive a personal correspondence from London's most sought-after criminal. Bachert could then say his Three Tuns story was true, but he was wrong in having met the Ripper, allowing him to produce future concoctions with the latest, most up-to-date description. It might also be read as a confession that he was a 'seeker of the limelight' with the line 'Yer only tried ter get yer name in the papers'.

The Ripper wasn't done with Bachert yet. On November 19th, the day of Mary Kelly's funeral, Bachert was awakened by an unnamed policeman and informed there was graffiti on the wall of his house at 13 Newnham. The chalk graffiti read: 'Dear Boss, - I am still about: Look out. – Yours, JACK THE RIPPER.' When a crowd began to gather, Bachert's mother, Georgina, showed up playing the poor man's Commissioner Warren and washed it away. Bachert claimed the graffiti matched the writing of the

Dear Boss letter, which would be an impressive feat even for the Dear Boss author himself, if working with chalk on a wall.

In July of 1889, Bachert was finally able to prove his muster and may actually have saved a young woman's life. On July 17th, the body of Alice McKenzie was found in Castle Alley, believed to have been murdered by Jack the Ripper. The *Times* of July 20th reported that a second murder would have taken place on the same spot had it not been for Albert and his band of vigilantes.

It was about a quarter to 10 when a woman was seen walking with a man. They stopped at a corner and only a moment later the woman began crying out, "No! I won't." The man grabbed her, dragged her a short distance away, and threw her down. He pulled out a knife and hit her with it. The woman continued screaming and a crowd gathered. The report continues: 'Amongst those who arrived on the scene were several members of the local vigilance association, who have only just recommenced their work, and before the man had time to get far he was seized, and a struggle ensued.'

During the struggle, the woman crawled away and was not seen again. Bachert was eventually able to wrestle the knife away from the man, who soon found himself subdued by the gathering crowd. Members of both the City and Metropolitan police forces arrived and took the man into custody. He was charged at the Commercial Street station. The report continues:

When asked whether he had anything to say in reply to the charge he replied, "The woman robbed me." When asked why he drew the dagger, he replied, "In self defence." He said he was a sailor and gave a Scotch name, and said he arrived from South Shields about a week ago. When asked where he was on the morning of the 17th inst. he said he could not say. He did not know where he had stayed whilst in London. On being searched a smaller knife was found in his possession, together with a seaman's discharge.

Albert Backert [sic], of 13 Newnham street, Whitechapel, one of the Vigilance Committee, who seized the knife and whose clothes were blood stained, has made a statement which tallies in every respect with the foregoing account and in the course of which he says that the assailant held the woman's hair in the right hand and the knife in the left.

Other newspapers reported additional details, including the rather unbelievable claim by the *Scotsman* that the struggle was witnessed by about 800 people. Debra Arif researched the event and discovered the additional details that Bachert had been standing at the corner of Goulston Street and Wentworth Street at the time he first saw the couple and that the actual attack occurred outside a butcher's shop near Aldgate East Station.

This event begs for more research but it seems it may have been a legitimate act of heroism on Bachert's part. However, that the woman scurried away (amidst up to 800 onlookers) and therefore could press no charges open possibility that Bachert engineered the entire assault as a façade to get his newly reformed 'committee' back in the papers. However, if the newspaper account is accurate, then there were other witnesses to the entire saga who corroborated everything, including the attack itself. It would be a testament to Bachert's powers of persuasion if he could convince a woman to bleed and the man playing the part of the attacker to willfully allow himself to be attacked and arrested, but more than likely, Albert Bachert — for once in his life — earned the press ink that was spilled on him. This being the case, it would be nice to know more about the man Bachert apprehended and where he may have been docked on the morning of Sept. 30th, 1888.

While the knowledge that Bachert may have risked injury to save the life of an unfortunate could to some cast doubt on the possibility that he might himself take a woman's life, it might be wise to remember that Ted Bundy was made a hero after saving the life of a drowning child, and is reported to have saved more lives than he took while working as a suicide help line operator. If good people can do bad things then the opposite must hold true as well.

It would be worth considering the strange death of a boy that occurred in Bachert's presence. The *Times* of November 19, 1891, reported that on Nov. 11th, Bachert was passing through 'the Poultry', walking along behind Arthur Charles Puleston, a printer's boy of only 14. As they were about to pass Pimm's restaurant, gale winds loosened some boards of Nos. 1

and 2, Poultry; these boards struck an ornamental 'griffin', made of cast iron, which fell and struck the boy dead. Some falling boards struck and injured Bachert.

The inquest was held Nov. 19th at St. Bartholomew's Hospital, presided over by City coroner, Samuel Langham. Bachert was the sole witness so the jury returned the only verdict it could, which was 'accidental death'.

While it may only have been his bad luck, some might regard it as rather suspicious that when no one but Bachert was around, a young boy found his head bashed in by a piece of ornamental metal, resembling a griffin no less. Arguably, it would have been less suspicious had Bachert not suffered any injuries of his own. We have no idea what suspicions the investigators may have held against Bachert, but without contradictory witness testimony, their hands would have been tied in pursuing any kind of case against him.

There is no evidence allowing me to suggest that Bachert killed the boy Puleston; Bachert has the same right as anyone to be presumed innocent. But many of the so-called Ripper suspects, with full volumes devoted to establishing their guilt, cannot claim so many suspicious circumstances in such a short amount of time. And there is yet more to consider.

The next piece of evidence we will look at is an extraordinary find from the *Birmingham Daily Post* of February 16, 1891:

Mr Albert Backert [sic], writing on Saturday from 13 Newnham Street, Whitechapel, says:- The woman who has been murdered [Frances Coles] was seen by a friend and myself last night at a quarter past twelve, outside Leman Street Railway Station, speaking to a man, and when I arrived home (only a few yards from the scene of the murder), it being then five minutes past one, the same woman was talking to a man opposite my house. I went inside, and later I heard some loud talking. I looked out of the window, and heard the man say, "Well, you won't come home with me?" She made some reply which I did not understand. He then said, "If you don't you will never go home with another man." They then walked off in the direction of the arches in Chambers Street. I have been called upon to serve on the jury tomorrow afternoon, and it is my intention to enquire into this case. If evidence is brought forward which can prove that it has been committed by the late Whitechapel Fiend, I shall at once reform the Vigilance Committee, and appeal to the public for aid.[109]

Considering how suspicious Bachert's behavior has been throughout the Autumn of Terror, having a woman murdered "only a few yards" from his house and then admitting to having seen her not once but twice, might be an indication of complicity. The Newnham Street address he wrote the letter from was his parents' house and the usual address he included on communications. Newnham Street could not even remotely be described as "a few yards away" from Swallow Gardens, the scene of Coles' murder. Albert was no fool and would expect Londoners to know as much, so it seems he was staying at another address, close to Swallow Gardens. Perhaps at his friend's house, or he may have temporarily had his own place. What is important is that he places himself so near the murder scene at the time it was committed.

While we're considering this communication from Albert, his address of 13 Newnham Street, and his hangout by the Leman Street Railway station, let's turn back the clock all the way to the night of Emma Smith's murder on April 3rd. Also assaulted that night was a 33 year old woman named Malvina Haynes.[110] She was received at the London Hospital and put under the care of Dr. George Haslip, who was also tending to Emma Smith. Haynes survived her injuries, but they were extensive and there was concern she might suffer permanent brain injury, although there's nothing on record to suggest that was the case. Considering that her assault occurred within hours of Smith's and both received blows to the head, there has long been speculation that the two events might be related.

What interests us now about the Haynes assault is that at this time she lived with her husband, Henry, a house painter, at 29 Newnham Street. They had gone out to enjoy the evening with some friends and later returned home. Malvina later went out, without her husband, but possibly not alone, and was near the Leman Street Railway when screams were heard. A constable found her unconscious by the railway and got her prompt medical attention. Her attacker was never discovered, although there was a clue; newspapers reported that 'a man who was said to have been near the unfortunate woman at the time of the occurrence, and who resided in the district, has left the neighbourhood. The police hope that he may come forward, as his testimony might aid the ends of justice, by relating what he saw of the outrage.'[111]

Bachert's next move was to try to get seated on the inquest into the murder of Frances Coles, but coroner Wynne Baxter would have nothing of it.

From the *Times*, February 16, 1891:

On the names of the jurymen summoned being called out by the Coroner's officer, it was found that only eight answered, the remainder of those present being substitutes. Some of the latter were accepted, but when Mr. Backert [sic], the chairman of the so called Whitechapel Vigilance Committee, offered himself as a substitute in place of a Mr. Fielder, the Coroner declined to allow him to serve.

Mr. Backert: Why?

The Coroner: Because I decline.

Mr. Backert: You decline simply because I happen to be chairman of the Vigilance Committee and you think I shall fully investigate this matter. I have a right to be on the jury.

The Coroner: I have decided you are not to serve on this jury.

Mr. Backert: Yes – because you know I shall inquire into this case.

The Coroner: You have already been told I shall decline to accept you.

Mr. Backert (walking to the back of the court): You will hear more of this.

The jury, having been sworn, proceeded to view the body. On their return, Mr. Backert, addressing the Coroner, said, "It was only after you heard who I was that you would not allow me to serve on the jury."

The Coroner: If you do not keep quiet I will have you ejected from the room.

Coles was murdered in a similar fashion to Liz Stride and some researchers who have sought to 'clear' the Ripper of Stride's murder have suggested that the same man was responsible for both. Could that man have been Albert Bachert, who placed himself at the scene of the Coles murder and seemed to have possessed insider knowledge relating to the murder of Liz Stride?

Nothing is known about Bachert after 1893, and before that time he does not appear to have had much of a criminal record, but that's mainly because the authorities could get nothing to stick. In December of 1889, Bachert and three of his friends — Albert Waple, Henry Norman, and John Smith, were indicted for uttering counterfeit florins. The jury acquitted Bachert and Norman but sentenced Waple to four months' hard labor and Smith to 15 months' hard labor. In September, 1892, Albert's own father, John Bachert, charged him with stealing at least £300, a very lofty sum in those times [at least £25,000 in today's money]. However, finding no evidence against Albert, the magistrate dropped the charges.

Bachert was very busy in the year 1892 trying to get a political career going and continuing to foster his hatred for anarchists and socialists. In May of that year he took the chair (which is meant literally as the speakers would all stand on a chair) at a meeting of London anarchists in Hyde Park. The *Times* of May 9th gives the story:

A man named Backert mounted the chair which serviced for a platform, and, addressing the crowd as "Friends and lovers of life," began a bitter attack on anarchy. Amid considerable interruption he said that the Anarchists were men who publicly and privately advocated force and murder. They were men whom honest persons should shun. He knew all about them from personal experience. Persons who advocated the use of dynamite to destroy life and property were dangerous to the country and should be kept in hand.

He was not going to stand by and see his fellow men torn to

pieces and terribly injured, while property was ruthlessly wrecked. Anarchists were people who had no hearts. They set men to execute the vilest crimes and then were proud of the fact. He trusted that in the near future the workers would stamp out of existence such a class of people, who were in reality only the scum of the earth.

He would move the resolution "That this meeting of English men and women, assembled in Hyde Park, views with horror the action of the so called London Anarchists, and condemns the principles of anarchy, which are in reality murderous and unmanly." Only half of a dozen hands were held up in favour of the motion. Then Backert invited all those present who were in favour of blowing up houses and murdering innocent people to hold up their hands. He soon afterwards left the meeting amid hoots and jeers.

This article gives us great insight into how deeply he hated anarchy and socialism, which seem to have been one and the same to his mind. On the fourth anniversary of Mary Kelly's murder, at a meeting at Tower Hills, Albert Bachert assumed the title of President of the Anti-Socialists, also known as the Anti- Socialists Unemployed Committee. In this capacity, he finally got a taste of the success he had so long for craved. His support grew until he was able to get a private audience with the Lord Mayor at the Lord Mayor's mansion. By December, Bachert was able to parlay his success into a salaried position with the Unemployed Relief Committee, which was comprised of three socialists and three anti-socialists. Alas, with power often comes corruption, and it didn't take Bachert long at all to bring about his own downfall.

Only two months after obtaining his position with the committee, which paid him 25s per week, Bachert forged the chairman's name on a large order of bread and flour, obtaining it illegally. Currently, the last known press mention of Bachert, from the Times of March 8, 1893, reads thus:

London County Sessions:

Before Sir P.H. Edlin, Q.C., Albert Backert [sic], 25, engraver, formerly salaried secretary of the Unemployed Investigation

Committee, was convicted of having obtained a quality of bread and flour by false pretences, and was sentenced to three months' imprisonment with hard labour.

And it is here that we lose all track of Bachert in the press reports. The last we see of him is in the 1901 census reports, living with his sister. It is possible that he retired from public life altogether, but no death notices have been discovered, so he may have changed his name, moved away from the area, or both. As he was only 25 to 32 in 1893, there is sure to be much more to find on this very intriguing man, if only we knew where to look.

SUMMATION

Albert Bachert, as early as 1885, harbored a deep hatred for socialists and anarchists, and seems to have made it his life's mission to bring them down. He had a personal conflict with members of the Berner Street club that he claimed led them to damage his property and threaten his life. Three weeks before Stride was murdered in the yard of this club, Bachert wrote a letter to the editor of the *Evening News* stating his belief that the Whitechapel murderer was a member of such a club and offered to provide them a list of the clubs he felt should be investigated. On the night of Stride's murder, Bachert was drinking at the Three Nuns (or Three Tuns) pub in City territory, but seems to have left just after midnight, with plenty of time to make it to Berner Street. As he seems to have been politically opposed to establishments offering alcohol for sale, it's curious we should find him in one an hour before a woman is murdered in the yard of his enemies.

Bachert inserts himself into the investigation the next day with a concocted tale involving a suspect culled from the legitimate evidence of Fanny Mortimer of 36 Berner Street. Her account had not been made public when he presented his tale to the police and press, so it's possible he was in Berner Street in the first few hours following the murder.

In 1891, another Whitechapel murder victim, Frances Coles, is found murdered only "a few yards" from where Bachert was staying and where he claims to have been at the time of the murder. He states that he saw the victim not once, but twice in the company of a man that evening. Some researchers feel the circumstances between the murder of Coles and Stride, to the exclusion of all other Whitechapel murders, are similar enough to suggest the same hand.

Bachert was not above stealing large sums from his own father, believed the police would conspire against him, and was alone with a 14-year-old boy when cast iron griffin 'fell' on his head, killing him.

Somebody murdered Elizabeth Stride. The police investigation cleared Michael Kidney, her only known lover, and the quick, passionless dispatch of the victim in a public place points decidedly away from it having been a 'domestic' homicide. Many researchers feel this same evidence clears Jack the Ripper of the murder.

But somebody murdered Elizabeth Stride.

We've read a lot about Albert Bachert. We like him, we think we know him. But how much do we really know about him?[112]

AUTHOR'S NOTE: This work is a continuation of 'A Berner Street Rogues Gallery' that appeared in *Casebook Examiner* No. 7. When *Casebook Examiner* ended its short run, Editor Don Souden created a wonderful journal with the purposefully non-descriptive name of *The New Independent Review*. His intention was to eventually offer authors the opportunity to stretch out beyond the Ripper murders and present research and theory on other historical mysteries. Unfortunately, a downturn in health forced Don to terminate the journal after only seven editions. But many journals that lasted ten times as long could not have hoped to have offered readers the visually and cerebrally stimulating research pieces that Souden managed to turn out with seeming ease. It was once again my honor to have been able to take part in a new venture of Don's, and the 'Bachert in Berner Street' appeared in the first issue of *The New Independent Review* in September of 2011. It has been updated with additional information regarding Albert Bachert. The author does not personally believe that Bachert murdered Liz Stride, or anybody, but admits the circumstances as presented here are eerie and unsettling and hopes researchers will continue to unearth more information about Albert Bachert, a truly enigmatic young man and argu-ably the original Ripperologist, or perhaps just an irritator. For readers newer to the case who might not be aware of just how active Bachert was as an investigator and agitator, I highly recommend reading Chris Scott's *Jack the Ripper: A Cast of Thousands*, the text of which is available for free at Casebook.org.

ADDITIONAL NOTE: As the manuscript of this book was being finalized, and after having written the foregoing, I received a copy of a new book authored by Ripper researcher and tour guide extraordinaire, Mick Priestley. The book is titled *Jack the Ripper: One Autumn in Whitechapel* and argues for Bachert as the Ripper. Mr. Priestley was unaware of my earlier article or research into the case and so his presentation and conclusions are entirely his own. Readers who found this essay intriguing might find it worthwhile to seek Mr. Priestley's book, which also offers a very in-depth survey of the murders he believes are attributable to the Ripper.

Or, the Case of the Fruiterer Who Sold Stride Grapes and Handed Us Lemons

F OLLOWING THE DISCOVERY of Annie Chapman's body in the yard of 29 Hanbury Street and an impassioned plea in the Sept. 8th, 1888 edition of the *Star* calling for citizens to form themselves 'at once into Vigilance Committees', a handful of local businessmen wasted no time in rising to the challenge, and the Whitechapel Vigilance Committee (heretofore referred to as the WVC) was born.

The *Daily Telegraph* of Sept. 11th reported the formation of the committee and that 'meetings were held at the various working men's clubs and other organisations, political and social, in the district, at most of which the proposed scheme was approved and volunteers enrolled.' Low on funds, all the patrolmen hired on by the committee were previously unemployed[113], and the headquarters for this newfound venture was located at the Crown Tavern at 74 Mile End Road, owned and operated by committee treasurer, Joseph Aarons.

The largest collection of able-bodied unemployed men to be found near the committee headquarters was the International Working Men's Educational

Society (also 'Club', heretofore referred to as the IWMES) at 40 Berner Street, which was both a political and social club. The men of the IWMES would have been very familiar to Aarons and his colleagues as they regularly held outdoor rallies in Mile End Road, and it is unavoidable that the IWMES would have been among their first stops in gaining support and recruits. Although it has yet to be discussed in Ripper literature, outside of my published essays[114], there would have been a strong link between the WVC and the IWMES, with some men being involved in both organizations simultaneously.

Feeling themselves unqualified for the task of investigation, the WVC at some point in September hired two private detectives[115] who '[held] themselves out as experts in the unraveling of mysteries.'[116] The men gave their names as Charles Le Grand and J. H. Batchelor.

On Saturday, September 30th, at 1 o'clock in the morning, Louis Diemshitz discovered the body of 45 year-old prostitute, Elizabeth Stride, in the pathway leading into the backyard of 40 Berner Street. She had expired from a single cut to the throat. Eight hours later, at approximately 9am, Police-Sergeant Stephen White, of H Division, knocked at the door of 44 Berner Street, where lived Matthew Packer, a fruiterer by trade, along with his wife, and two lodgers: Sarah Harrison and Harry Douglas. White's interrogation was short and uneventful, and whatever answers he received were recorded in a notebook he carried for that purpose. The particulars are provided below from a report prepared by White on Oct. 4[th.]

> I asked him what time he closed his shop on the previous night. He replied half past twelve [Note in margin reads:-? Half past 11] in consequence of the rain it was no good for me to keep open. I asked him if he saw anything of a man or woman going into Dutfield's Yard, or saw anyone standing about the street about the time he was closing his shop. He replied "No I saw no one standing about neither did I see anyone go up the yard. I never saw anything suspicious or heard the slightest noise, and know [sic] nothing about the murder until I heard of it in the morning.
>
> I also saw Mrs. Packer, Sarah Harris[on] and Harry Douglas

residing in the same house but none of them could give the slightest information respecting the matter.[117]

What prompted PS White's superiors to request this report was a sensational article that appeared earlier that evening in the *Evening News*, to the effect that Matthew Packer had spoken to Elizabeth Stride and a man (presumably her killer) and sold them grapes. If true, it meant that Packer had likely spoken to Jack the Ripper and the investigators had missed him, a fact that would deal a heavy blow to the already suffering reputation of the Metropolitan Police. This spectacular, though lengthy, report from the *Evening News* of October 4th was actually two reports – the first written on the information turned in by the private detectives, the second a follow-up interview with Packer by the newspaper's 'Special Commissioner'.

It is highly unlikely the *Evening News* were in on the trick with Le Grand and Packer, or were even aware of the subterfuge, but the scoop was so good that they're sure to have turned a blind eye to any mutterings or details that otherwise should have set off alarm bells. It is also possible that Le Grand was himself the 'Special Commissioner', as it would be odd for the newspaper to commission yet another person outside of their offices when they could have sent a trusted staff reporter.

The substance of Packer's story as related in the first section of the report (that belonging to the private detectives), describes 'Messrs. Grand & J.H. Batchelor' arriving in Berner Street and going almost straight to number 44 where Packer, apparently with no inducement, started telling them everything he knew. He stated that at 11:45pm on Friday, the 29th, a man and a woman came to his window and purchased some grapes. He described the man as '…middle aged, perhaps 35 years; about five feet seven inches in height, stout, square built; wore a wideawake hat and dark clothes; had the appearance of a clerk; had a rough voice and a quick, sharp way of talking.' Regarding the woman, he said she was middle-aged and wearing dark clothing. Because it was dark outside and the only light available came from an oil lamp he had burning inside, a white flower she wore on her bosom stood in contrast to the darkness and drew his particular attention. He had the following conversation with the man:

The man asked his companion whether she would have black or white grapes; she replied "black."

"Well, what's the price of the black grapes, old man?" he inquired.

"The black are sixpence and the white fourpence," replied Packer.

"Well then, old man, give us half a pound of the black," said the man. Packer served him with the grapes, which he handed to the woman. They then crossed the road and stood on the pavement almost directly opposite to the shop for a long time more than half an hour.

Watching the couple across the street, Packer remarked to his wife, "What fools those people are to be standing in the rain like that." The wet couple shortly crossed the road and stood in front of the IWMES, apparently listening to the music. According to the report, it was now ten or fifteen minutes after midnight, although if the couple came to his window at 11:45 and stood across the road for more than 30 minutes, it could have been no earlier than 12:20am that they crossed the street to the club. Packer says he fixed the time by the closing of the public houses, by which he would have meant the Nelson beerhouse a few doors down from him at the corner of Berner and Fairclough Street or the George IV pub further down Berner Street.

Following three interviews, the private detectives had Packer sign a sworn statement to the foregoing and then, to test his accuracy, told him they were taking him to identify Stride's body. They instead took him to view the body of Catherine Eddowes. He denied she was the woman he saw, but immediately identified Stride when shown her corpse. It was here that PS Stephen White made first contact with Packer and the PIs. His report recalls the meeting:

On 4th Inst. I was directed by Inspr. Moore to make further inquiry & if necessary see Packer and take him to the mortuary. I then went to 44 Berner St. and saw Mrs. Packer who informed me that two Detectives had called and taken her husband to the mortuary. I then went towards the mortuary when I met Packer with a man. I asked where he had been. He said, "this detective asked me to go to see if I could identify the woman.["] I said "have you so," he said "Yes, I believe she bought some grapes at my shop about 12. o clock on Saturday.["] Shortly afterwards they were joined by another man. I asked the men what they were doing with Packer and they both said that they were Detectives. I asked for their Authority one of the men produced a card from a pocket Book, but would not allow me to touch it. They then said that they were private detectives. They then induced Packer to go away with them.

Back in Berner Street, the two PIs set about finding corroborative evidence for Packer's tale, and this they found in abundance and in record time. Knocking at 14 Berner Street, the men spoke to Mrs. Rosenfield and her sister, Eva Harstein. Mrs. Rosenfield stated that she passed through Dutfield's Yard early on Sunday morning and saw a bloody grape stalk. Ms. Harstein, who apparently was present in the yard before Stride's body was removed, corroborated her sister's story and added that after removal of the body she saw 'a few small petals of a white natural flower' near where the body had been. Knowing that the yard had been washed down following the removal of Stride's body and following a hunch, the detectives searched the club's gutter and amidst the refuse discovered a grape stalk.

Their case was closed.

Regarding the 'Special Commissioner' of the *Evening News*, he conducted a rather leading interview with Packer and relayed it in the most dramatic terms possible. Packer's man's age regressed a bit to 30-35, and Stride now carried the flower in her hand as opposed to wearing it in her bosom. The couple's movements also changed a bit, with them first going in front of the club for a few minutes before passing to the other side of the street to stand in the rain for a half an hour or so. But the most sensational part of the interview is as follows:

"Well, Mr. Packer, I suppose the police came at once to ask you and your wife what you knew about the affair, as soon as ever the body was discovered."

"The police? No. They haven't asked me a word about it yet!!! A young man in plain clothes came in here on Monday and asked if he might look at the yard at the back of our house, so as to see if anybody had climbed over. My missus lent him some steps. But he didn't put any questions to us about the man and the woman."

"I am afraid you don't quite understand my question, Mr. Packer. Do you actually mean to say that no detective or policeman came to inquire whether you had sold grapes to any one that night? Now, please be very careful in your answer, for this may prove a serious business for the London police."

"I've only got one answer," said the man "because it's the truth. Except a gentleman who is a private detective. No detective or policeman has ever asked me a single question nor come near my shop to find out if I knew anything about the grapes the murdered woman had been eating before her throat was cut!!!"

This would certainly have been news to PS White, who, intent on having his meeting with Packer, returned to Packer's residence later that same day. His report, filed later that evening, records yet another abortive attempt:

About 4p.m. I saw Packer at his shop and while talking to him the two men drove up in a Hansom Cab, and after going into the shop they induced Packer to enter the Cab stating that they would take him to Scotland Yard to see Sir Charles Warren.

From inquiry I have made there is no doubt that these are the two men referred to in attached Newspaper cutting, who examined the drain in Dutfield's Yard on 2nd Inst. One of the men had a letter in his hand addressed to Le Grand & Co., Strand.

While the idea that Packer could simply waltz in and demand an interview with the Commissioner of Police is laughable, it nevertheless has become largely accepted in Ripper lore through repetition. The two 'detectives', for good reason, would not have accompanied Packer inside the station, so he would now for the first time have to stand on his own legs and deliver his story to people most familiar with the particulars of the crime. The results are quite telling:

Matthew Packer

Keeps a shop in Berner St. has a few grapes in window, black & white.

On Sat night about 11p.m. a young man from 25-30 – about 5.7. with long black coat buttoned up – soft felt hat, kind of Yankee hat rather broad shoulders – rather quick in speaking. rough voice. I sold him ½ pound black grapes 3d. A woman came up with him from Back Church end (the lower end of street) She was dressed in black frock & jacket, fur round bottom of jacket a black crape bonnet, she was playing with a flower like a geranium white outside & red inside. I identify the woman at the St. George's mortuary as the one I saw that night –

They passed by as though they were going up Com-Road, but – instead of going up they crossed to the other side of the road to the Board School, & were there for about ½ an hour till I shd. say 11.30. talking to one another. I then shut up my shutters.

Before they passed over opposite to my shop, they wait[ed] near to the club for a few minutes apparently listening to the music.

I saw no more of them after I shut up my shutters. I put the man down as a young clerk. He had a frock coat on – no gloves. He was about 1 ½ or 2 or 3 inches - a little higher than she was.

Packer's middle-aged man has now become a 'young man from 25-30'; unless Jack the Ripper was Benjamin Button, it's safe to say that Packer, when having to act on his own, was not a sufficient liar. Only hours earlier Packer had told PS White that the man bought grapes at 'about 12am', but here it becomes 11pm. This would probably have less to do with Packer's poor memory and more to do with the police knowledge of the circumstances surrounding the murder; the moment that Packer stated the couple bought grapes at 'about midnight' and stood for 30 minutes in the rain, he would have been reminded that the rain let up after 11pm and stopped altogether around 11:30pm, forcing Packer to back-peddle and concede that his conversation with Stride and her man must have happened at 11pm. His interrogator also would also have been aware that Stride's clothing was bone-dry when found at 1am, meaning she could not have stood in the rain for any length of time only an hour or two before her discovery. For these reasons, Packer could not be believed, not even by the men who would later accept George Hutchinson's statement at face value.

When further questioning of Louis Diemshitz and others present in Dutfield's Yard revealed that no grapes were seen in the hand of the victim, and the medical reports proved she had not consumed grapes (the idea given by some writers that she unfailingly spit out all seeds and skins is, in my opinion, preposterous), it would become clear beyond a doubt that Packer's entire story was a fabrication.

In Chief Inspector Donald Swanson's well-known and crucial report of Oct. 19th, he summarizes Packer's statement and offers the following consensus:

> Mr. Packer when asked by the police stated that he did not see any suspicious person about, and it was not until after the publication in the newspapers of the description of man seen by the P.C. that Mr. Packer gave the foregoing particulars to two private enquiry men acting conjointly with the Vigilance Comtee. and the press, who upon searching a drain in the yard found a grape stem which was amongst the other matter swept from the yard after its examination by the police & then calling upon Mr. Packer whom they took to the mortuary where he identified the body of Elizabeth Stride as that of the woman. Packer who is an elderly man[118], has unfortunately made different statements so that apart from the fact of the hour at which he saw the woman (and she was seen afterwards by the P.C. & Schwartz as stated) any statement he made would be rendered almost valueless as evidence.

If Swanson was being generous to Packer in his summary, his superior, Assistant Commissioner, Dr. Robert Anderson, did not mind revealing his bitter annoyance in a report dated Oct. 23rd, which read in part, '... the activity of the Police has been to a considerable extent wasted through the exigencies of sensational journalism, and the action of unprincipled persons, who, from various motives, have endeavoured to mislead us.' It is not known if the police spoke with Mrs. Rosenfield and Eva Harstein regarding their roles in the mystery play, but as their names and addresses were made available in the *Evening News* report, it would be remarkable if they had not. Whether the sisters kept with their story or sang like birds can only be guessed at, but Anderson's comment referencing the press, various 'unprincipled persons', and different motives, is a strong indicator they traced the entire subterfuge back to the two private detectives. This should not have been hard to figure out, as it was they who sought out Packer, sought out the sisters, 'found' the grape stalk, and sold the story to a newspaper. The question the police should have asked at the time, but wouldn't until much later, is '*Why* did the two men go to such trouble to perpetrate this hoax'? That's a question too big for this present work and will have to wait until my next book. Our purpose here is take a long hard look at Matthew Packer, and fortunately, his motive was obvious.

Money.

For more than 100 years, writers on the case have either accepted Packer's story at face value, or, deciding it well and truly quashed by the police at the time, ignored it in favor of more reliable evidence. Nobody gave it much thought or took a closer look at the people involved. That is, until August of 1998 and the publication of issue 18 of *Ripperologist* magazine, which contained a short piece by researcher Gerry Nixon entitled 'Le Grand of the Strand'.

Nixon published the details of some newspaper reports he had uncovered regarding private detective Charles Le Grand. He revealed that Le Grand had been known to police among many aliases, had been convicted numerous times for theft, blackmail, and writing threatening letters. Subsequent research revealed that among his many other criminalistics exploits, Le Grand was also in the habit of paying people to give false testimony.

It occurred to me how absurd it was to think that Matthew Packer could have engineered the deceit that had attached itself so firmly to his name. He was, after all, a simple fruiterer and family man who was getting on in years. It simply isn't conceivable that he could have dreamt up such a tale, convinced the two sisters to go along with it, and most importantly, have succeeded in deceiving a career criminal such as Le Grand.

Grapes played a pivotal part in at least two of the most popular Ripper films, including 2001's *From Hell*, and countless Ripper books. Indeed, Sir William Withey Gull's love for grapes was one of the key points of evidence used to falsely identify him as the Ripper. That the 'grapes of myth' are so ingrained in Ripper lore well over a century after the murders is testament to the impact it must have had while the investigation was afoot.

With much to lose and nothing apparent to gain, it appears possible that Le Grand's sole motive in orchestrating the Berner Street conspiracy was to present the world with a phantom suspect; one who never existed, and therefore could never be found, and one who, it must be said, looked nothing like himself.

Le Grand, Packer & the Batty Street Lodger

The Batty Street Lodger should be familiar to most Ripper readers, having been the 'title character' of Stewart Evans and Paul Gainey's seminal 1995 best-seller, *The Lodger* (U.S.A. title *Jack the Ripper: First American Serial Killer*). Evans and Gainey argued that a mysterious foreign man lodging in the house of Mrs. Kuer, a German laundress, at 22 Batty Street, had left behind a bloodstained shirt following the 'double event' murders of Catherine Eddowes and Liz Stride, and that this man must have been the American quack doctor and Ripper suspect, Francis Tumblety. A good portion of the book was devoted to developing this thesis, and it's fair to say that the Batty Street Lodger theory formed one of the three pillars of evidence upon which the argument for Tumblety as Ripper stands; the other two being the well-known 'Littlechild letter' and the vast amount of reportage in American papers concerning Scotland Yard inspectors following Tumblety to America and shadowing his every move.

In a series of articles for *Ripperologist* magazine[119], researcher Gavin Bromley expertly demonstrated reasons why we might conclude (without actually stating as much himself) that the Batty Street Lodger had never existed and had largely been little more than the press making a mountain out of a molehill. More recently, Robert House resurrected the Batty Street Lodger for his book arguing Aaron Kozminski as the Ripper.[120]

Bromley wrote that the Lodger story broke in the papers on October 16th, although subsequently he was able to find one report from the day before, and it had previously been accepted that this was the first report-age of the Batty Street Lodger. However, a recent bombshell discovery by Debra Arif comes a full five days earlier, on Oct. 10th, and is the first and possibly last word on the Batty Street Lodger:

A BLOODSTAINED SHIRT.

Messrs Grand and Batchelor, private detectives, received informa-tion yesterday afternoon which induced them to make enquiries in Batty-street, Whitechapel. They ascertained that a man, name unknown, recently left with Mrs. Kail [sic] a shirt, the sleeves of which were stained with blood. Information was sent to the police, who at once instituted enquiries, with what result is not known. Mrs. Kail was able to give a good description of her mys-terious customer; but the authorities do not consider it advisable to make it public. Little importance is attached to the incident, it being pretty obvious that if the murderer wished to dispose of his blood-stained garment, he would get rid of it in a more effective manner than by leaving it with a laundress to be washed.[121]

This means that not one but two long-standing ruses can be laid at the feet of Charles Le Grand, who not only had the police running in every direction but his own, but also modern researchers likewise look-ing with misguided suspicion at the wrong men. Mrs. Kuer could only speak German, which posed a problem for reporters, so it's likely that the German-speaking Le Grand – the original source for the story – was also the person responsible for the otherwise mundane story becoming a press sensation, while being careful to keep his name out of the press once the story took hold. Le Grand's stooge, Matthew Packer, turned up to provide a link between his two tall tales. The *Echo* from Oct. 18th, 1888, reports:

An Echo reporter called yesterday afternoon upon Mr. Packer, the Berner-street fruitier, where the murderer bought the grapes for Elizabeth Stride. It now appears that the man was known by Mr. Packer, who positively asserted, "I had seen him in this dis-trict several times before, and if you ask me where he lives I can tell you within a little. He lodges not a great way from the house where Lipski, who was hanged for poisoning a woman, lived." "How many times have you seen him?" was asked Mr. Packer. "About twenty; and I have not seen him since the murder."

Since Israel Lipski lived at 16 Batty Street, only 3 doors down from Mrs. Kuer/Kail at number 22, there can be no doubt that Packer is here tying together Le Grand's two stories and offering them up as one, with the added information that he'd known this extraordinary suspect well by sight. Any writer now wishing to invest either the Lodger story or the Packer grape episode with any evidential value will certainly have an uphill battle. But it gets better.

The Further Misadventures of Matthew Packer

Matthew Packer, in a modern Ripper book, would make a brief appearance in the course of a chapter covering the Liz Stride murder, and swiftly exit stage left following the author's treatment of his evidence regarding the sale of the grapes. However, such was not the case in 1888, when Packer developed into sort of a Whitechapel Kato Kaelin.[122]

Packer remained a media constant throughout October on account of the widespread belief that he was the man most likely to have seen the Whitechapel Murderer, who himself was on the cusp of worldwide infamy by the exposure afforded the 'Dear Boss' letter that had rechristened him 'Jack the Ripper'. According to the press of Oct. 8th, Packer had been working closely with the police to produce a sketch of Stride's escort to whom he'd sold the grapes. That the police bothered to work with Packer in creating sketches for a suspect they didn't believe existed is doubtful; there's certainly no evidence for it in the surviving reports. However, there's no question that he participated in such an exercise with the press.

Identikits, as they're known today, didn't really exist in 1888, so in a way it was a rather innovative, if futile, exercise. First, numerous sketches were made from the descriptions given by Packer, Henry Birch[123], Albert Bachert[124], and PC Smith[125], which appeared in the press. A series of photographs were also prepared. Packer and Birch 'at once rejected the faces of men of purely sensuous types and thus threw aside the portraits of several noted American criminals.'[126]

When a copy of this sketch was made available to Packer he said it bore 'no resemblance whatsoever' to the man he'd endeavored to describe and looked more like a 'mere boy' than the man of at least 30 years of age he'd spoken with. Tellingly, he also 'complained very bitterly that he had wasted nearly the whole week in trying to help the police, had neglected his business, and had not received the least remuneration, though promises had been made to him that his time would be paid for'.[127]

Packer was to see his Ripper again on Saturday, October 27th when the fruiterer was tending his mobile fruit stand at the corner of Greenfield Street and Commercial Road. His adventure was detailed in numerous newspapers, but it were his friends at the *Evening News* who found themselves blessed with a personal interview with the reluctant Ripper hunter:

"Between seven and eight o'clock, on Saturday evening last, I was standing with my barrow at the corner of Greenfield-street, Commercial-road, when I saw a man pass by on the opposite side of Greenfield-street, near the watchmaker's shop. I recognized him in a minute as the man I had seen outside my shop on the night when Elizabeth Stride was murdered in Berner-street. It was the man who bought the grapes and gave them to the woman that was afterwards found murdered in the yard. I shall never forget his face and should know him again amongst a thousand men.

"I can tell you what it was. I was pretty right knocked over with fright. It gave me such a turn as I have never had in my life. I was too frightened and staggered to know what I was about, and I saw in a minute that the man knew me as well. He looked hard at me as he passed, and then turned round and passed again, with a most vicious look on his face, that made me think I should not have liked to have been with him in any quiet corner. I'm sure he'd have killed me. He walked by four times altogether, and I thought he wanted to get close to me, so I kept moving round to the north side of my barrow. I then called to a young chap that I knew who was standing at the coroner of the street, and asked him to keep an eye on the man, as I was afraid he meant mischief. There were no policemen in sight, and I was afraid to lose sight of the man. I sent the young chap for a policeman, and the man seeing there was something up jumped into a tram that was going to Blackwall."[128]

Packer recovered sufficiently from the shock of seeing the Ripper again - as well as the financial loss he suffered at the hands of an ungrateful police force - to have by November expanded his business to include live stock. No doubt his local celebrity had driven much custom his way and he meant to capitalize on it to the fullest.

On Tuesday, November 13th, two men came to his shop to purchase 12 shillings' worth of rabbits. In the course of their transaction the men asked him about the man to whom he'd sold grapes on the night of the 'double event' murders. Packer would have mastered the telling of the story through repetition by this point and provided the men with his stock description. He was surprised by their response, but his contact at the *Evening News* was soon on hand to take up the clue:

In reply to some questions by Packer, one of the men said, 'Well, I am sorry to say that I firmly believe it is my own cousin. He is an Englishman by birth, but some time ago he went to America, stayed there a few years, and then came back to London about seven or eight months ago. On his return he came to see me, and his first words were, 'Well, Boss, how are you?' He asked me to have some walks out with him, and I did round Commercial Street and Whitechapel. I found that he had very much altered on his return, for he was thoroughly harem scarem.

We met a lot of Whitechapel women, and when we passed them he used to say to me, 'How do you think we used to serve them where I came from? Why we used to cut their throats and rip them up. I could rip one of them up and get her inside out in no time.' He said, 'We Jack Rippers killed lots of women over there. You will hear of some of it being done over here soon, for I am going to turn a London Jack Ripper.' The man then said, 'I did not take much notice then of what he said, and I thought it was only his swagger and bounce of what he had been doing in America, at some place which Packer says he mentioned, but he forgets the name. 'But,' continued the man, 'When I heard of the first woman being murdered and stabbed all over, I then began to be very uneasy, and to wonder whether he really was carrying out his threats. I did not, however, like to say anything about him, as he is my own cousin. Then, as one murder followed another, I felt that I could scarcely rest.

He is a perfect monster towards women, especially when he has had a drop of drink. But, in addition to what he said to me about these murders in America, and what was going to be done here, I feel certain it is him, because of the way these Jack Ripper letters which have appeared in the papers begin. They all begin 'Dear Boss,' and that is just the way he begins his letters. He calls everybody 'Boss' when he speaks to them. I did not want to say anything about him if I could help it so I wrote to him, but he did not answer my letter. Since this last murder I have felt that I could not remain silent any longer, for at least something ought to be done to put him under restraint.[129]

Packer felt sure the men were speaking the truth; so sure, in fact, that he bypassed the police station in favor of selling it to the reporter, who took Packer's statement and mailed a copy to both Home Secretary Henry Matthews and Sir James Fraser, the Commissioner of the City of London Police. It doesn't appear that the Metropolitan Police (who were in charge of the Stride investigation and with whom Packer would have been most familiar) were contacted, probably on account of their animosity towards Packer. Although Packer's personal evidence was questionable at best, because of the notoriety it brought him, it's not outside the realm of possibility that someone with real evidence might seek him out and share it. According to the *Evening News*, Sir James Fraser sent Detective-Sergeants White[130] and Mitchell to take Packer's statement and set themselves upon the trail of the mysterious rabbit men.

The results were disappointing. Four days after the original article ran, the *Manchester Guardian* reported that Packer's information 'is still being investigated by the detectives, who are inclined to doubt the veracity of the greater portion of the details. They, however, believe they have found the cousin referred to, and attach little importance to what was at first supposed to be a substantial clue.' The Aberdeen *Weekly News*, writing on the 16th (only a day after the initial *Evening News* report), was even more succinct in their coverage, bluntly stating 'The Central News says the statement made by the Berner Street fruiterer, Matthew Packer, has been fully investigated by the police and proved to be worthless.'

The police were no doubt annoyed by Packer, as such statements had to be investigated, which took valuable resources away from following up more promising clues, particularly the avalanche of information that followed in the wake of the murder of Mary Kelly. In the same article that discussed this latest Packer episode, one newspaper reported 'the police are now to a great extent concentrating their efforts upon an endeavour to find a man so vividly described by George Hutchinson, and they do not doubt that they will be successful. It is understood that the police authorities are somewhat annoyed at the widespread publicity and complain that its immediate effect will be to put the assassin on his guard.'[131]

The 'American Cousin' story quickly petered out, but it hardly had time to do so before Packer was once again back with a new sighting of the murderer, this time in concert with fellow witness, the milkman Henry Birch, and Birch's son. This episode is more fully discussed in the chapter 'Henry Birch and the Cambridge Heath Road Incident' in Chapter 6 of Section 1 of this book, but in short their story amounted to them having formed their own vigilance league, and upon spotting the Ripper in Commercial Road on Friday, November 23rd, they quietly followed him, witnessed him accost a woman, and then mysteriously disappear down a dark turning once he realized he was being sleuthed.

Henry Birch claimed to have given a statement to the police on September 1st, but there's no evidence that he had said a word about the suspicious man who entered his milk stall until October, when he showed up in the press, backing Packer's description of the 'assassin'. He may have been another stooge paid by Charles Le Grand, or may have been a friend of Packer trying to get a piece of the action after seeing the celebrity

Packer had gained. There's always the off chance that Birch really did see what he says he saw on September 1ˢᵗ, but his later affiliation with Packer must cast doubt on that.

November did not end well for Matthew Packer, seeing him receive a threatening letter as well as a physical beating. The *Echo* of November 24ᵗʰ[132] carried the story:

THE ASSAULT ON THE FRUITERER

A few evenings ago Packer received an anonymous threatening letter. On this a murder was represented, drawn in blood. It was posted at Tottenham. At all events, it bore the Tottenham post-mark. He took it to the police. In the course of this week while standing one night outside his shop he was set upon by a gang of roughs. Two of them seized him and punched him in the ribs, and then threw him to the ground. His wife ran out to his assistance, and, on raising an alarm, they hurried away. A policeman who was at the bottom of the street captured one of the men, and he was taken to the police-station. He admitted there were nine in the gang, but said he had nothing to do with the assault, and he was allowed to go. Packer was last night still suffering from the injuries he has received.

It's interesting to note that Packer's various escapades seem to take place just after a major event. He first entered the scene in the wake of the Stride murder, and is next heard from when the mysterious 'Batty Street Lodger' makes the front pages, proclaiming his man and the lodger to be one and the same. His 'American Cousin' story came in the wake of Mary Kelly's murder, and his 'threatening letter' and beating are to have con-curred with the alleged assault upon Annie Farmer at the now-notorious 19 George Street.[133]

1889 would prove an even more trying year for Packer, who more or less kept his nose clean, but still managed to make the press in September of that year:

Shortly after the commission of the murder preceding the

Pinchin street discovery, Packer again expressed an opinion that the criminal did not live "very far from Batty Street," which is within three minutes' walk of the railway arch. Not long after that Packer averred that, while he was standing near his door-step, two men rushed upon him and knocked him down, with the remark, "Know where Jack the Ripper lives, do you?" The unfortunate man was, as a result, admitted to the London Hospital, where he was detained for three weeks. A reporter has since seen Packer. He declares that this story is quite true, and that he was seriously injured by the attack. "But I don't wish to say any more," said he. "I've had quite enough of this Whitechapel business already – too much for me."[134]

Thus ends Matthew Packer's involvement with the investigation. The murder preceding the discovery of the Pinchin Street torso was that of Alice Mackenzie in July of 1889, so it was around this time that this last assault on Packer would have occurred. Researcher Rob Clack checked the London Hospital admission and discharge records from November 9th, 1888 to the end of January, 1889, and then from June 1889 to the middle of September, 1889, and found no mention of Packer having been admitted there, let alone for three weeks.[135]

Packer would live on into the 20th century, selling fruit out of the window of 44 Berner Street. I'm not certain when he died, but he would continue to be visited by the children and grandchildren from his first marriage and appears never to have been disturbed by the Ripper again.

Some writers find Packer to have been a credible witness, but this might be a case of wanting to see what isn't there. What I see when I look at the full story of his prolonged self-involvement with the investigation is an opportunist who was paid cash by Charles Le Grand to back up a story about a man who never existed, and then, finding some measure of notoriety from this, wanted to stretch his proverbial 15 minutes into as long a time as possible. And this he did.

AUTHOR'S NOTE: When I wrote my 'Berner Street Mystery' essays for *Ripper Notes* some years ago I took for granted that it was universally understood that the fruiterer, Matthew Packer, was a dishonest witness and had never actually sold Liz Stride and her eventual murderer grapes on that rainy, fateful evening. However, two popular Ripper books arrived in 2015 that argue vehemently for Packer as a credible witness and further suggest that there was a police conspiracy to cover up his sale of and Liz's consumption of the grapes. In 'Jack and the Grape Stalk' I went through the eyewitness evidence and explained how it came about that the 'oblong clots' of blood on Stride's wrist were mistaken for clutched grapes. I thought that for the sake of accuracy it was also important that we take an intimate look at Packer himself and the many sequels his grape story spawned. Big chunks of this piece were first published in a lengthy essay I'd written about Packer's tempter, Charles Le Grand, and published in the *Casebook Examiner* #2, June, 2010; but the latter portion covering Packer's subsequent exploits was compiled and written fresh for this book.

New Insights on Crucial Witnesses – Smith, Brown & Mortimer

F ANNY MORTIMER, DEPENDING on which book you read, was a confused old woman, an attention-seeking gossiping busybody, or a crucial witness. And that's when she's not excluded all together. The evidence of what she saw and when she saw it is important in helping provide a timeline for the more contentious witnesses. However, she also tended to use the attention she received from reporters to pass on gossip she'd picked up in the huddle outside Dutfield's Yard. It's my intention to sort all that out and place her evidence into its proper historical perspective.

Fanny Skipp, aged 21, married 22 year-old William Mortimer on March 3rd, 1861. By 1871 they had set up house at 36 Berner Street and were raising three of their eventual five children. William worked as a car man and may have been the Mr. Mortimer who had appeared in court just the day before the 'double event' when an employee of his attempted (without Mortimer's complicity) to steal a van load of goods.[136] Whatever the case, the salad days were certainly behind him; William would pass away within six months, the cause currently unknown.[137] But on the final night of Liz

Stride's life he was alive and attempting to sleep when all hell broke loose on their tiny, narrow street.

The Mortimers lived only two doors away from the Berner Street club. Fanny was wide awake with her door open for much of the hour leading up to 1am and the discovery of Liz Stride's murder. Because of her proximity to the scene of the crime and her early arrival after the cry was raised by the clubmen, her statements necessitate careful consideration.

There are two press articles purporting to emanate from Fanny that receive the most attention from modern readers. The first was a syndicated press release and was carried in many newspapers beginning October 1st:

> Mrs. Mortimer, living at 36, Berner-street, four doors from the scene of the tragedy, says: I was standing at the door of my house nearly the whole time between half-past twelve and one o'clock this (Sunday) morning, and did not notice anything unusual. I had just gone indoors, and was preparing to go to bed, when I heard a commotion outside, and immediately ran out, thinking that there was another row at the Socialists' Club close by. I went to see what was the matter, and was informed that another dreadful murder had been committed in the yard adjoining the clubhouse, and on going inside I saw the body of a woman lying huddled up just inside the gates with her throat cut from ear to ear. A man touched her face, and said it was quite warm, so that the deed must have been done while I was standing at the door of my house. There was certainly no noise made, and I did not observe anyone enter the gates. It was just after one o'clock when I went out, and the only man whom I had seen pass through the street previously was a young man carrying a black shiny bag, who walked very fast down the street from the Commercial-road. He looked up at the club, and then went round the corner by the Board School. I was told that the manager or steward of the club had discovered the woman on his return home in his pony cart. He drove through the gates, and my opinion is that he interrupted the murderer, who must have made his escape immediately under cover of the cart. If a man had come out of the yard before one o'clock I must have

seen him. It was almost incredible to me that the thing could have been done without the steward's wife hearing a noise, for she was sitting in the kitchen from which a window opens four yards from the spot where the woman was found. The body was lying slightly on one side, with the legs a little drawn up as if in pain, the clothes being slightly disarranged, so that the legs were partly visible. The woman appeared to me to be respectable, judging by her clothes, and in her hand were found a bunch of grapes and some sweets. A young man and his sweetheart were standing at the corner of the street, about 20 yards away, before and after the time the woman must have been murdered, but they told me they did not hear a sound.[138]

The other well-known report comes from the *Evening News* of the same date:

When the alarm of murder was raised a young girl had been standing in a bisecting thoroughfare not fifty yards from the spot where the body was found. She had, she said, been stand-ing there for about twenty-minutes, talking with her sweetheart, but neither of them heard any unusual noises. A woman who lives two doors from the club has made an important statement. It appears that shortly before a quarter to one o'clock she heard the measured, heavy tramp of a policeman passing the house on his beat. Immediately afterwards she went to the street-door, with the intention of shooting the bolts, though she remained standing there ten minutes before she did so. During the ten minutes she saw no one enter or leave the neighbouring yard, and she feels sure that had any one done so she could not have overlooked the fact. The quiet and deserted character of the street appears even to have struck her at the time. Locking the door, she prepared to retire to bed, in the front room on the ground floor, and it so happened that in about four minutes' time she heard Diemschitz's [sic] pony cart pass the house, and remarked upon the circum-stance to her husband.

Much of what Fanny reports is hearsay information, such as the bit about the young couple (which will be discussed shortly) and the 'bunch of grapes and some sweets' that she must have heard about some time later, as she would not have been present in the locked yard when Stride's hands were opened. It has been described that Fanny witnessed a young couple standing on the corner, but her statement makes clear that she learned this information second hand from the young woman, who was known to her. Fanny would have certainly seen the body with her own eyes and her description of Stride's position corresponds with the most reliable reports. What causes confusion are her seemingly contradictory statements about when and for how long she was at her door:

> **Syndicated Press:** 'I was standing at the door of my house nearly the whole time between half-past twelve and one o'clock this (Sunday) morning, and did not notice anything unusual.'

> **Evening News:** 'It appears that shortly before a quarter to one o'clock she heard the measured, heavy tramp of a policeman pass-ing the house on his beat. Immediately afterwards she went to the street-door, with the intention of shooting the bolts, though she remained standing there ten minutes before she did so.'

It seems that at one moment she's putting herself in the doorway for half an hour and then the next moment is saying it had only been ten minutes. It was not unheard of then and is not now for a minor witness to 'guild the lily' when speaking to the press in an effort to bolster their own newsworthiness, and it's quite possible that Fanny - who, as we shall see, dressed better than the other women of the street – was given to such van-ity. But there might be a more innocent explanation.

In the *Evening News* report she mentions that her intention had been to bolt the front door when instead she ended up standing in her door-way. This indicates that the door had been open for some time with Fanny moving around inside. Perhaps when she said that she'd been at the door of her house for most of a half hour she simply meant that she was inside and had a view through her open front door. After all, the *Daily News* puts her bedroom in the front room of the ground floor. However, if this is the case, she couldn't have been at the door the entire time or she would have seen the person, assumed to be a constable, who walked with a heavy tramp by her door. It should also be noted that there was no public clock visible from her vantage point and her times must be estimates; if any of us have ever seen 15 minutes pass that felt like 10 or knew 20 minutes to drag on like a full 30, then we should extend to Fanny the benefit of the doubt that her estimates of time were honest but possibly inaccurate. It also should be mentioned that we're not studying signed statements given to objective law enforcement officers, but press reports hurriedly scribbled in the street, written up later, and then chopped or rewritten at the whim of the copy editor. Errors or discrepancies across news reports are not necessarily the fault of the subject being interviewed, so we can't be certain as to what Fanny actually said.

What makes Fanny's evidence so crucial is that it puts her on the scene when some of the most important events of the Berner Street mystery are said to have played out: the Schwartz stand-off; James Brown passing by the couple on the corner; and the murder of Liz Stride itself. Fanny saw none of it, and some would argue that meant either she was lying or other witnesses were lying or mistaken. We're going to consider the various angles and we'll start with the man who walked into Leman Street station and proved that Fanny Mortimer was good to her word.

The Man with the Black Bag

Mortimer's description of a man with a black bag strolling along Berner Street in the minutes before the discovery of Stride's body excited the imagination of the press, the public, and at least a couple of the more questionable witnesses who would come forward in its wake. If the speculation as to the Ripper's medical prowess is what put a top hat and cloak on the mythical Whitechapel phantom, then it was Fanny Mortimer's curbside utterings that put the infamous black bag firmly in his grasp. Shortly after the wide publication of her statement, Albert Bachert came forward with his story of a similar man at the Three Nuns (or Three Tuns) and Henry Birch stepped forward with his retroactive information about a man with a black bag coming into his milk stand at the time of the Cambridge Heath Road incident (discussed in the first section). Both of these stories are highly suspect and probably fabricated, but they illustrate the immediate impact that Mortimer's evidence had on the investigation. This is in spite of the fact that the 'man with the black bag' himself marched into the Leman Street police station late on the night of Tuesday, Oct 2nd and identified himself. Without missing a beat he then marched over to the offices of the *Daily News* for a midnight visit. He was escorted about by William Wess, the secretary of the Berner Street club

Wess and his fellow club leaders had been in damage control mode since the discovery of the murder. Although they had intentionally courted controversy for some time and regularly made foes of authorities, they had not banked on the body of a murdered gentile woman turning up in their yard, and there was strong anticipation that the police would use the momentum from the murder as a means to close them down. The following report, if true, illustrates the wide divide between the police and the socialists:

What the Police were Doing.

In the midst of the excitement following on the Berner-street murder, some of the police were mean enough to try to purchase tobacco and drink from some of the members of the Jewish club. Money was tendered when request was made, but was, of course, refused. The police were not so entirely absorbed in endeavoring to catch the criminal but that they could attempt to inveigle innocent persons into committing a petty crime for the sake of securing a paltry conviction.[139]

The Berner Street club, as with the many gentleman's clubs across the city, did not hold a permit to sell alcohol and tobacco, but could provide such things to their members freely as part of their membership dues. This was a bugaboo for Chief Commissioner Sir Charles Warren, who days after the murder of Elizabeth Stride, released his report for the year 1887 and stressed that such clubs were little better than public houses and 'should be placed under supervision.' He also argued that publicans should be held legally responsible if someone they serve alcohol to should then go out and commit a crime. Such pressures upon the club were not new, and in at least some instances were not undeserved, but in October of 1888 they found themselves facing a potential accusation of murder, and it's understandable that they were keen to subvert that. Not helping matters was Mortimer's honest but inconvenient testimony of a young man with a black bag being on the scene, and her added speculation that the man belonged to their club.

In a rarely seen interview with Mrs. Mortimer, published in the *Evening News*, Fanny is presented in full force:

> Some three doors from the gateway where the body of the first victim as discovered, I saw a clean, respectable-looking woman chatting with one or two neighbours. She was apparently the wife of a well-to-do artisan, and formed a strong contrast to many of those around her. I got into conversation with her and found that she was one of the first on the spot.

> "I was just about going to bed, sir, when I heard a call for the police. I ran to the door, and before I could open it I heard somebody say, 'Come out quick; there's a poor woman here that's had ten inches of cold steel in her.' I hurried out and saw some two or three people standing in the gateway. Lewis [sic-Louis Diemshitz], the man who looks after the Socialist Club at No. 40, was there, and his wife.

> "Then I see a sight that turned me all sick and cold. There was the murdered woman a-lying on her side, with her throat cut across till her head seemed to be hanging by a bit of skin. Her legs was drawn up under her, and her head and the upper part of her body was soaked in blood. She was dressed in black as if she was in mourning for somebody.

> "Did you see no sound of quarrelling, no cry for help?" I asked.

> "Nothing of the sort, sir. I should think I must have heard it if the poor creature screamed at all, for I hadn't long come in from the door when I was roused, as I tell you, by that call for the police. But that was from the people as found the body. Mr. Lewis, who travels in cheap drapery things a bit now and again, had just drove

into the yard when his horse shied at something that was lying in the corner. He thought 'twas a bundle of some kind till he got down from his cart and struck a light. Then he saw what it was and gave the alarm."

"Was the street quiet at the time?"

"Yes, there was hardly anybody moving about, except at the club. There was music and dancing going on there at the very time that that poor creature was being murdered at their very door, as one may say."

"I suppose you did not notice a man and woman pass down the street while you were at the door?"

"No, sir. I think I should have noticed if they had. Particularly if they'd been strangers, at that time o'night. I only noticed one person passing, just before I turned in. That was a young man walking up Berner-street, carrying a black bag in his hand."

"Did you observe him closely, or notice anything in his appearance?"

"No, I didn't pay particular attention to him. He was respectably dressed, but was a stranger to me. He might ha' been coming from the Socialist Club. A good many young men goes there, of a Saturday night especially."

That was all that my informant had to tell me. I wonder will the detectives think it worth while to satisfy themselves about that black bag?

It should be noted that this interview was published on the same day and in the same journal (Evening News) that one of the two most cited articles on Mortimer appeared. Curiously, the well-known *Evening News* report omits all mention of the man with the black bag. It's probable that one came first and the other was carried in a later edition that day. Although longer and more vulgar, this interview actually presented fewer details than the more sober paragraph that appeared in the same journal. We should be cautious in accepting that these were the actual words used by Fanny Mortimer and not a sensationalized and fictional rendering of her statement. Unfortunately, we're left none the wiser about her doorway vigil. What we are offered that is new is Fanny's speculation about the identity of the black bag man, which she had probably been circulating around Berner Street long before it saw print, bristling the neck hairs of the Berner Street club hierarchy. They knew who the black bag man was and they knew that he wasn't Stride's killer, but if they came forward, would people believe them? They decided it was a chance worth taking and Wess escorted a 22 year-old Russian cigarette maker[140] named Leon Goldstein to the police station to identify himself and give his statement.

> Mr. W. Wess, Secretary of the International Working Men's Club, Berner-street, called at our office at midnight and made the following statement:-It having come to my knowledge that the man who was seen by Mrs. Mortimer, of 36, Berner-street, passing her house "carrying a black shiny bag," who walked very fast down the street from the Commercial-road about the time the murder was supposed to have occurred, was a member of the club, I immediately went with him, between 10 and 11 to-night, to the Leman-street Police-station, where he made a statement as to his whereabouts on Saturday evening which was completely satisfactory.[141]

That Wess ushered Goldstein straight from the station to the *Daily News* office underscores the desperation with which he wanted to clear the air regarding the suspicious 'black bag man' speculated to be one of his brethren. Although some other papers such as *Lloyd's* offered a line or two towards dispelling the myth, most reporters were happier to perpetuate the myth and the papers continued to fill with speculation about such a figure roaming the East End alleyways. Indeed, Inspector Walter Dew, who as a detective-constable participated in the Whitechapel murders inquiry, would fifty years after the fact write in his memoir that Fanny Mortimer was 'the only person ever to see the Ripper within the vicinity of his crimes.'[142]

Chief Inspector Donald S. Swanson, in his Oct. 19th report to Home Office, made the following reference to Goldstein:

About 1 a.m. 30th Leon Goldstein of 22 Christian Street

Commercial Road, called at Leman St. & stated that he was the man that passed down Berner St. with a black bag at that hour, that the bag contained empty cigarette boxes & that he had left a coffee house in Spectacle Alley a short time before.

This information is crucial to our understanding of the timing of events because Swanson drew his information from the police reports and Goldstein put himself in Berner Street mere minutes before Louis Diemshitz discovered the body. Fanny doesn't say at which point during her vigil she saw Goldstein come along the roadway, but she does state from the time she shut the door it was about four minutes before she heard Diemshitz pass by with his pony and cart, so to say she closed her door at 12:56am would be the best estimate. Goldstein stated that he passed along the road at about 1am, and we know it was before 12:56, so we'll say he trekked through at 12:55am. As far as Goldstein, Diemshitz, and Mortimer are concerned, their timings and statements dovetail nicely, but this is where Mortimer's harmony with other witnesses ends.

Fanny tells us that 'shortly before' 12:45am she heard what she took to be the footsteps of a constable on patrol and went to her door "immediately afterwards," remaining there for ten minutes. This puts her at her door at some point between 12:45am and 12:56am during which time she saw nothing and no one, excepting Goldstein. This would be fine except for all the things she *should* have seen but didn't, namely Israel Schwartz, the broad-shouldered man (BS Man) he was tailing, the pipe-smoking man (Pipe Man), Liz Stride, and the brief dramatic episode this foursome are supposed to have participated in.

Schwartz stated that at 12:45am he turned from Commercial Road onto Berner Street and found himself walking behind another man who stopped at the gates to Dutfield's Yard and spoke with a woman in the gateway for a few moments before he began pulling her towards the street. Schwartz walked to the other side of the road but turned as he got to the curb and saw the man throw Stride down, turn in his direction, and shout the word 'Lipski'. At this point, a taller man emerged from around a corner, lighting a pipe. Feeling threatened, Schwartz ran away, followed by Pipeman. It's impossible that Fanny could have missed this had it occurred while she was at her door, so we're left with three possibilities: it happened prior to her coming to her door; it happened after she went back inside at 12:56 and before Diemshitz's arrival at 1am; or, it never happened at all.

Extending Schwartz the benefit of the doubt, we'll see what we can do with Fanny's timings, because there's one other discrepancy to consider – the heavy treading constable.

PC William Smith was 36 years old on that evening, in his fifth year with the Metropolitan police, and well into his second year with H Division. He walked a long beat that went as far as Gower Walk, along Commercial Road, round Christian Street and Fairclough Street to Grove Street, then along Grove Street as far as Backchurch Lane, and up the latter into Commercial Road again, taking in all the interior streets, including Berner Street.[143] He stated his beat took him 25 to 30 minutes to complete. On the night of the 29th he had last been through Berner Street at some time between 12:30 and 12:35am and was certain he'd seen a woman he later identified as Stride standing on the pavement across the street from the club, where a large Board School took up half of lower Berner Street. She was talking with a young man who was holding a relatively substantial parcel wrapped in newspaper (Parcel Man).[144] He did not overhear any conversation between them, but they seemed sober and did not particularly attract his attention. He did not get a good look at the man's face but stated at the inquest that he 'had no whiskers'; curiously, in the Oct. 19th report by Chief Inspector Swanson, Smith's man has grown a small dark moustache that was missing from the original description circulated by police.

Smith testified that his beat next took him to the top of Berner Street in Commercial Road around 1am when he noticed a crowd outside the club. Upon investigating he learned of the murder and found two constables (PC Henry Lamb and PC 426H, identified by author Neil R. A. Bell as PC William Ayliffe) already on the scene and a third (Reserve PC Albert Collins) had already been sent for a doctor. Upon seeing the body, Smith left to fetch an ambulance, and as he was leaving, the third constable arrived with Edward Johnston, the assistant to Dr. Blackwell.

There's an obvious problem with Smith's timeline if he believed that he found this crew already in place at 1am, since Diemshitz was only discovering the body at that time, and the events that must have transpired between the discovery of the body and Smith's eventual arrival on the scene are: Diemshitz informing the people inside the club of the murder and returning to the yard to inspect the body; Diemshitz, Kozebrodski, and other clubmen spreading out to find police; Edward Spooner following the men back from his spot outside the Beehive pub at the corner of Christian Street and Fairclough Street; and Reserve PC Albert Collins returning with Edward Johnston, Dr. Blackwell's assistant.

These events need not have taken a great deal of time, but they must have consumed some minutes. In fact, PC Henry Lamb was at the head of Berner Street in Commercial Road when two of the clubmen informed him of the murder and pointed him towards the club yard. This was just after 1am and PC Smith was somewhere else on his beat, too far away to hear the cries of 'Police!' The best gauge we have would be Dr. Blackwell, who was working from a time piece. He stated that PC Collins arrived at his home at 1:10am. He had been sleeping so he sent his assistant on with the constable while he got dressed. His home and practice were quite nearby on Commercial Road so when he arrived at the yard it was 1:16am. Johnston would have arrived about four minutes prior to this, at 1:12am, just after Smith himself had arrived. This means that Smith's timing was off by about ten minutes.

Researcher and essayist Gavin Bromley published a detailed analysis of what he believed to be Smith's movements along his beat and concluded that Smith was likely unaware of what time he had seen Stride and her man in Berner Street and had reached his timing of 12:30 or 12:35 by deducting 25 and 30 minutes from 1am, which he believed to have been the time he first noticed the crowd gathering outside 40 Berner Street. Bromley reasoned that if he was ten minutes off then we should expect he had actually passed through Berner Street between 12:40 and 12:45am, and it was at this time that he saw Stride with Parcel Man.

It's not usually advisable to play with accepted timings in a historical event, particularly when they've been accepted as accurate by the authorities recording them; times that, in this case, were submitted by PC William Smith and accepted by his superiors as well as Chief Inspector Swanson. However, it's unlikely any of these men thought to sit down and compare the movements and timings of the various player - a luxury enjoyed by modern investigators. But when an obvious discrepancy is presented in the testimony itself, it requires we consider an alternative timeline. The timing of 12:40-45 ties in nicely with Fanny Mortimer's recollection that 'shortly before a quarter to one o'clock [I] heard the measured, heavy tramp of a policeman passing the house on his beat,' but it forces a reconsideration of other events.

If not for Mortimer's recollection of when she heard the constable pass, and her accuracy in regards to the other timings she offered (i.e. Goldstein and Diemshitz's passing), it would be tempting to conclude that Smith passed through Berner Street at 12:35 and made his way back to the top of the street closer to 1:05 than 1:10. After all, there were many public clocks from which he could mark his time as he walked, just as Diemshitz had noted the time at a baker's clock on Commercial Road before he turned onto Berner Street. It might be expected Smith would make use of the clocks if for no other reason than to know how much longer he had on his shift. But his estimation of 1am for finding the crowd at Berner Street is provably inaccurate and brings his earlier timings into question. Mortimer's timing only serves to cast further doubt, and so we must consider that the following all occurred around or within the five minutes between 12:40 and 12:45am:

PC Smith witnessed Stride standing across the street from the club talking to Parcel Man.

Morris Eagle returned to the club after walking his sweetheart home and entered by the side kitchen door via the gateway. He estimated the time as 12:40 and this was loosely corroborated by Sarah Diemshitz and others in the club. He was the last person to enter before Diemshitz's return. He stated there were men and women on the street, but no more than usual for the time. He took no particular notice of them.

Joseph Lave, a Russian from America, temporarily staying at the club, went for a short stroll going 'as far as the street', which might have meant he only went just past the gateway, or he might have meant he walked up to where Berner Street intersected with Commercial Road. He thought he had gone out about 20 minutes before the alarm was raised (i.e. 12:40am) and walked about for five minutes. He said the street was quiet and he noticed nothing wrong. It should be noted that his timing must have been off since he was known to have reentered the club prior to Eagle's return at approximately 12:40am.

Israel Schwartz witnessed BS Man assault Stride in front of the club gates while Pipe Man stood by. He approximated the time as 12:45am.

James Brown witnessed Stride standing on the Fairclough side of the Board School with yet a third man (Overcoat Man). He approximated the time as 12:45am.

James Brown and the couple he saw would likely have been out of Mortimer's line of sight, so it's possible this event could have occurred while Fanny was in her doorway, but the other events must have occurred before or after Mortimer was at her door.

It has been argued that Mortimer's evidence and the restructured timing of PC Smith's might compel us to conclude that the Schwartz event never actually happened. But if we consider the very short amount of time it would have taken to walk from Commercial Road to the club, cross the street, and then run away, the entire event would have occurred in less than two minutes. Smith and Eagle both observed that there were people in the street, whereas Mortimer, Schwartz, and Brown describe the area as nearly desolate, so it's likely that Eagle and Smith passed through the street prior to the others.

We receive some additional information, albeit third hand, from Charles Letchford, whose family lived a few doors down from Fanny at #30. He stated to a reporter that his sister was at their door at 12:50am and did not see anyone pass by.[145] This indicates that the street was clear at that time and corroborates Mortimer. It isn't odd that Mortimer would not recall having seen the young woman since neither stated they were outside their doors.

A timeline based on our new understanding of the evidence would suggest that Smith and Eagle passed along the street at roughly the same time which would be 12:40am. Stride may very well have been in place with Parcel Man at the time and Eagle simply didn't take particular notice, aside from observing that there were people about. Fanny believed she had gone to her door 'almost immediately' after the passing of what she took to be the constable, but enough time must have passed to allow Stride and

Parcel Man to walk out of view, so here we find what might be a kink in Mortimer's armor. Of course, this presupposes that her assumption is correct that the plodding footsteps belonged to a constable and not one of the other known players, or a player as yet unknown.

Although Schwartz's part in the story was brief, we must assume that action was still taking place on Berner Street after his departure, with Stride on the pavement and an angry BS Man towering over her. When we further consider that somewhere in these few minutes we must also find time for Stride to be around the corner on Fairclough Street for Brown to witness her, we begin to find ourselves almost impossibly cramped for time. Something has got to give, and for many writers that 'something' is James Brown.

It's frequently written that the couple he saw was not Stride and a man, but the young couple referred to by Fanny Mortimer. While this proposition would lighten the load of the modern researcher (it would mean one less place Stride needed to be in a tight timeframe), information was uncovered during the course of my research that allows us to conclude that although there was, in fact, a young couple on Berner Street that night, they could not have been the couple witnessed by James Brown at or after 12:45am.

The Couple on the Corner

James Brown is something of an enigma. All we know about him, aside from his name, is that in late September/early October of 1888 he lived at 35 Fairclough Street.[146] We don't know his age, his history, or what became of him after his brief testimony on the fourth day of the inquest into Stride's murder. We can't even be certain of his profession because some reporters heard him say 'box maker' and others heard 'dock labourer'. Brown is completely missing from the surviving police reports and did not make the cut for Swanson's Oct. 19th catch-all, possibly because it was perceived his evidence might conflict with or devalue that of Israel Schwartz. It's apparent that he was considered credible and honest by the police who submitted his statement to Coroner Baxter, who in turn called him to give evidence at the inquest. Such was not the case with Matthew Packer, who was not considered credible, nor Israel Schwartz, whose evidence the police apparently preferred to keep under wraps at the time.

The story James Brown told was a brief one. He stated that he headed out from his home, which would have been about a minute's walk away, and went to the chandler shop on the corner of Fairclough and Berner Street to fetch his supper. This would have been cater-corner from the Board School outside of which he would shortly witness his couple. After spending about three or four minutes in the shop he headed out and crossed to the Board School side of the street and noticed a woman with her back to the wall of the school and a man leaning with one arm against the wall, close to the woman. This would have been just around the corner of Berner Street and outside of Fanny Mortimer's view. He heard the woman say "No, not tonight; some other night," which caused him to turn his head and take notice. After viewing the body in the mortuary he stated he was almost certain it was the woman he had seen.

Whether or not the woman Brown saw was Stride continues to be hotly debated. The time at which he saw the couple is consistently marked at 12:45am in Ripper books and this is generally accepted as accurate. However, that time was set in stone decades ago when few contemporary newspapers other than the *Times* were readily accessible and is now repeated out of tradition. In the course of my research I learned that some reporters heard differently and for the sake of transparency I thought it wise to present these different interpretations for consideration:

The Times: I saw the deceased about a quarter to 1 on Sunday morning. At that time I was going from my house to get some supper from a chandler's shop at the corner of Berner-street and Fairclough-street. As I was going across the road I saw a man and woman standing by the Board School in Fairclough-street.

Daily Telegraph: (Brown) I have seen the body in the mortuary. I did not know the deceased, but I saw her about a quarter to one on Sunday morning last. (Coroner) Where were you? (Brown) I was going from my house to the chandler's shop at the corner of Berner-street and Fairclough-street, to get some supper. I stayed there three or four minutes, and then went back home, when I saw a man and woman standing at the corner of the Board School.

Morning Advertiser: On Sunday morning last, about 12.45, I went from my own home to get something for supper at the corner of Berner-street, and was in the shop three or four minutes and then went back home. As I was going home I saw a man and woman standing against the wall by the board school in Fairclough-street.

The Star: [Brown] said that at about a quarter to one on Sunday morning he went out to get some supper at the corner of Berner-street, where there is a chandler's shop. He was gone three or four minutes, and as he returned he saw a man and woman standing by the Board School (which is just opposite the scene of the murder).

The *Times* seems to state that Brown saw the couple at 12:45, but confuses matters by then marking this as the time he left his house. This reporter also suggests that Brown saw the couple upon leaving his house, which was not the case. The *Daily Telegraph* reporter, who was somewhat more thorough, tells us that Brown saw the woman at *about* 12:45, but when asked where he was, Brown tells the story of how he'd left his house for the chandler shop, making it unclear what he was doing at precisely 12:45 – leaving his house or passing the couple. The reporters for both the *Morning Advertiser* and the *Star* have Brown leaving his home at 12:45, walking the short distance to the store, spending three or four minutes inside, and discovering the couple upon leaving and crossing the street. This timing effectively places the actual witnessing at approximately 12:50 or 12:51am.

It might be worth noting that Brown apparently had a clock at his home, which is not surprising, as most people did. In answering questions posed by coroner Baxter, he offered "I did not look at any clock at the chandler's shop. I arrived home first at 10 minutes past twelve o'clock."[147] 12:10 would have been the time he arrived home from work, and this he notes with precision. He did not notice the time at the chandler's shop and so estimates he was in there three or four minutes. Although we cannot be sure about any witness's timing – particularly one as imprecise as Brown – it seems as though he was rather aware of the time from the clock at his house and so would not be very wide of the mark. The sources agree that when he gave the time of 12:45 he was giving the time he left his house, which means he witnessed the couple on the corner at 12:50 or 12:51am.

If Brown was correct in his identification of Stride then it would require us to reconsider what we think we know about the Berner Street murder. To prevent confusion, Fanny Mortimer's second-hand information about the young couple on the corner is often promoted to personal observation and submitted as a good reason to ignore Brown. That would certainly be more convenient for all of us who struggle with the crowded timeline, but, as it would happen, it is not accurate.

To review, what has led many modern commentators to believe that Fanny witnessed the young couple was her comment that "a young man and his sweetheart were standing at the corner of the street, about 20 yards away, before and after the time the woman must have been murdered, but they told me they did not hear a sound." Anyone standing on the Fairclough side of the Board School would not have been visible to Fanny, and she does not claim to have seen them, but does indicate that she had a conversation with one or both of them after the fact. The *Evening News* reported that 'when the alarm of murder was raised a young girl had been standing in a bisecting thoroughfare not fifty yards from the spot where the body was found. She had, she said, been standing there for about twenty-minutes, talking with her sweetheart, but neither of them heard any unusual noises.' We're now out to 50 yards, which puts the couple at the corner of Berner Street and Commercial Road and nowhere near the Board School. Fortunately, this is no longer a point that we need to debate over, as I uncovered an interview with the 'young girl' herself that proves they could not have been Brown's couple:

> It is established almost beyond doubt that the poor creature met her death some time between twelve and one o'clock. And yet no one seems to have heard a struggle, or a groan, or the slightest indication of what was going on. From twelve o'clock till half-past a young girl who lives in the street walked up and down, and within twenty yards of where the body was found, with her sweetheart.
>
> "We heard nothing whatever," she told a reporter this morning. "I passed the gate of the yard a few minutes before twelve o'clock alone. The doors were open, and, so far as I could tell, there was nothing inside them." "I met my young man (she proceeded) at

the top of the street, and then we went for a short walk along the Commercial-road and back again, and down Berner-street. No one passed us then, but just before we said "Good night" a man came along the Commercial-road; and went in the direction of Aldgate."[148]

In the first hours after the murder it was not known that Stride had been killed close to 1am. With Fanny claiming it could not have happened from 12:30 to 1am, both Fanny and the young couple concluded that they had been out and about at the time the murder was committed. In turn, this confusion led to modern speculation that they were Brown's couple.

With the young couple removed from the scene, we're left with Stride and an unknown man as the likely couple standing on the Fairclough Street side of the Board School around 12:50. This does not conflict with either Mortimer (who could not have seen them) or PC Smith, who spotted Stride only feet away, on the Berner Street side of the school, some minutes prior. With this in mind, we'll consider the couple that Brown saw.

Brown did not go into any detail about the features of the woman – it was not necessary since he had seen the body of Stride at the mortuary and believed them to be one and the same – but in response to the inquisitive Baxter he stated that he did not see any flowers on Stride's dress, or, indeed, anything 'light in colour' about either of the people. This might be because the woman he saw was not Stride, or it might be that the angle at which the couple were standing did not allow for Brown to see the flowers; he stated that the man was 'standing with his arm against the wall' and the woman was 'inclined towards his arm, facing him, and with her back to the wall.' Brown was rather close, walking in the street along the curb nearest the couple.[149] Brown replied 'Yes' to the question "You are sure it was not her dress that you chiefly noticed?" This is crucial because it tells us that Brown identified Stride by her features and not merely by her dark clothes; Mitre Square witness, Joseph Lawende, was able to identify Catherine Eddowes only by her clothes, and this might have been on Baxter's mind as he questioned Brown.

Regarding the man, it seems Brown did not get a good look at him. What attracted his focus was the woman's comment "No, not tonight;

some other night," and being a man, it stands to reason that he'd take more notice of the woman. He was certain the man wore a long, dark coat that seemed like an overcoat and went almost to his heels; he was of average build and Brown guessed his height at 5'7". He looked more like a clerk than someone used to hard labor. Brown evidently did not get a good look at the man's face as he wasn't sure if he wore a hat and couldn't say if he had whiskers, but felt he did not.

Coroner Baxter might have suspected that Brown was mistaken in his timing and attempted to uncover this by asking about the rain, knowing full well that the rains had stopped much earlier. Brown replied it was not raining and further qualified his timing by offering that he had just finished eating the supper he'd purchased when he heard cries of 'Murder!' and 'Police!' from people moving in the direction of Grove Street. He opened his window and saw a policeman standing on Christian Street who was then summoned to Berner Street by another man.[150] Brown said this took place about 15 minutes after he'd seen the couple. If we give enough time from the discovery of the body for Diemshitz to alert his fellow clubmen, gather in the yard to view the body, and take off in search of constables, then it would be approximately 1:05 when Brown heard the passing screams; counting 15 minutes back from this puts it at 12:50am when he saw the couple. This is by no means scientific, but it's a second method of timing that puts us in the prescribed time frame of 12:50-51am.

That Brown was an honest witness has never been in question; there's only ever been a question of accuracy. He believed the woman he saw was Stride and it must be said that Stride did not have an average face. It cannot be stated that there were no other women in the area at that time, but as has been demonstrated, there was not another couple known to have been in the area and by all accounts the streets were nearly barren after 12:45am. Brown's evidence, as inconvenient as it may be, cannot be set aside or dismissed simply because it conflicts with other evidence. It does not conflict with the evidence of PC Smith, who passed through Berner Street between 5 and 10 minutes prior to Brown's entry. Although Parcel Man and Overcoat Man are apparently not one and the same, it's reasonable to expect that not all of the men Stride approached or spoke with would have gone off with her, and if Parcel Man departed after Smith had passed, then Stride would continue to approach men, and in doing so, she met Overcoat Man. In fact, since Fanny Mortimer did not see either Parcel Man or Stride upon opening her door, shortly after the passing of Smith, it stands to reason that Parcel Man went on his way and Stride wandered onto Fairclough Street, where she remained until after Mortimer had gone inside.

The reason this scenario is not discussed in Ripper literature is that it comes into conflict with that most sacred of Berner Street cows – Israel Schwartz. Added weight is given to Schwartz's evidence both in Swanson's report and in modern literature largely because he witnessed an act of violence committed against a woman he identified as Stride. In most works on the case Schwartz is placed front and center and the rest of the evidence either rises or falls in his wake. I've made the choice in this present work to make Fanny Mortimer my Rosetta stone, primarily because the most sensational element of her story – the man with the black bag – proved true and was corroborated by Leon Goldstein. None of the other witnesses command this sort of confidence. That is not to say that she couldn't have been mistaken in her estimates of time, or that we shouldn't remain cautious, but where she can be put to the test (Goldstein's passing, Diemshitz's arrival) she fairs rather well, so if any witness is going to become our center wheel, it should be Fanny Mortimer.

Where we hit a snag in this approach is when it comes to Israel Schwartz's evidence. He stated that at about 12:45am he followed BS Man into Berner Street and witnessed the assault on Stride, after which he was chased or followed by Pipeman. This event would only have consumed 2-4 minutes. But which two to four minutes? This is a significant question that we will return to after we take a fresh look at the man at its center.

ISRAEL SCHWARTZ – A CRITICAL ANALYSIS

STEPHEN KNIGHT'S *JACK the Ripper: The Final Solution* (1976) was a well-written work of faction propelled by perfect timing to the top of the bestseller lists. Knight's book not only gave rise to what is now regarded (or disregarded) as the 'royal conspiracy' theory, but also provided information-starved Ripperologists with some of their first and best glimpses into the secret vaults of Scotland Yard. Knight was afforded access to the still private police files from which he faithfully reproduced a portion of a report written by Chief Inspector Donald S. Swanson on Oct. 19th, 1888. It was here that - almost 90 years after the murders - interested researchers were first introduced to Israel Schwartz.

What follows is the portion of the Oct. 19th Swanson Report most relevant to our discussion of Schwartz.

12:45 a.m. 30th Israel Schwartz of 22 Helen [sic-Ellen] Street, Backchurch Lane stated that at that hour on turning into Berner St. from Commercial Road & had got as far as the gateway where the murder was committed he saw a man stop & speak to a woman who was standing in the gateway. The man tried to pull the woman into the street but he turned her round & threw her down on the footway & the woman screamed three times, but not very loudly. On crossing to the opposite side of the street, he saw a second man standing lighting his pipe. The man who threw the woman down called out apparently to the man on the opposite side of the road "Lipski" & then Schwartz walked away, but finding that he was followed by the second man he ran as far as the railway arch but the man did not follow so far. Schwartz cannot say whether the two men were together or known to each other. Upon being taken to the mortuary Schwartz identified the body as that of the woman he had seen & he thus describes the first man who threw the woman down: - age about 30 ht. 5 ft. 5in. comp. fair hair dark, small brown moustache, full face, broad shouldered, dress, dark jacket & trousers black cap with peak, had nothing in his hands.

Second man age 35 ht. 5ft. 11in. comp. fresh, hair light brown, moustache brown, dress dark overcoat, old black hard felt hat wide brim, had a clay pipe in his hand.

The description of the man seen by the P.C. [Smith] was circulated amongst Police by wire, & by authority of Commissioner it was also given to the press. On the evening of 30th the man Schwartz gave the description of the man he had seen ten minutes later than the P.C. and it was circulated by wire. It will be observed that allowing for differences of opinion between the P.C. and Schwartz as to apparent age & height of the man each saw with the woman whose body they both identified there are serious differences in the description of dress: - thus the P.C. describes the dress of the man whom he saw as black diagonal coat, hard felt hat, while Schwartz describes the dress of the man he saw as dark jacket black cap with peak, so that it is at least rendered doubtful whether they are describing the same man.

If Schwartz is to be believed, and the police report of his statement casts no doubt upon it, it follows if they are describing different men that the man Schwartz saw & described is the more probable of the two to be the murderer, for a quarter of an hour afterwards the body is found murdered. At the same time account must be taken of the fact that the throat only of the victim was cut in this instance which measured by time, considering meeting (if with a man other than Schwartz saw) the time for the agreement

& the murderous action would I think be a question of so many minutes, five at least, ten at most, so that I respectfully submit it is not clearly proved that the man that Schwartz saw is the murderer, although it is clearly the more probable of the two.

Before concluding in dealing with the descriptions of these two men I venture to insert here for the purpose of comparison with these two descriptions, the description of a man seen with a woman in Church Passage close to Mitre Square at 1.35 a.m. 30th by two men coming out of a club close by: - age 30 ht. 5ft. 7 or 8in. comp. fair, fair moustache, medium build, dress pepper & salt colour loose jacket, grey cloth cap with peak of same colour, reddish handkerchief tied in a knot, round neck, appearance of a sailor. In this case I understand from City Police that Mr. Lewin [sic-Lawende] one of the men identified the clothes only of the murdered woman Eddowes, which is a serious drawback to the value of the description of the man. Ten minutes afterwards the body is found horribly mutilated & it is therefore reasonable to believe that the man he saw was the murderer, but for purposes of comparison, this description is much nearer to that given by Schwartz than to that given by the P.C.

In the wake of Home Office's receipt of the Swanson report there was much discussion about Schwartz's evidence, some of which is preserved penciled in the margins of the report itself. These questions instigated the following Nov. 1st report written by Inspector Frederick George Abberline, who personally oversaw the interrogation of Schwartz:

With reference to the annexed copy extract from Home Office Letter.

I beg to report that since a jew named Lipski was hanged for the murder of a jewess in 1887 the name has very frequently been used by persons as mere ejaculation by way of endeavouring to insult the jew to whom it has been addressed, and as Schwartz has a strong jewish appearance I am of opinion it was addressed to him as he stopped to look at the man he saw ill-using the deceased woman.

I questioned Israel Schwartz very closely at the time he made the statement as to whom the man addressed when he called Lipski but he was unable to say.

There was only one other person to be seen in the street and that was a man on the opposite side of the road in the act of lighting a pipe.

Schwartz being a foreigner and unable to speak English became alarmed and ran away. The man whom he saw lighting his pipe also ran in the same direction as himself, but whether this man was running after him or not he could not tell he might have been alarmed the same as himself and ran away.

A house to house inquiry was made in Berner street with a view to ascertain whether any person was seen acting suspiciously or any noise heard on the night in question but without result.

Inquiries have also been made in the neighbourhood but no person named Lipski could be found.

What Swanson provides us in relation to Schwartz is sometimes generically referred to as the 'police report' but is in fact a summary of the actual report provided by Abberline which is no longer extant. A signed witness statement is more or less an objective report, composed simply to record information. The same cannot be said about Swanson's Oct. 19th report to Home Office, which was composed by subordinates for the consideration of their superiors. In today's parlance it might be thought of more as a quarterly report.

On Oct. 13th, two weeks following the double murder of Elizabeth Stride and Catherine Eddowes, Commissioner Charles Warren received a letter from the Home Office requesting that a report be furnished to Secretary of State Henry Matthews detailing 'all the measures which have been taken for the detection of the perpetrator of the Whitechapel Murders and of the results.'[151] The request was passed on to Assistant Commissioner Robert Anderson, who in turn assigned it to Chief Inspector Donald S. Swanson, the man in overall charge of the investigation into the murders. This resulted in the Oct. 19th report.

Although lengthy and detailed by the standards of documentation-starved Ripperologists, the Swanson report is no more than a brief summary of the investigation in its first few weeks; a collection of 'highlights' designed to give Home Office the impression that they were making progress towards identifying the murderer.

The murder of Catherine Eddowes brought the City Police squarely into the fray and they wasted no time in plastering the city with reward notices and freely speaking to members of the press, winning both the press and public over in their favor. By contrast, it was the Met Police's policy not to issue rewards, and as the investigation progressed, they became more and more antagonistic towards the press. Although both forces would work together as well as possible in their shared goal of catching the Ripper, there can be no doubt that their efforts were guided in some measure by a long standing competitive spirit. If the City Police, with their comparatively minimal resources and late start in the 'game' were successful in capturing the Ripper, the Metropolitan Police would be dealt a powerful and tragic blow that at the very least would cost many men their positions.

This 'home turf' attitude might have colored the vision of H Division surgeon, Dr. George Bagster Phillips, who voiced the opinion that Eddowes had been the victim of a copycat killer. If Eddowes was seen as a copycat [i.e. unrelated] murder then the City Police could still be excluded from the official Whitechapel Murder inquiry. But the undeniable similarities inherent in the butchery of Eddowes and Annie Chapman rendered moot any serious argument for Eddowes's exclusion from the Ripper's tally. Nevertheless, in drawing a comparison between the men witnessed in Berner Street by PC William Smith and Israel Schwartz with that of the man seen by Joseph Lawende near Mitre Square, Swanson writes, '…I understand from the City Police that Mr. Lewin [sic] one of the men identified the clothes only of the murdered woman Eddowes, which is a serious drawback to the value of the description of the man.' Although his point is logically sound, and he goes on to concede that it's 'reasonable' to believe Lawende saw the murderer, the fact that he took an opportunity in a report to his superiors to undervalue the competence of the City Police's key witness reeks of professional rivalry.

These observations are important if we're to understand the genesis of the 'Swanson Report', which remains our only surviving official account of the Schwartz story.

Perhaps no one at Scotland Yard – short of the commissioner himself - felt such searing pressure to capture the Whitechapel murderer as did Assistant Commissioner Robert Anderson. Before turning Swanson's report over to his superiors, Anderson penned a brief cover letter. Dated October 23rd, 1888, the letter makes for interesting reading:

At the present stage of the inquiry the best reply that can be made to the Secretary of State's request for a report upon these cases is to send the accompanying copy of detailed reports prepared by Chief Inspector Swanson, who has special charge of the matter at this office.

I wish to guard against its being supposed that the inquiry is now concluded. There is no reason for furnishing these reports at this moment except that they have been called for.

That a crime of this kind should have been committed without any clue being supplied by the criminal, is unusual, but that five successive murders[152] should have been committed without our having the slightest clue of any kind is extraordinary, if not unique, in the annals of crime. The result has been to necessitate our giving attention to innumerable suggestions, such as would in any ordinary case be dismissed unnoticed, and no hint of any kind, which was not obviously absurd, has been neglected. Moreover the activity of the Police has been to a considerable extent wasted through the exigencies of sensational journalism and the action of unprincipled persons, who, from various motives, have endeavoured to mislead us. But on the other hand the public generally and especially the inhabitants of the East End have shown a marked desire to assist in every way, even at some sacrifice to themselves, as for example in permitting their houses to be searched as mentioned at page 10 of the last report.

The vigilance of the officers engaged on the inquiry continues unabated.

R. Anderson

Oct. 23/88

This brief letter represents the assistant commissioner at his political best. In its first paragraph Anderson reminds the Home Office that Chief Inspector Donald Swanson - and not he - has 'special charge' of investigating the Whitechapel murders. His frustration both with the failure of the investigation to catch its prey and the increasing pressure from the press, public, and Home Office, is candidly evident in the second paragraph; and the entirety of the third, longer, paragraph, is devoted to drawing attention to how far the police were willing to go in solving the mystery. Appearing on the surface to unselfishly praise the denizens of the East End for their cooperation, Anderson reveals his true motive by abandoning subtlety altogether and referring his bosses to 'page 10' of the report to review a list of investigative exertions designed to impress.

While it is not my intention to suggest that Warren, Anderson, or – by proxy – Swanson, were working to deceive their superiors, I believe it should be kept to the front of every researcher's mind that documents such as the Oct. 19th report were composed by human beings under tremendous pressure, whose very jobs depended on their being able to justify their actions to the men who signed their pay checks. Such personal biases and behind-the-scenes politics strongly influence the written record left to us and should be considered by any researcher hoping to effectively analyze the available data.

So what can we learn about the Oct. 19th report? Only a relatively short amount of space is devoted to summarizing the investigative measures as requested by the Home Office while the lion's share of Swanson's ink is spilled on detailing the evidence of only four witnesses: PC Smith, Israel Schwartz, Leon Goldstein, and Matthew Packer.

Leon Goldstein, in company with IWMES secretary, William Wess, came to the Leman Street police station to clear up the matter of Fanny Mortimer's 'man with the black bag' whom she watched saunter through Berner Street just prior to the finding of the body. Other than this, he was of no significance to the investigation whatsoever. Matthew Packer provided nothing but inconsistencies and had been dismissed by the police in the first week of October. Only Smith and Schwartz can be considered bona fide witnesses with possibly pertinent information. So why were these four men singled out by Swanson for discussion? The only thread that ties them together is that they each were prominently represented in newspaper reports, so this must have been Swanson's (or Anderson's) criteria.

Swanson assumed Secretary Matthews would be familiar with and curious about these stories and concocted his report in order to satisfy this curiosity. However, the handwritten marginalia that appears throughout the document makes it clear that the senior officials at the Home Office were ignorant of events that even the most illiterate of East Enders had been fully aware of for weeks. For instance, they were unaware of Fanny Mortimer and any sighting of a man with a black bag, even though the papers had been full of it. There was also presupposition that Pipeman's name must be 'Lipski' and Home Office wondered if the police had attempted to track down a man with that name. This is what instigated the report from Abberline as to his belief that BS Man had directed his call of 'Lipski' to Schwartz as either a threat or an epithet, and not to Pipeman, who Assistant Commissioner Anderson characterized as the 'supposed accomplice'.

Swanson notes that that descriptions of BS Man and Parcel Man were circulated by wire to the various police stations as well as to the press. The *Echo* printed the circulated description on Oct. 1st but made little out of the story:

> The police authorities have received an important statement in reference to the Berner-street crime. It is to the effect that a man between 35 and 40 years of age, and of fair complexion, was seen to throw the murdered woman to the ground. It was thought by the person who witnessed this that it was a man and his wife quarrelling, and consequently no notice was taken of it.

The *Manchester Guardian* followed suit the next day, including even less information:

> During the day all sorts of stories were brought to the police. Another story was to the effect that a man of light complexion had been struggling with the woman Stride in Berner Street and that he threw her down, but it being thought that it was a man and wife quarrelling nobody interfered with them.

Curiously, and intentionally, left out of the wire, was Pipeman's description. Home Office recognized the exception and observed in the marginalia that 'the Police apparently do not suspect the 2nd man whom Schwartz saw on the other side of the street & who followed Schwartz.' Author Paul Begg offered in the way of explanation that the identity of Pipeman may have already been known to police.[153] However, the speculation of officials as to his name and complicity, three weeks following the murder, argue strongly against this. What I believe the police chose to do was to utilize official channels to find BS Man and unofficial channels in their pursuit of Pipeman.

In Search of Pipeman

Swanson tells us that Schwartz came to the police station on the evening of September 30th. The next day the *Star* published the following:

> Information which may be important was given to the Leman Street police yesterday by an Hungarian concerning this murder. The foreigner was well-dressed, and had the appearance of being in the theatrical line. He could not speak a word of English, but came to the police station accompanied by a friend, who acted as interpreter. He gave his name and address, but the police have not disclosed them. A *Star* man, however, got wind of his call, and ran him to earth in Backchurch Lane. The reporter's Hungarian was quite as imperfect as the foreigner's English, but an interpreter was at hand, and the man's story was retold just as he had given it to the police. It is, in fact, to the effect that he saw the whole thing.
>
> It seems that he had gone out for the day, and his wife had expected to move, during his absence, from their lodgings in Berner Street to others in Backchurch Lane. When he first came homewards about a quarter before one he first walked down Berner Street to see if his wife had moved. As he turned the corner from Commercial Road he noticed some distance in front of him a man walking as if partially intoxicated. He walked on behind him, and presently he noticed a woman standing in the entrance to

the alleyway where the body was found. The half-tipsy man halted and spoke to her. The Hungarian saw him put his hand on her shoulder and push her back into the pass- age, but feeling rather timid of getting mixed up in quarrels, he crossed to the other side of the street. Before he had gone many yards, however, he heard the sound of a quarrel, and turned back to learn what was the matter, but just as he stepped from the kerb a second man came out of the doorway of a public house a few doors off, and shouting out some sort of warning to the man who was with the woman, rushed forward as if to attack the intruder. The Hungarian states positively that he saw a knife in the second man's hand, but he waited to see no more. He fled incontinently to his new lodgings.

He described the man with the woman as about 30 years of age, rather stoutly built, and wearing a brown moustache. He was dressed respectably in dark clothes and felt hat. The man who came at him with a knife he also describes, but not in detail. He says he was taller than the other but not so stout, and that his moustaches were red. Both men seemed to belong to the same grade of society. The police have arrested one man answering the description the Hungarian furnishes. The prisoner has not been charged, but is held for inquiries to be made. The truth of the man's statement is not wholly accepted.

The differences between the Swanson summary and the *Star* report have been discussed and debated endlessly since the advent of internet message boards. The crux of these debates is typically Schwartz's own veracity, with one side attempting to explain away the differences in defense of Schwartz (usually by pointing at the unknown interpreter or suggesting the reporter spiced up the story), and the other side indicting Schwartz as a liar who told conflicting stories.

Following are the points where the Swanson summary and the *Star* report conflict: Swanson has BS Man pulling Stride away from the club gates, whereas the *Star* has him pushing her back into the yard; Swanson has BS Man shouting 'Lipski' whereas the *Star* has Pipeman shouting a warning to BS Man; Swanson has Pipeman holding a pipe whereas the *Star* replaces the pipe with a knife; Swanson describes Pipeman as having light brown hair and no moustaches are mentioned, whereas the *Star* describes him as having red moustaches.

The *Star* report also provides details that did not conflict with the Swanson summary but also were not supported by it, which include Schwartz's having lived on Berner Street up until that day; his reason for being in the street at that time; and the description of BS Man as having appeared to be partially intoxicated or 'half-tipsy'.

Israel Schwartz's name would never appear in the press and he would never give another interview regarding his crucial role in the Ripper investigation. This behavior stands in stark contrast to that of most other witnesses, such as Matthew Packer and Fanny Mortimer. This should raise questions as to how the *Star* reporter landed the interview and why Schwartz agreed to participate when the police had just handed him a gag order. The reporter notes that the police have not disclosed the witness's name, but that would not have stopped the reporter from providing it to his readers, and it doesn't explain how the reporter tracked him down in the first place. It also stands to reason that if one reporter could so easily locate Schwartz, so could have others, but that didn't happen. The police were so keen to keep Schwartz a secret that they must have worked to gain coroner Baxter's compliance in keeping him out of the inquest proceedings. Indeed, they were so successful in isolating Schwartz that the better part of a century would pass before his name would be entered into the known historical record.

The *Star* interview is an anomaly. I believe the explanation for its existence is that it was planted by the police in order to draw Pipeman out into the open.

Pipeman would have been unaware of what Schwartz actually told the police and would be scouring the press to see what information had been gleaned. The police knew this, and the *Star* was the most widely read newspaper in the East End (Stride even had a portion of the Sept. 28th edition stuffed inside her bonnet to help it fit). Leon Goldstein had just come to the station to identify himself as Mortimer's black bag man, so why wouldn't Pipeman do the same? That would have been the thinking. I believe this is the best explanation not only for why Schwartz's name and actual street were kept from the report, but also why Pipeman is portrayed as a knife-wielding redhead working as an accomplice to the man throwing Stride around. The police were hedging their bets: if Pipeman were simply an innocent bystander, he'd feel an urgency to step forward and set the record straight about what really had happened, allowing the police to gain an extra eye witness and crucial corroboration for Schwartz's story. On the other hand, if Pipeman really was an accomplice to BS Man, he'd feel relieved at seeing Schwartz describe him as a redhead and would not be so quick to flee the area. BS Man would likewise breathe easier seeing Pipeman portrayed as the more villainous of the two and might even be inclined to present himself to the police as a witness, not knowing that he'd then be arrested as a suspect.

The theory is not as radical as it might seem. The police had planted information in papers many times, one example discussed earlier in this book relates to the Nichols case. There was, for a time, a genuine belief that the slaughtermen of Barber's Yard were complicit in the murder, and the police used the papers to play on their presumed paranoia by suggesting that one of them was on the verge of turning on the others. Likewise, articles were planted that warned unnamed suspects against fleeing the area, lest they be arrested on the spot.

Newspapers in London in 1888 numbered in the dozens if not hundreds and were fiercely competitive. The *Star* was perhaps more competitive than most and was quick to make the most of any scoops in high profile cases that came their way. If the scoop was less than genuine, such as with the 'Leather Apron' fiasco of a couple of months earlier, then all the better. Therefore, it beggars belief why an exclusive interview with the man most likely to have come face to face with the Whitechapel murderer would not be plastered on the front page and milked for all its worth over the coming week until a new story should present itself. The editor instead chose to all but bury the story under puff pieces attacking the police and stock descriptions of Berner Street. When the interview does appear it is beneath the underwhelming headline of 'INFORMATION WHICH MAY BE IMPORTANT'. What's more, this edition of the paper starts off with an editorial in which the editor undermines his own scoop, observing that 'the story of a man who is said to have seen the Berner-street tragedy, and declares that one man butchered and another man watched, is, we think, *a priori* incredible.'

The day following the publication of their interview, instead of trumpeting it from the rafters with sensationalized follow-ups, the *Star* offered their readers this bit of cynicism:

Inquiry at the Bishops-gate and Leman-street police-stations this morning developed the fact that there was no clue whatever. The threads that had been taken up on the possible chance of their leading to something tangible have been laid down again. It is but fair to say that the police have clutched eagerly at every straw that promised to help them out, but there is nothing left to work on. People have come forward by scores to furnish the description of a man they had seen with some woman near the scene, and not a great while before the commission of one or the other of Sunday morning's crimes, but no two of the descriptions are alike, and none of the accompanying information has thus far been able to bear investigation. In the matter of the Hungarian who said he saw a struggle between a man and a woman in the passage where the Stride body was afterwards found, the Leman-street police have reason to doubt the truth of the story. They arrested one man on the description thus obtained, and a second on that furnished from another source, but they are not likely to act further on the same information without additional facts. If every man should be arrested who was known to have been seen in company with an abandoned woman in that locality on last Saturday night, the police-stations would not hold them. There are many people in that district who volunteer information to the police on the principle of securing lenient treatment for their own offences, and there are others who turn in descriptions on the chance of coming near enough the mark to claim a portion of the reward if the man should be caught, just as one buys a ticket in a lottery. Even where such information is given in good faith, it can rarely be looked upon in the light of a clue.

It was the *Star's* counterintuitive way of handling their scoop – quite out of keeping for a paper known for its sensationalism – that some time ago led me to suspect that something else was going on behind the scenes. Also, the article seemed to be worded to achieve a specific effect, not so much in the casual reader, but in two readers in particular – Pipeman and BS Man. Instead of simply noting that the second man held a knife, it's written that 'the Hungarian states positively that he saw a knife in the second-man's hand,' as though to leave no doubt that this 'fact' was not an error of translation.

None of the articles or editorials came with bylines, so we can't be certain they were written by the same men. However, the two editorials panning Schwartz's evidence seem to share the same 'voice'. What wasn't so obvious was if the editor was downplaying Schwartz's story in order to play along with the police ruse, or if it was because he was not in on the ruse and smelled a rat. His fuming editorial the next day suggests the latter. The relevant portion reads:

> In investigating a crime, detectives proceed very quietly – often too quietly, it might be thought – and frequently through the agency of too credulous reporters lead the really suspected person to believe that the scent lies quite in another quarter, while in reality his every movement is being closely watched. In some instances, the reluctance of witnesses to come forward with evidence is a great stumbling block in the way of success.[154]

The brief but venomous expose begins with this telling paragraph: 'A few words here as to the general system adopted in setting about the investigation of a murder mystery, such as the latest Whitechapel one and the others that have preceded it, may not be out of place.' The editor is singling out the Stride murder by calling it the 'Whitechapel one' in spite of the fact that a second murder in the series occurred at the same time. This is perhaps because the *Star* did not have a beef with the City Police. Published, as it was, only two days following the Schwartz interview, it's difficult to imagine the expose was a mere coincidence and did not refer to the paper's one and only exclusive involving a witness description of a suspect. None of the other witnesses in the case fit the bill: Packer's story had not yet broken; Albert Bachert's tale was clearly of his own making; Fanny

Mortimer was on the pavement within an hour or two of murder speaking with anyone who'd listen, so there would have been no time and no need for police involvement in publicizing her story.

The *Star* expose does not constitute proof of anything other than the editor's suspicions, but it certainly bolsters the argument that the *Star* interview was concocted by the police to draw out Pipeman and/or BS Man. It's possible that the reporter in question was merely 'credulous' as suggested by the editor, but it's more probable that he was paid well to submit the plant as a legitimate article and would have been proud to do so as it was an exclusive. What the editor learned or what sparked his suspicions can only be guessed at.

This new perspective explains not only the discrepancies in the *Star* article and the contradictory reports that Schwartz was not believed by the police, but also why Schwartz was absent from the inquest and why Pipeman's description was left out of the published circular.

Israel Schwartz & the Berner Street Club

We know very little about Israel Schwartz the man. Abberline's Nov. 1st report tells us that he was of 'strong Jewish appearance' and did not speak English. The *Star* report adds that up until the day of the murder Schwartz had lived *on Berner Street*, a potentially significant but generally overlooked detail. It also tells us that Schwartz was Hungarian and 'was well-dressed and had the appearance of being in the theatrical line.' If Schwartz was indeed an actor, his inability to speak English would require that he performed in the Yiddish theater. If this were the case, the fact that he was interviewed in costume suggests the possibility that he had a performance scheduled somewhere in the area that day, and therefore a search for reviews and advertising might prove fruitful. He might also have been described that way because that's how he appeared to BS Man and Pipeman. However, it should go without saying that information in the *Star* report must be approached with caution. It's most likely that Schwartz worked in the clothing industry, as did so many immigrant Jews in the East End. Perhaps he was a new arrival in London who had enjoyed better circumstances in his home country and still dressed in fine apparel that would have been alien to the English reporter. In any event, Schwartz's manner and dress suggests he was not a Hassidic Jew, a detail that will become significant later on in our study.

Having exhausted our known sources of information on Schwartz, we turn to the census for further enlightenment. Fortunately, this work has already been done for us by author Chris Scott for his 2004 e-book, *Jack the Ripper: A Cast of Thousands*[155], and presented later by authors Paul Begg, Martin Fido, and Keith Skinner, in their compendium *The Comprehensive Jack the Ripper A-Z*.[156] Surprisingly, the 1891 census index contain very few entries for 'Israel Schwartz' or similar variations, and only one emerges that both sources site as the possible (though by no means definite) identification of Schwartz and family:

22 Samuel Street, St. George's in the East

Head:
Israel Schwartz aged 27 born Poland - Tailor's presser
Wife:
Eva Schwartz aged 27 born Poland
Children:
Dinah E aged 6 born Poland
Louis aged 1 months born St George's.

The only real hurdle in settling on this man as 'Schwartz the witness' is the fact that he and his family are described as Polish and not Hungarian. This could be explained either as an error on the part of the census taker or *Star* reporter, or it could be that Schwartz was in fact Polish and described as Hungarian in the paper in order to make it difficult for others to locate him. The police files do not give Schwartz's country of origin. The age of the daughter suggests the Samuel Street family moved to London at some point in or after 1885, which is in keeping with the notion that Schwartz was a recent arrival in London at the time of the murders.

If all the above is correct, then Israel Schwartz was a relatively recent immigrant from either Poland or Hungary, aged about 24, with a 'strong Jewish appearance,' and was probably Jewish, though not Hassidic. He had been gone (according to the *Star*) from the area on Sept. 29th while his wife spent the day moving from Berner Street to their new residence in nearby Ellen Street. Schwartz was on his way home at approximately 12:45am on the morning of the 30th and his reason for being in Berner Street at that time was to make sure that his wife had moved. That he was walking along the pavement on the western side of the street suggests his destination would have been on the same side. According to Swanson, Schwartz got 'as far as the gateway where the murder was committed,' so it is reasonable to infer that he had not already passed the house where his wife might be waiting. This means his destination was somewhere on the western side of Berner Street from #40 on to the street's end at #82. Further excluding businesses within this radius, we have effectively eliminated about 80% of the street as having been the likely location of Schwartz's previous residence.[157] This still leaves us with close to three dozen possible addresses for the Schwartz family. The most obvious place where we might expect to find a young Jewish immigrant family enjoying a temporary stay is at the International Workingmen's Educational Society at #40 Berner Street.

The Berner Street club was very active in the Match Girl Strike of 1888, the headquarters of which was the Christ Church Hall at 22 Hanbury Street, only a stone's throw from where Annie Chapman would soon be found murdered. As a result of their efforts and publicity the club gained a great amount of respect from the immigrant sweater population. The Berner Street club was also "the nucleus of the radical and trade union movement in both the East and West Ends of London"[158] and was chiefly responsible for the Jewish Tailors and Sweaters Unions. Their public gatherings were well attended and their weekly Yiddish publication, *Der Arbeter Fraint* (the Worker's Friend), was quite popular amongst the non-English speaking Jewish population.

With this in mind, imagine that you're a young Jewish man, unable to speak English, probably in the tailoring trade, living on the same small street as a club consisting of men such as yourself. Not only is it reasonable to suggest that Israel Schwartz would have visited the club, it's difficult to imagine that he would not have. The club was a magnet for Jewish immigrants and Israel Schwartz would have been no exception. However, having made this point it needs to be said that no proof has yet surfaced to show that Schwartz was a visitor to the club. This is hardly surprising, considering the papers of the Berner Street club may no longer exist. I inquired at Warwick University, where are held the papers of club secretary, William Wess, but very little material relating to his time at the club is to be found there.

Even if a member roll were to be found it is doubtful that Schwartz's name would be on it. Full-fledged card-carrying members of the club were very few, the majority of their supporters being casual attendees. A better bet would be the records of the tailor and sweaters unions managed by Wess or the Berner Street club if they could be located. In the meantime, we must work with what we have, and a rather tantalizing piece of evidence surfaced in the form of a newspaper report that appeared in the *Echo* on the day following the murder:

A MAN PURSUED. - SAID TO BE THE MURDERER.

In the course of conversation (says the journalist) the secretary mentioned the fact that the murderer had no doubt been disturbed in his work, as about a quarter to one o'clock on Sunday morning he was seen- or, at least, a man whom the public prefer to regard as the murderer- being chased by another man along Fairclough-street, which runs across Berner-street close to the Club, and which is intersected on the right by Providence-street, Brunswick-street, and Christian-street, and on the left by Batty-street and Grove-street, the two latter running up into Commercial-road. The man pursued escaped, however, and the secretary of the Club cannot remember the name of the man who gave chase, but he is not a member of their body.

The timing of the incident ('a quarter to one') and the description of a desperate chase from Berner Street leave no doubt that the story told to the *Echo* reporter by the club secretary, William Wess, is a variation on the Schwartz incident. On its surface the report suggests that an unnamed witness watched as Pipeman chased Schwartz from Berner Street, and goes on to make the even more remarkable claim that Pipeman's identity was known, although Wess could not remember his name.

Considering that this report was apparently written not by the journalist who attended the club meeting but a second journalist working from his notes (suggested by the reference to 'the journalist' as a third party), it's not surprising that errors and omissions were made, although we can't be certain who was responsible – the speaker, the reporter, the writer, or a combination. However, there are a few things of which we *can* be certain: The interviewee was William Wess, the secretary of the Berner Street club, who was firmly on damage control mode in the hours and days following the murder of Liz Stride in his club's yard. Pipeman's identity was never discovered, or at least not by the day following the murder, and no other witness came forth to corroborate Schwartz's tale. Therefore, when Wess made the claim that he knew - but could not remember - the name of the man who 'gave chase', he could only have been referring to Israel Schwartz.

The *Star* man who interviewed him wrote that Schwartz 'gave his name and address, but the police have not disclosed them.' No doubt the reporter ached to reveal Schwartz's identity to the world, yet something compelled him not to do so. Schwartz did not appear publicly at the inquest and his name remained unknown to researchers until 1976. While it is probably true that the Metropolitan Police did not accept Schwartz's evidence at face value, they reasoned it wise to keep his identity completely secret, a unique move with Ripper witnesses. With secrecy the order of the day, William Wess was almost certainly being disingenuous when he told the reporter that he could not remember the name of the man who may have seen the Ripper, in lieu of revealing the more dramatic truth that he'd been sworn to secrecy, if not by the police then by Schwartz himself.

How did Wess come to know Schwartz's tale so soon after the murder and only hours after the police first heard it? While it could be argued that Wess caught the 'word on the street', there's no evidence that such word was making the rounds so soon after the murder. The only plausible explanation is that he heard it either from the police or Schwartz himself. If the police had a hunch that Schwartz might be associated with the club, or even knew for a fact that he was, it makes sense that they'd inquire about his character. But in probing Wess for insight into Schwartz's character, would they be so sloppy as to divulge such guarded information to a known radical and agitator with press connections? Stranger things happened during the investigation, but still it seems unlikely. With Schwartz having been a neighbor (or even resident) of a club catering to a demographic to which Schwartz belonged, it seems most probable that Wess learned of these events from Schwartz himself.

Wess, it will be remembered, escorted Leon Goldstein to the same police station Schwartz visited to act as interpreter (and moral support), so that Goldstein could clear himself of any suspicion after recognizing himself as Fanny Mortimer's black bag man. Goldstein, like Schwartz, was a young Jewish immigrant unable to speak English. If Wess had served as Schwartz's escort as well, it would explain his inside knowledge.

Whether Wess learned his information from the police or from Schwartz himself the conclusion is the same – Israel Schwartz was probably familiar with the Berner Street club and possibly a friend. If such were the case, then it means his wife might have been waiting for him in one of the cottages in the yard, across the path from the club house. A *Star* man, early on the scene in Berner Street, spoke with anyone willing in hopes of picking up scraps of information. One woman had little to offer but he wrote about her anyway: 'A woman living just opposite says that she was waiting up for her husband and listening for his coming, and she heard nothing to arouse her suspicion.' (The *Star*, Oct. 1ˢᵗ, 1888.)

The Great Schwartz Debate

Recent years have seen more voice put to the notion that Israel Schwartz was not an honest witness. The theory has even made its way into the published literature, often by authors who find merit in being contrary for contrary's sake. I confess I myself have played a part in fuelling the debate, having on many occasions shared on internet message boards my theory that Schwartz was affiliated with the Berner Street club. It is a legitimate theory, with real possibilities.[159]

Going a step further I observed that Schwartz's evidence was rather convenient for the club, who at that time would be viewed with the direst of suspicion. Many already believed the Ripper Jewish and here was a club full of angry young Jewish radicals playing host in their yard to the Ripper himself. It might have seemed to the police a bit convenient that a witness with associations to the club should present himself (possibly accompanied by William Wess) with a statement that casts suspicion upon an alleged anti-Semite (BS Man) and the obviously gentile Pipeman. An objective study of the material means one must often assume perspectives that oppose his personal biases, so I presented this information in spite of my general belief that Schwartz was an honest witness. It's as much a mistake to blindly accept the Schwartz story as factual as it is to disregard it (or any similar evidence) because it is inconvenient or because one chooses to believe that everything police officials wrote or said were lies. If Schwartz was a friend of the IWMES, and even if his evidence shifted suspicion away from the club, it does not mean that he didn't see what he said he saw.

The *Star* reported within two days of the murder that Schwartz was not wholly believed. Some have interpreted this to mean that Schwartz was a liar. As already noted, there appears to have been an agenda behind how the *Star* treated the Schwartz story, so we can't be certain this was not placed in the paper by the police wishing to put the suspects at ease; or that it was a vengeful editor hoping to undermine the police's star witness. Whatever the case, it's probably true that Schwartz's statement was not wholly accepted. The police did not simply take all witnesses at their word, nor should it be expected that they would. It must have occurred to more than a few of them (and, in particular, Abberline) that they'd heard a similar story before.

In the wake of the Annie Chapman murder, when 'Leather Apron' fever was at its pitch, a 63 year-old immigrant named Emmanuel Delbast Violina provided the police with a statement to the effect that he had been walking along Hanbury Street when he bore witness to a man abusing Chapman. Upon further questioning he added a second man to the mix and stated one of them held a knife. Inspector Abberline, among others, interrogated Violina and quickly exposed the story as a lie.[160] The press had this to say about Violina: 'The conduct of the man who professed to identify Pizer has caused much indignation, it having kept several experienced officers from prosecuting inquiries in other directions. His statement, clear enough at first, utterly failed to stand the test even of ordinary questioning.'[161]

If the police routinely treated sensational statements with a healthy amount of skepticism, then Schwartz's strikingly similar tale, coming less than three weeks after Violina, must have set alarm bells ringing. Matthew Packer's statement, much like Violina's, was discredited largely because he could not remain consistent in his details. Schwartz, whom we might assume would have been viewed with more than the usual amount of suspicion, passed the interrogation test and the police were not able to disprove his story. They were also not able to corroborate it.

If we study the Berner Street murder in a bubble and don't look beyond October, we would be compelled to conclude that Schwartz was the person most likely to have seen the Ripper – or, at the very least, the killer of Stride. However, if we widen our scope and consider what the people in the best position to know had to say in the years to come, after all the hands were played and the chips were in, we might not feel so certain.

Chief Inspector Swanson, in comparing Schwartz's evidence with PC Smith's, observed: 'I respectfully submit it is not clearly proved that the man that Schwartz saw is the murderer, although it is clearly the more probable of the two.' Schwartz's man was different enough in description to Smith's as to suggest they must be two different people, and as Schwartz was the latter of the two witnesses, logic dictated he was most likely to have seen Stride's killer. However, Swanson's observation regarding the value of Schwartz's evidence is crucial and often overlooked; because of the time that lapsed between Schwartz's sighting and the finding of the body, Schwartz's evidence could not constitute proof of guilt against a suspect, even if the correct person could be identified.

Regarding Joseph Lawende in Mitre Square, Swanson tells us that he 'identified the clothes only of the murdered woman Eddowes, which is a serious drawback to the value of the description of the man. Ten minutes afterwards the body is found horribly mutilated & it is therefore reasonable to believe that the man he saw was the murderer.' The inference here is that Lawende is the most likely to have seen the murderer, but observed so little that his evidence would be valueless; Schwartz, by contrast, got a good look at his man, but there's question as to if the man he saw was actually Stride's killer; it would not stand up in court but could be an excellent investigatory tool if they were able to find the right man for Schwartz to view.

Swanson also observed in his summary that Abberline's report 'casts no doubt' upon Schwartz's veracity, which is not the same as saying that the police had succeeded in corroborating or otherwise proving Schwartz true, but it does indicate that Abberline's techniques of sniffing out a false witness had proved fruitless with Schwartz and the seasoned investigator was inclined to believe him. However, statements made by Abberline 15 years later suggest he may have altered his opinion.

By 1903, Frederick Abberline had been retired for a decade but had maintained contact with Scotland Yard and had not lost interest in the Ripper case. The trial and conviction of George Chapman had come and gone and Abberline formed an opinion that the serial wife poisoner made for a convincing Ripper suspect. Along with Chapman's willingness to murder women, Abberline was most influenced by the fact that he had lived in the Whitechapel area throughout the time of the murders. Also impressing Abberline was Chapman's appearance: "…the height of the man and the peaked cap he is said to have worn quite tallies with the descriptions I got of him. All agree, too, that he was a foreign-looking man – but that, of course, helped us little in a district so full of foreigners as Whitechapel.' Both Schwartz and Lawende had described their men as wearing peaked caps, so this sentence has often been seen to support a continued belief in Schwartz by police. However, with his next sentence, Abberline qualifies his favored descriptions: 'One discrepancy only have I noted, and this is that the people who alleged that they saw Jack the Ripper at one time or another, state that he was a man about thirty-five or forty years of age. They, however, state that they only saw his back, and it is easy to misjudge age from a back view.'

The witnesses that Abberline seems to be referring to are Elizabeth Long and Joseph Lawende. Although Lawende did not see his man from behind[162], he admittedly did not get a good look at him and was specific in his description of a 'peaked cap'. 47 year-old Elizabeth Long, walking along Hanbury Street around 5:30am on the morning of Annie Chapman's murder, described having seen Chapman talking with a man outside the shutters of #29. Chapman's mutilated body would soon be discovered in the backyard of this address and it was believed by some that Long had seen the murderer. She'd only seen the mystery man from behind but guessed his age at over 40 and described him as wearing a brown deer-stalker hat, which possessed peaks both front and back. There was and is some debate over the relevance of Mrs. Long's testimony since it conflicts to some degree with that of Albert Cadosch, who reported having heard what is assumed to be Chapman and her murderer in the backyard of #29 at a time previous to that which Long saw her couple. That Abberline would accept this evidence in favor of Schwartz is confusing if he still considered Schwartz a key witness. Even more bewildering is his preference for Joseph Lawende, a City Police witness with whom he would have had little or no personal communication.

Inspector Edmund Reid was firm in his belief that no one had witnessed the Ripper[163], whereas the officials of both forces believed that one man only had emerged from all inquiries as the most likely to have seen Jack the Ripper. Sir Henry Smith, Chief Constable of the City Police and Acting Commissioner at the time of the Stride and Eddowes murders, published his memoirs in 1910. In his book he touched upon the evidence of Joseph Lawende, whom he describes as 'honest, apparently, and intelligent also.' Smith accepted as fact that Lawende had seen Eddowes with her murderer but observed with regret that the witness had only seen the man for a moment and would not recognize him again.

Prior to the publication of Smith's book, former Assistant Commissioner Sir Robert Anderson's memoirs were serialized in *Blackwood's Magazine* and later published in book form, with alterations, as *The Lighter Side of My Official Life*. The portion relevant to our discussion from both sources is presented below:

'I will only add that when the individual whom we suspected was caged in an asylum, the only person who had ever had a good view of the murderer at once identified him, but when he learned that the suspect was a fellow-Jew he declined to swear to him.'

— *Blackwood's Magazine*

'I will merely add that the only person who had ever had a good view

of the murderer unhesitatingly identified the suspect the instant he was confronted with him; but he refused to give evidence against him.'

— The Lighter Side of My Official Life

The *Blackwood's* version of Anderson's memoirs had been available at the time that Henry Smith was penning his memoirs and Smith had the opportunity to respond to Anderson's confident assertion that the Ripper had been discovered and placed safely away in an asylum. Interestingly, Smith did not take this opportunity to argue over the Ripper's identity, the merits of Anderson's suspect, or to suggest that the identification didn't take place. What he took issue with were Anderson's accusations against the Jews of the East End, whom the Met man felt had sheltered the criminal and kept him out of the reach of 'Gentile justice'. Smith was aware that his book was being published very closely to Anderson's, and thanks to *Blackwell's Magazine*, Smith was also aware of Anderson's assertions that the only person who had ever seen the Ripper was the key to his alleged solution to the mystery. Smith shared Anderson's belief that only one man had seen the Ripper, but was unequivocal in stating that the man would be useless for identification purposes. This may have been Smith's way of undermining Anderson and in doing so identifies Anderson's witness as Joseph Lawende.

Frances Coles was murdered in February of 1891 and there was strong speculation that she may have been a victim of Jack the Ripper. Her beau, James Sadler, was the prime suspect, and Joseph Lawende failed to identify him as the man he'd seen near Mitre Square. There's no mention of Schwartz being used, even though he was still living in London at the time (if, indeed, the Israel Schwartz of the 1891 census is our man). The *Daily Telegraph* fashioned the description given by Lawende as 'probably the only trustworthy description of the assassin.'[164] In 1892, murderer Frederick Deeming was all the talk as a possible 'Ripper' and much use was made of Joseph Lawende's evidence by the press, who once again singled him out as the ultimate Ripper witness.

It is believed that Lawende was used as late as 1895 to view potential Ripper suspects. William Grant (aka Grainger) was arrested for stabbing Alice Graham and was positively identified by an unnamed witness described in the press as 'one person whom the police believe to have actually seen the Whitechapel murderer with a woman a few minutes before the woman's dissected body was found in the street.' However, it's been argued that Lawende could not have identified both Grainger and Anderson's suspect named by Donald Swanson as 'Kozminski', therefore Schwartz is the most likely candidate to have been the witness in one of these instances. As Schwartz witnessed two men in the street, it's not outside the realm of possibility that he was the witness in both cases – identifying Kozminski as BS Man and Grainger as Pipeman. However, there's no actual evidence to support the contention that Schwartz was ever utilized as a witness.

In February of 1894, Assistant Chief Commissioner Melville Macnaghten, who did not begin working with the police until 1889, penned a document now referred to as the 'Macnaghten Memoranda', which remained preserved with the other Home Office reports. The document is most notable for naming three suspects (M.J. Druitt, Michael Ostrog, and 'Kosminski') and prescribing the Ripper with only five murders. Regarding witness evidence, Macnaghten firmly states that 'no one ever saw the Whitechapel Murderer'. This is technically correct in that there was no witness who stated they had seen the Ripper in the course of murdering a woman. Any man seen previously with a victim could only be regarded as a suspect. Many years later, Macnaghten's daughter, Lady Aberconway, had her secretary type up what must have been an earlier draft of the memoranda. This typed version (with some pages handwritten by Aberconway herself) is all that remains of this draft. The Aberconway version adds this caveat to Macnaghten's assertion that no one had seen the Ripper: 'unless possibly it was the City P.C. who was a beat [sic] near Mitre Square'. That Macnaghten saw fit to strike this from his final version might indicate he realized he'd been mistaken. Or he may have reconsidered the witness evidence and decided it was unlikely the man had seen the Ripper.

There was, of course, no City constable who had witnessed a possible Ripper near Mitre Square, so Macnaghten was either confused about PC Smith in Berner Street or (most likely) had muddled Joseph Lawende with PC Ernest Thompson, who had discovered the body of Frances Coles. Although Thompson had not seen a man fleeing the scene, he'd heard his footsteps, and made the decision to follow protocol and remain with the victim instead of pursuing the likely murderer. In any event, Macnaghten was either unaware of Israel Schwartz (which might suggest that Schwartz had been disregarded as unreliable by officials prior to Macnaghten's joining of the force in 1889) or he was aware of Schwartz's evidence but felt inclined to discount it.

The complicated reality is that there exists no reference, direct or oblique, to Schwartz having been used as a witness at any time. In fact, there's no suggestion that he was viewed as a significant witness after November 1st, 1888. It has been argued that he had moved from London and was thus not available, but this would not explain the absolute lack of reference to him or his description. Abberline could have pointed to BS Man as a possible sighting of George Chapman, but he did not do so. Macnaghten could have argued BS Man was Druitt, but he did not. Henry Smith discusses the Berner Street murder in his book but states no one heard or saw a thing. All of these men must have been aware of Schwartz but for one reason or another thought of him as inconsequential.

There likewise exists no statement to the effect that Schwartz was proved a liar or untrustworthy. He may have been, but there are other explanations. Lawende's evidence was corroborated by Joseph Levy and Harry Harris, whereas Schwartz was corroborated by no one. This, of course, does not prove that Schwartz was a liar but in the absence of proof to the contrary there must naturally remain some doubt. The evidence of PC Smith was accepted without question but its value as evidence was hampered by its occurring so far before the murder. The same might be said of Schwartz. The murder of Stride would have taken only seconds, so the 15 minutes between Schwartz's pass through the street and the time her murder was believed to have occurred would have raised doubts that what Schwartz saw related to her murder. The murder and mutilation of Eddowes, by contrast, would have consumed many minutes, so Lawende's sighting of her with a man 10 minutes before the discovery of her body made it likely that he'd seen the Ripper. There's also the outside possibility that the police had come to learn the identity of BS Man and he was able to provide an alibi for the Eddowes murder and thus remove himself from suspicion.

All we can say for sure is that Schwartz is not referenced as a witness after November, 1888, and the various surviving accounts point to the most viable (if not only) witness being someone associated with the Mitre Square murder, apparently Joseph Lawende. The rest is speculation.

The Square Peg

It could be argued that if the police discounted Schwartz then so should we. But it's a little more complicated than that. We cannot be sure that the police did discount Schwartz. As mentioned before, we do not have a statement to that effect, although the absence of reference to him post 1888 is confusing and unsettling. But it's happened before that a witness had told the truth and was not believed or a truthful witness has had doubt cast upon them by a character flaw or an inconvenient but perhaps coincidental association (the Berner Street club, for instance). Schwartz, a stranger in a strange land who did not speak the language, succeeded in winning the confidence of a seasoned investigator and the distribution of his description in the *Police Gazette* proves (as does the Swanson report) that weeks after he came forth he was considered a key witness. So, if Schwartz was a liar, he was a skilled liar. He was also quite lucky.

If we assume the stance that Schwartz fed the police a fib, we should consider what that would mean. Schwartz described an empty street at a specific time and two rather specific fictional characters. He had no idea what other intelligence the police had received but must have known, or at least assumed, that they had knocked on every door in the street and that other people who'd been in the area had come forth to reveal whatever they had or had not seen at that particular time. A story such as Schwartz's would in most instances have been quite easy to disprove. But that was not the case. Fanny Mortimer and others stated the street was desolate for much of the time surrounding Schwartz's trip through. A liar might also be tempted to put a weapon in the hands of one of his men or have the assailant ushering the victim to the spot where she was murdered, as opposed to pulling her away from it. A liar might also have expected better footing if he'd placed his timing a few minutes prior to the ascribed time of death and not a quarter of an hour before. It's also worth noting that neither the clerkly BS Man nor the shabby genteel Pipeman bore any resemblance to the stooped, beady-eyed 'Leather Apron' who the whole of the East End was looking for. If Schwartz wanted the police to believe his fiction it might be expected that he'd provide descriptions in keeping with ones they'd already received.

If we consider our revised timeline of significant events prior to 1am and omit Schwartz from the narrative, here is what we get (times approximate):

12:40-12:45am – PC Smith passes through the street and sees Stride with Parcel Man. Morris Eagle comes from Commercial Road and enters the club via Dutfield's Yard. He believed there were other people about but took no notice of them.

12:46-12:55am – Fanny Mortimer is at her door and sees no one pass by.

12:50-12:51 – James Brown leaves the chandler's shop on the corner of Berner and Fairclough and passes by a woman he believes was Stride standing with Overcoat Man on the School Board side of the street.

12:55-12:56am – Leon Goldstein passes through Berner Street and is witnessed by Fanny Mortimer. Goldstein sees nothing unusual. Fanny Mortimer closes her door and retires.

1:00am – Louis Diemshitz arrives home and discovers the body of Elizabeth Stride.

These timings, *sans* Schwartz, are quite harmonious with one another and would leave precious little to debate over. Spotted only 9 minutes prior to the finding of her body, Overcoat Man emerges as the likely slayer. Now to see what happens when Schwartz is inserted back into the fold.

Schwartz's time in the street would have consumed roughly two minutes. Leaving time for the other characters to retire to their corners before the next witness happens onto the scene we should double that time and allow four minutes for the entire episode to play out. This is not scientific in the least but I believe it's reasonable and fair. So, in our timeline above, we're looking for a four-minute block of time where no one else was on the street and the series of events that Schwartz describes would make sense. Traditionally, the Schwartz event is placed before James Brown in the timeline because it's assumed BS Man murdered Stride and because a misinterpretation of Brown's evidence had up to now led us to believe that he'd witnessed Stride at 12:45am, the same time provided by Schwartz.

If we want to follow tradition and place Schwartz after Brown then we have Schwartz and BS Man entering from Commercial Road at 12:51am, which would mean that Stride must have abandoned Overcoat Man at this time in order to take her position in Dutfield's Yard prior to BS Man's arrival at the gate. Overcoat Man would pull out his pipe and become Pipeman and four minutes later, the Ripper (presumably BS Man) would be in the deep shadows of the yard's passageway, murdering Stride, as Leon Goldstein makes his way through the street, Pipeman and Schwartz having already fled. This timeline would be quite cozy except for the fact that Fanny Mortimer was in her doorway during this time and saw nothing of the sort.

If we move the Schwartz episode back in time to just before Fanny came to her door we'd be looking at a timeframe of 12:41 to 12:45am, which dovetails nicely with the time of 12:45am provided by Schwartz himself. This new timeline would require us to squeeze Morris Eagle's and PC Smith's passing back a few minutes to 12:38 to no later than 12:40am, but that's no insurmountable hurdle. However, this scenario is not without its problems. For starters, Fanny Mortimer recalled that she went to her door just after hearing the PC pass. We do not know how many seconds or minutes this would have constituted in Fanny's mind, but we know there must have been ample time for Stride and Parcel Man to have made their exit. In the last chapter we allowed two minutes for this. But with Schwartz's episode taking place after Smith's passing and before Fanny's entrance, and leaving enough time for Smith to get out of ear/eyeshot, we must allow a bare minimum of five minutes from Smith's passing her doorway to Fanny coming to stand in it. This is a significant alteration to the historical record, but it pales in comparison to the challenge it places on our accepted wisdom of Schwartz being the last witness to have seen Stride alive and BS Man as her likely killer.

If Schwartz exits the street at 12:45am, then that means Stride is still alive and perched just around the corner of the Board School on Fairclough Street, speaking with Overcoat Man. This would make James Brown the last witness to see her alive and Overcoat Man her probable killer.

If we assume the perspective that Brown was the final witness, then the scenario would look something like this: PC Smith passes along and sees Stride across the street from the club talking with Parcel Man. Shortly after he passes, Stride enters Dutfield's Yard, where she remains for only a couple of minutes before she engages a passing BS Man in conversation. Schwartz crosses the street to avoid the noisy couple, is yelled at by BS Man as Pipeman rounds the corner, lighting his pipe. Schwartz takes off running with Pipeman in pursuit for only a part of the way. BS Man either enters the club (assuming he was Morris Eagle) or exits Berner Street (assuming he was not). Stride dusts herself off and walks away from the club and into Fairclough Street. Fanny Mortimer comes to her door. Pipeman returns to find Stride (or a similarly dressed man comes upon her) and holds her in conversation for several minutes. James Brown passes during this time. Leon Goldstein hurries pass them, taking no notice, and they hear a door close on the street. Looking around the corner, Overcoat Man sees the coast is clear and coaxes Stride to follow him into Dutfield's Yard. He murders Stride and exits the yard just before or just after Diemshitz's arrival.

I suggest that Pipeman and Overcoat man were one and the same because of the similarity of their descriptions and because they were observed by two witnesses in the same location (around the corner on Fairclough Street) within minutes of each other. Schwartz described Pipeman as age 35, 5' 11" inches in height, with light brown hair, a brown moustache, wearing an old black hard felt hat with a wide brim and a dark overcoat. The admittedly less observant Brown was certain that his man wore a long, dark coat that seemed like an overcoat and went almost to his heels, was of average build and about 5' 7". He didn't get a good look at the man's face but felt that his appearance was more of clerk than a laborer. Aside from the difference in height, which could be attributed to Brown's inattentiveness or the angle of his view from the street to the pavement, there's little to distinguish Pipeman from Overcoat Man.

The only concession we have to make in order to accept this sequence of events is that Fanny Mortimer didn't go directly to her doorway after she heard the constable pass. By contrast, the traditional scenario where Schwartz follows Brown requires not only moving Schwartz's given time up at least 10 minutes but, more significantly, eliminating Fanny Mortimer's testimony altogether. A third alternative, of course, would be to decide that Schwartz is the least believable of the witnesses and to exclude him altogether. However, he got too many things right to simply be disregarded. A person arguing for Schwartz as a liar would have to explain how he could have known that a man in a dark overcoat was lurking just around the corner.

There are too many missing pieces to allow for us to feel too certain about anything, but given the available scenarios I'd propose it's most likely that Stride remained alive after Schwartz fled Berner Street and that Overcoat/Pipeman was most probably her killer. This might seem a radical move away from accepted wisdom, but it is not. Our accepted wisdom comes to us largely from Ripper books written in previous decades when there was far fewer contemporary accounts available, or when detailed analysis of minutia was not yet a standard in true crime books. The information I provided regarding James Brown's inquest testimony as reported by a variety of newspapers reveals that he left his rooms at 12:45 and it was not until some minutes later that he witnessed Stride with Overcoat Man. It's an adjustment of only six minutes – hardly radical – but it does force a reconsideration of the timeline. I've also demonstrated that the 'young couple' offered in earlier works as an alternative for Brown's couple were long gone by the time he left his house. We have to accept Fanny Mortimer as an honest witness, and James Brown gives us no reason to question his integrity.

With Schwartz we should exercise more caution, but without a firm case to dismiss him, we should work with what he gives us. And for the most part his evidence dovetails rather nicely with that of the other witnesses once the fog clouding their timelines is swept away. Here's the amended and definitive timeline:

12:38-12:40am – PC Smith and Morris Eagle (assuming he wasn't BS Man) make their way along Berner Street. Eagle notices nothing and Smith sees Stride with Parcel man on the sidewalk across from the club.

12:41-12:45am – Israel Schwartz witnesses BS Man pull Stride from the gateway and throw her down. He's chased from the scene by Pipeman. Stride brushes herself off and goes around the corner of the Board School. Brown leaves his house.

12:46am - Fanny Mortimer comes to her door.

12:46-12:50am – Stride meets Overcoat Man, who may be a returning Pipeman. They stand against the Board School talking.

12:50-12:51am – James Brown witnesses Stride with Overcoat Man and hears her say "Not tonight, some other night."

12:55am – Leon Goldstein walks through Berner Street and is witnessed by Fanny Mortimer.

12:56am – Fanny Mortimer retires and closes her door.

12:56-1am – Stride returns to Dutfield's Yard with her killer, probably Overcoat Man, and is murdered.

1:00am – Louis Diemshitz discovers Stride's body.

The venomous *Star* editorial of October 3rd, outing the police for tricking newspapers into printing false stories in order to draw witnesses or suspects out, sheds light on some of the other mysteries surrounding Schwartz – namely the discrepancies in the *Star* interview and why Schwartz did not give evidence at the inquest. If Schwartz were called he'd be compelled to tell the truth and the police were anxious to take full advantage of what they believed to be an eye witness to the Whitechapel murderer. Some have suggested that they hid Schwartz from the inquisitive coroner, Wynne Baxter, but there's nothing to support that and plenty to argue against it.[165] It's quite reasonable to assume that if they could convince Baxter that calling Schwartz would be more advantageous to the murderer than to investigators, he'd agree and go along with it. Showing him the Oct. 1st *Star* report would have provided them leverage.

Researching history means you're working with scraps. Writing history means you're only telling part of the story. The best we can say at the present moment is that Israel Schwartz was taken seriously by police in October of 1888, but disappears from the historical record shortly after this point; although many officials make reference to significant witnesses in the years and decades that followed the murders, Israel Schwartz is never referenced as one. This could be for any number of reasons, but because one of them is that he was somehow discredited, a certain measure of doubt must be entertained when handling his evidence. I've seen many researchers discount Stride as a Ripper victim largely because they accept as fact that Schwartz was the last person to have seen Stride alive and that the arguably unRipper-like BS Man was her killer. Swanson, writing only a few weeks later, did not make such leaps, so it's advisable we shouldn't either. It is more likely that James Brown was the last witness to have seen Stride alive, in which case, BS Man is exonerated.

With so many possibilities and so few certainties, it's comforting to know that interest in Israel Schwartz and his role in the Berner Street mystery is not waning. As long as there is uncertainty there will be debate, and as long as there is debate there will be people looking for answers. That's Ripperology.

SECTION THREE

Curios & Oddities

Just the Facts…and Then Some

IT IS MORE likely that we will discover the identity of the Ripper than it is likely we will ever know who wrote what author Martin Fido dismissively termed the 'Goulston Street graffito'. This is because the police didn't know. There were no witnesses to its creation and no two people who saw it remembered it the same. A photographer was ordered but no photograph was made.

We swim in envy of those Ripper authors blessed with the preternatural insight that allows them to claim – finally and indisputably – to know who the Ripper was. There's no mystery for these gifted souls, for their knowledge of the Ripper's identity tells them the whole story. If your man is the teacher Montague Druitt, then the existence of a cryptic piece of chalk writing makes perfect sense. If you're more inclined to an immigrant suspect (that is, one who is unlikely to boast of an English school boy's hand), then it's easy to discount the writing as a pre-existing happenstance under which the bloodied portion of Catherine Eddowes's apron happened to drop. However, for us workaday writers, groping in the dark without a pet theory to light the way, we have only our study of the historical record for any hope of enlightenment.

Here we will look at the facts, as few as they are, and tease what we can out of them. We will also give careful consideration to contemporary opinion on the writing and juxtapose this with more modern trends of thought that have influenced the current debate.

The What, When, and Where

At approximately 1:45am on September 30th, City PC Edward Watkins shone his lamp into the dark corners of Mitre Square and discovered the ravaged remnants of a woman. He summoned the help of a retired constable working nearby as a night watchman and an alarm was raised. The hunt was on. What the police didn't yet know was the woman's name – Catherine Eddowes – or that her killer had cut off a portion of her apron and fled with it. What they were all too well aware of was that this was the second murder of the night and there was little reason to suppose there wouldn't be a third.

Alfred Long had been a baker by trade and a distinguished member of the 9th Lancers before joining the Metropolitan Police in 1884. He was four years into what would be his five year career with the police when he was pulled from his regular beat in A Division (Whitehall) to help aid the beleaguered H Division in their hunt for the Whitechapel murderer.[166]

Long was only hours into his first night's patrol in H Division territory when he made the most significant find of his short police career. The time was 2:55am and the place was one of the numerous passageways into the Wentworth Model Dwellings on Goulston Street. Long saw a bundle in the entry to numbers 108-119 and upon investigation discovered it to be a bloodstained portion of apron. Above it was some chalk writing. Long's first thought was not that there might be a killer lurking nearby but that there might be a victim somewhere in the shadows of the deep stairwells. He found nothing. Upon fetching PC 190H Willie Bettles from a neighboring beat to prohibit anyone from entering or leaving the property, he was off to notify his superiors. Long reported his find to an inspector at Commercial Street, who returned with him to inspect the writing and gather the apron. Together they went to the Leman Street station where the apron piece was handed over to Dr. George Bagster Phillips. PC Long was kept waiting for more than an hour before he was allowed to return to duty at Goulston Street at about 5am.

Just before Long's discovery of the apron, Detective Constable Daniel Halse, a 25 year veteran of the City Police, passed through Goulston Street on his hunt for the Mitre Square murderer. He'd just stopped two men walking together in Wentworth Street and let them go after they were able to satisfy him as to why they were in the streets at that hour. The identity of these men is not known. After leaving the men, Halse went through Goulston Street on his way to Mitre Square. The time was about 2:20am and he did not see the apron or chalk writing. If the writing and apron were in place at this time, it's unfortunate that Halse did not take notice.

The timing is important because we know that by 1:45am Catherine Eddowes was dead and her killer was fleeing. The trek from Mitre Square to Goulston Street is only four minutes, so if he fled directly from the square to the model dwellings we would expect the apron to have been discarded around 1:50am. However, PC Long claims not to have seen the apron in place when he'd previously investigated the spot at 2:20am. This means either he was mistaken, lying, or the killer went elsewhere with his loot before reemerging to place the apron and (possibly) write the chalked message. Author Stewart P. Evans, himself a retired constable, observed that if a constable were to be found negligent in his duty he could lose his post and so would be encouraged to lie. Evans suggested such might have been the case with Long. This suggestion is certainly sensible, but it's impossible to confirm or refute.

No matter how inconvenient Long's evidence might be, it would be unfair to write him off as a liar without good reason. DC Halse, who was not a colleague of Long's and was on the opposite side of the argument from Long's superiors over the erasing of the writing, could have put the lie to Long had he mentioned spotting the apron as he passed through Goulston Street at about the same time as Long had. But he didn't see the apron either. Halse was not leisurely patrolling the street as was Long, but he was on the hunt for a murderer and his senses would have been heightened. That neither man saw the apron cannot be seen as proof that it wasn't already there, but it does tip the scales of logic in that direction.

Modern mainstream Ripperology has moved away from its acceptance of the Goulston Street writing as a legitimate clue left behind by the Ripper. A healthy seed of skepticism has been there since 1888, but the movement away from considering the writing relevant didn't take root until around the Ripper centenary. Writing in 1987, author Martin Fido described the apron piece as an 'insignificant discarded rag' and suggested Long and Halse had simply overlooked it (The Crimes, Detection and Death of Jack the Ripper). More recently, author Neil Bell similarly characterized it as a 'dirty rag' (Capturing Jack the Ripper (2014). Although in the technical sense any piece of cloth might be called a 'rag', the word seems designed to suggest small dimensions, or in the words of Fido, something 'insignificant'. But the cloth in question would have been more than that.

A woman's apron such as the one in question was worn outside the clothes and would have extended from just under the neck to nearly the ankles, or else would have tied only at the waist and extended down to beneath the fall of the dress. The former would have tied off with a string at the back of the neck and another string around the waist, the latter just one string at the waist. Writing 22 years after the murder, Major Henry Smith, who was Acting Commissioner of the City Police on the night of the double event, recalled that 'about one-half of the apron was missing. It had been severed by a clean cut.'[167] Author Paul Begg estimates from this that the apron piece found in Goulston Street was 'a sizeable piece of material, possibly 3-4 feet square.'[168] In fact, it may have been larger. Dr. Frederick Gordon Brown, who performed the autopsy on Eddowes, appeared as a witness at the inquest and gave extensive details about her post mortem, which were recorded by Coroner Samuel Langham and survive to the present. Dr. Brown did not provide any details about the dimensions of the apron piece found in Goulston Street, but regarding the portion remaining with the body, he said 'it was the corner of the apron, with a string attached.' Interestingly, the small portion remaining with the body was also spotted with blood of recent origin.[169]

What would have been waiting for PC Long in the entryway of 108-119 Goulston Street was not an 'insignificant rag' but a large and rather obvious expanse of material. This makes it rather less likely that DC Halse would have missed or failed to investigate something so obvious while in pursuit of a murderer. He wouldn't have yet known that a portion of apron was missing, but he knew that two women had been murdered and a third body might pop up anywhere and at any time. It likewise stretches credulity that Long would have overlooked such an item in the course of his patrols, which would have included stepping over the cloth to cast his lantern into the dark entry. Either he saw the apron piece at 2:20am and failed to investigate it, in which case he lied under oath, or it was as Long said and the apron piece was not in place at that time, which would mean that the Ripper had absconded to a bolt hole with the apron as well as Eddowes's uterus and one of her kidneys, and emerged later to deposit the apron.

Constables being lax on duty was not a rare or strange thing and was well-illustrated in the wake of the Buck's Row murder of Polly Nichols. However, unlike PC Mizen and the men of J Division, Long was already aware that there had been a murder in Berner Street that evening and had been drafted into H Division for the sole purpose of catching Jack the Ripper. If there was one night where we'd expect him to be alert and less likely to be delinquent, it would have been this night.

It's not possible to say with any certainty when the apron piece was dropped in Goulston Street. We must each decide for ourselves whether PC Long was telling the truth or if he was lying to protect himself. If he was lying, it was to his great fortune that DC Halse failed to notice the mass in front of the entryway as he passed. Some additional insight might be gained when we consider the curious circumstance of the chalk writing.

Later we'll discuss some ideas about what the writing might actually have said, but for now we'll go with the most accepted version, which is 'The Juwes are the men that will not be blamed for nothing'. There is ongoing debate as to where this writing was located, although a few of those who saw it were rather clear in their placement. PC Long, in his November 6th report to Home Office, writes 'I found a portion of an apron covered in blood lying in the passage of the door-way leading to Nos. 108 to 119 Model Dwellings in Goulston Street. Above it on the wall was written in chalk "The Juews are the men that will not be blamed for nothing."' Long's use of the word 'wall' has led some to believe it was written on the wall proper beyond the entryway, but his placement of the apron inside the 'doorway' and the writing just above it is relatively clear. More succinct is Sir Charles Warren, writing a similar report on the same day: 'The writing was on the jamb of the open archway or doorway visible to anybody in the street.' If the writing had been on the wall inside the doorway it would not have been visible from the street, so it must have been written inside the entryway on the narrow jamb where a door might have closed had there been one. DC Halse added that the writing was on the black dado, which was a portion of the wall colored black that reached up only four feet from the ground, the bricks above this height being painted white. It would have been necessary for whoever held the white chalk to kneel and write on the black bricks where it would contrast and be seen. So, when Long says the writing was above the apron, he means that it was only inches to at most a few feet above it.

The authors of *The Complete Jack the Ripper A-Z* tell us that the jamb was only a brick and a half deep, which would have made it necessary for the graffitist to write small and stack his words. Indeed, DC Halse estimated the capital letters to have been only ¾ of an inch in height and the other letters proportionately smaller. Halse recalled the sentence occupied three lines whereas Warren gave it five lines.

The Warren Omission

The hours of furrowed brows and reams of heated words spent debating and speculating over the particulars of the Goulston Street writing would not have been necessary had a photograph been taken. It's not outside the realm of possibility that such a clue would eventually have aided in the identification of the Ripper himself. The decision to erase is attributed to Met Police commissioner, Sir Charles Warren, but his motives for doing so have continually been brought into question. Authors from Stephen Knight to Bruce Robinson have postulated that Warren's allegiance to his Freemasonic brotherhood usurped his commitment to the men he commanded and compelled him to enter into a dark conspiracy with the Ripper when faced with an arcane masonic message scrawled, undoubtedly by the killer, as a message to his masonic 'brothers' that he was one of their secret fraternity. The suggestion, disavowed by Masonic commentators, is that the second word, 'Juwes', is a cryptic reference to three men sacred to Masonic lore.

Critics of the theory point out that nothing in the graffiti alludes to the Masons and so it could not have been misconstrued by Warren – himself a

Masonic historian – as a plea for help by a brother in need. It's also effectively argued that a Mason who began a campaign of wholesale murder would no longer be accepted as a brother and could not expect help, let alone complicity, from the brotherhood he'd disgraced. Perhaps the most convincing evidence that Warren did not associate the Ripper with the Freemasons is that it's from his own internal correspondence that we're provided with what has been accepted by students as the most definitive rendering of the writing, complete with the controversial spelling of the second word as 'Juwes'.

It was not immediately obvious what the second word was and it was remembered differently by each person who saw it. Had Warren been anxious to hush up a secret clue to the Ripper's identity then we might expect he would have endorsed one of the versions other than the one featuring the 'Juwes' spelling. This very simple move would assure that the 'clue' wasn't revealed to the world at large. Instead, he did just the opposite, and it's from his own desk that we receive the 'official' and most widely accepted version of the writing. Warren unwittingly preserved the very evidence that would be used by the conspiracy theorists of later generations to point the finger of complicity at him. Warren, by anyone's measure, was not addlebrained nor simpleminded, so the very actions that a few see as suspicious surely appeal to the more rational mind as proof that Warren's motive for erasing the writing was not to protect a mysterious 'brother'.

So what did motivate him? The simple truth is that he made a decision based upon the advice and information provided him by one man – Superintendent Thomas Arnold, the head of H Division. Arnold had been on leave for the previous murders and arrived back to work just in time for the double event. When he caught word of the finding of the apron piece and writing in Goulston Street, he immediately dispatched a constable with sponge and bucket to the scene to await word of its erasure. He then sent a telegram to Warren. We do not know the contents of that telegram, but we can assume the immediacy with which it was worded by the fact that Warren went first Goulston Street before visiting either of the actual murder sites.

Warren conferred with Arnold upon his arrival and also discussed the matter with the present members of the City Police force. It appears that everyone with the exception of Arnold felt it prudent to preserve the writing until it could be photographed. The sun would rise within the hour and the street would begin filling with workers who, Arnold feared, might interpret the writing to mean that the Ripper was a Jew, and would then forego their day's pay in order to start a pogrom against the largely Jewish population of Goulston Street and surrounding environs. With Arnold adamant that it should be erased immediately, others present who knew the evidence should be preserved found it necessary to offer concessions, such as a temporary covering being placed over the writing until the photographer arrived, or that the potentially offensive word 'Juwes' be erased and the remainder photographed. None of this was acceptable to Arnold and Warren, and since they were standing on Met territory, their word was law. To the chagrin of the City Police (and many Met officials), one of the most controversial and potentially critical clues in the series of murders was obliterated.

The average person would find it nearly impossible to defend the actions of a police official choosing to destroy potential evidence in a serial murder case, yet a number of modern writers feel up to the task. These commentators point out the loud and public protests against the Jews that followed the murder of Annie Chapman and the overhyped press exposure of the Jewish 'Leather Apron' suspect, and feel that Warren was prudent in his choice. However, there had not been a pogrom against the Jews following the murder of Chapman and that there would be one at all was purely theoretical, whereas the message itself was quite real and a photograph of it might have yielded real results.

That Warren wanted to keep word of the message from getting out is evident by his actions which suggest that he (and by extension, the Met force) was not eager to inform the public that it had ever existed at all. Reports of the finding of the apron piece in Goulston Street appeared immediately in the press sans any mention of the writing. First mention of the chalk clue came on Oct. 2nd in the *Echo* where it was summarily dismissed as an unsubstantiated rumor.

Among the many discredited rumours current in the neighbourhood is the assertion that Sir Charles Warren on visiting the yard on Sunday morning last discovered some writing on the wall in chalk, which gave expression to very objectionable sentiments of a religious character, and which was supposed to have been the handiwork of the murderer. This was alleged to have given such great offence that Sir Charles, fearing a disturbance in the neighbourhood, directed the writing to be washed out. Investigation, however, has proved, so far as can be judged, the absolute fallacy of the story. A careful examination of the brickwork in the yard this morning has revealed beyond dispute the fact that there has been no effacement of chalk marks on the walls, certainly within recent date.

The reporters received accurate but incomplete information which led them to assume the writing had been at the murder scene in Mitre Square. It's therefore no wonder that no traces of any writing remained for them to see.

Almost a full week would pass before the press would again catch wind of the persistent rumor that the police had clandestinely abolished a rare clue left behind by the Whitechapel murderer. By that time the infamous 'Dear Boss' letter and 'Saucy Jacky' postcard were all the talk and the moniker 'Jack the Ripper' was already a household name. The press, usually eager to take shots at the police, couldn't conceive of even the worst of cops – let alone the commissioner himself – cleaning up behind the Ripper, and made no attempt to get any mileage out of a report they felt sure was a crock.

The *Star* of Oct. 8th reported: 'The Central News Agency, which first gave publicity to the original 'Jack the Ripper' letter and postcard now resuscitates the rumour – which has already been dismissed as false – that on a wall, within a few yards of the spot where the blood-stained part of an apron was found, were written the words, 'The Jews shall not be blamed for nothing."

On the same day, the *Pall Mall Gazette* carried the story and published in full the original Central News Report:

The following extraordinary story has been sent to us by the

Central News. We publish it with all reserve, and without at present attaching to it any special importance.

The Central News Agency says: 'A startling fact has just come to light. After killing Katherine Eddowes in Mitre Square, the murderer, it is now known, walked to Goulston Street, where he threw away the piece of the deceased woman's apron upon which he had wiped his hands and knife. Within a few feet of this spot he had written upon the wall, 'The Jews shall not be blamed for nothing.'

Most unfortunately one of the police officers gave orders for the writing to be immediately sponged out, probably with a view of stifling the morbid curiosity which it would certainly have aroused. But in so doing a very important link was destroyed, for had the writing been photographed a certain clue would have been in the hands of the authorities. The witnesses who saw the writing, however, state that it was similar in character to the letters sent to the Central News and signed 'Jack the Ripper,' and though it would have been far better to have clearly demonstrated this by photography, there is now every reason to believe that the writer of the letter and postcard sent to the Central News (facsimiles of which are now to be seen outside every police-station) is the actual murderer. The police, consequently, are very anxious that any citizen who can identify the handwriting should without delay communicate with the authorities…

Whoever was leaking the story to the press clearly did not want their identity revealed, but as the day of the Eddowes inquest drew nearer, the story became impossible to keep under wraps. The *Pall Mall Gazette*, who days earlier attached no importance to the rumor, had become convinced. On Oct. 11th they informed their readers that 'A very strange, startling rumour as to the manner in which Sir Charles Warren performs the duty of Chief Detective of Scotland-yard is current this morning in the City. Those who repeat it assert that it will be verified at the inquest which is now proceeding and report of which will be continued in succeeding editions. The rumour in question is to the effect that rather than face the danger of allowing a crowd to assemble in a public thoroughfare Sir Charles

Warren deliberately destroyed a clue – the only clue which the City Police believed to afford any guidance as to the identity of the assassin.'

This article suggests that the confidential informant was someone inside the City Police; this makes sense as the Met men had closed ranks and the City heads were fuming over the casual destruction of a clue to a murder that occurred on their territory. If the Gazette's source was confident that Warren would be outed at the inquest held later that day, they were to be left disappointed when the day came and went without a single mention of who had ordered the erasure. Even the City men who gave evidence didn't take the opportunity to point the finger at Warren. This cannot have been a mere happenstance and indicates some sort of gentlemen's agreement between the forces. The Met had failed to keep word of the writing from coming out and now it was simply a matter of minimizing the damage.

Keeping Warren's name out of the inquest did not keep his name out of the press. Continuing their coverage the next day, the *Pall Mall Gazette* held nothing back:

> The case against the Chief Commissioner is overwhelming. Strange, almost incredible though it appears, this excellent Major-General, whose first thought is ever how to repress disorder, and to whom the detection of crime is but a secondary consideration, actually persisted in destroying this clue, in face of the protests of the city police and at the suggestion of one of his own men… He was destroying evidence that might have been of priceless value, and hid that avowedly from a political motive… and so perished the only clue which the murderer has left us by which he might be identified.

Taking Warren to task not only for destroying evidence but also for the obvious attempt to hide his actions from the public, the article points out that Warren's primary interest was preventing unrest and not solving crime. As was the custom of the time, Warren had not risen through the ranks but had been appointed to his post as police commissioner and had no experience with the discipline of policing or the craft of detection. For such insight he depended on his immediate subordinates – real policemen with an ear to the ground. Although the ultimate blame for erasing the writing in Goulston Street must rest with Warren, it might be fairer to say that he was the victim of bad counsel from Superintendent Thomas Arnold, the head of H Division.

The Home Office, in early November, launched an inquiry into the Goulston Street affair and reports were requested from the primary players within the Met Police, namely PC Long, Supt. Arnold, and Commissioner Warren. Arnold's report was brief, succinct, and minced no words about the fact that he was fully prepared to have the graffiti erased on his own authority had Warren not been available. He referenced as his motivation the ill feeling towards the Jewish population that arose after a Jewish cobbler, John Pizer, had fallen under suspicion weeks before. The Englishman's ire towards foreigners in such closed quarters as the East End was an ongoing concern, but no riot had as yet occurred and it's not clear why Arnold felt so sure a piece of ambiguous chalk writing would elicit a riot that the largest police force in the free world could not keep under control for the 45 minutes or so longer it would take for the sun to rise sufficiently to allow for a photograph to be taken.

Arnold evidently didn't feel that the disposal of the victim's bloody apron in front of a tenement building populated largely by Jews and very near the well-known Jewish Baths would, on its own, be enough to cause a pogrom. What is evident from Arnold's report is that the passing weeks and bad press did not shake his confidence in his decision. Perhaps this is because his decision had landed squarely on the shoulders of his superior.

Warren's response to Home Office was more than twice the length of Arnold's and put off a faint scent of desperation. The first portion of his letter echoed Arnold's sense of immediacy in the need to erase the writing or else be faced with an angry mob. He then quoted a letter he received from the acting Chief Rabbi who expressed gratitude for the humanity Warren had shown in acting in the defense of the Jewish citizenship. The next paragraph is worth reproducing in full: 'I do not hesitate myself to say that if that writing had been left there would have been an onslaught upon the Jews, property would have been wrecked, and lives would probably have been lost, and I was much gratified with the promptitude with which Superintendent Arnold was prepared to act in the matter if I had not been there.' These words are often quoted by modern authors as representing Warren's approval of Arnold's advice and his firm belief that he'd done the right thing. On the surface that is how it appears, but the actual message being conveyed to Home Office is that had Warren not been available that morning the graffiti would have been erased anyway. In essence, he's 'throwing' Arnold 'under the bus' and removing himself from the situation altogether, in the hope, perhaps, that mercy will be shown him. It was not. Two days later Warren was out of a job. The next day, Mary Kelly was murdered and Superintendent Arnold was given a raise.[170]

Then and Now: What the Experts Say

The police never came to a consensus about Goulston Street - what was written, when, or by whom. But they were there and formed opinions, some of which were committed to print and left for us to ponder. It's odd then that so many of the books on our shelves can't agree on how the police perceived the graffiti. Up until a few decades ago, it's arguable that the majority of Ripperologists – casual or more involved – would have said they believed the Goulston Street writing to have been the Ripper's handiwork. Many, no doubt, would have taken that for granted. After all, it was still accepted that the Ripper wrote letters to the police and press, a notion that to date has not been supported by the evidence.

In more recent years there has been a noticeable shift in view regarding Goulston Street, and while no official poll has been undertaken, it is this author's observation that the field is split and there might now be a majority view that nothing more than coincidence placed that ambiguous piece of scribble over the bloodied cloth discarded by the Ripper as he fled in haste.

Part of studying history is understanding how and when ideas take hold and why they persist, particularly if they're not fully supported by the evidence. There were rare flashes of literary brilliance in the first hundred years following the murders – Dan Farson and Donald Rumbelow, among others – but Ripperology as we know it today began in earnest only in the months preceding the centenary. Martin Fido's 1987 offering, *The Crimes, Detection & Death of Jack the Ripper*, wowed readers with sharp logic founded more on solid research than the loose and careless theorizing that had long defined the field. The only new book published during the year of the centenary proved every bit as definitive -in spite of its provocative title, Paul Begg's *Jack the Ripper: The Uncensored Facts* was the driest and most sober narrative of the murders to that point.

Begg offered his readers a very direct 'just the facts' review of the murders, evidence, and investigation. As run-of-the-mill as that might sound now, it was a novel approach in 1988 and the author's high standing in the field today is testament to how fact-starved Ripper readers were in an era when the field was so dominated by supposition and folklore. Begg clearly made a conscious effort not to impose himself on his reader, so anyone hoping for a hard answer on the graffiti was to be disappointed to find the author concluding that 'the writing on the wall is not of any great significance because it was never certainly established that it was written by the murderer.'

Authors, even Ripper authors, cannot be without their biases, and one bias Begg felt rather confident about was that the most logical pursuit of investigation was to begin with the men who had actually been there and investigated the case. Of these men, he felt that Assistant Commissioner Dr. (later Sir) Robert Anderson was the most reliable, and perhaps crucially, was the only one who stated with any measure of certainty that the killer's identity had been known to him.

Martin Fido would subsequently team up with Begg and co-author (along with researcher Keith Skinner) the highly successful encyclopedia of the field, *The Jack the Ripper A-Z*. But in 1987 he was a lone gun with a contract to turn in a book solving the greatest unsolved murder series of all time. Remarkably, or perhaps not so, he'd had the same revelation regarding Anderson as had Begg - which was that the best Ripper suspect was Anderson's unnamed 'Polish Jew'. Although they would form their own individual ideas about who this suspect might have been, their belief that Anderson was on the right trail means they believed it likely (in Begg's case) if not probable (as in Fido's case) that the Ripper was an immigrant Polish Jew for whom English would be a second language. While Begg remained noncommittal in offering an opinion about the Goulston Street writing, Fido was not at all ambiguous: 'Bear in mind that there is no evidence that the writing and the apron appeared at the same time and it seems that the chalked clue lost for ever as day broke over the night of the double murder was no clue at all.'

The approaching centenary of the Ripper murders saw unparalleled promotion of the case as a classic whodunit for which a solution might be imminent. This attracted new readers and writers of all stripes. There were no shortage of sensational theories to engage the mind, but the more rational and logical of the set were no doubt attracted to the works that offered a seemingly more historical context, such as Fido and Begg, who represented the cutting edge of Ripper research at the time. This marked a significant movement within the field that I've often, and perhaps incorrectly, characterized as the 'minimalist' movement. In essence, the idea was formed to strip the Ripper case of all its lore; done away with was the myth of the foggy murder nights, the top hat and cloak, and the almost supernatural ability of the Ripper-as-super villain to appear and kill with impunity. Quite rightly, it was pointed out that the famous Ripper letters contained no information to show that any one of them had actually been penned by the Ripper. This is significant, because when it was largely accepted that the Ripper had written letters, it made sense that he might chalk up a message as well. Conversely, when doubt set in that the Ripper was a communicator, the doubt naturally spread to all purported writings, including Goulston Street.

Further supporting the case against the Ripper-as-writer was the burgeoning field of serial killer profiling. The biggest proponent and voice of profiling at the time, and perhaps to this day, was John Douglas, who was instrumental in getting the FBI to open its Behavioral Sciences unit in Quantico Virginia. He gained support for helping prosecutors secure the conviction of Wayne Williams for what has become known as the Atlanta Child Murders. It's now widely believed that Williams was not responsible for most, if any, of the murders for which his name has become synonymous.

Douglas also 'helped' with Washington State's investigation into a long string of prostitute murders dubbed the Green River killings, because some of the early victims were disposed in or near the Green River. Douglas and his team worked up a profile to help the beleaguered investigators tighten their burgeoning list of suspects. They believed the killer would be a white male, not married, unkempt, who could not maintain steady employment, and would be a smoker and heavy beer drinker. This profile helped investigators eliminate Gary Ridgway as a suspect. One intrepid policeman was not so sure and obtained DNA samples from Ridgway as he went off to enjoy two more decades of freedom before those DNA samples would finally be tested and lead to his prosecution for the murders.

Ridgway, who was below average intelligence, neat in his habits, kept the same job for over 20 years, did not smoke, do drugs, and rarely drank, was allowed to remain free at least in part because of an FBI serial killer profile. Because of popular TV shows and novels, it's widely accepted that profiling of this sort is effective. While there are many examples of other disciplines of profiling (geographic, linguistic, et al) helping investigators close cases, there is as of yet zero examples of behavioral profiling playing any part in the successful capture and conviction of a serial killer.

I discuss this not to disparage the field. In time and with more accurate information it's possible it will become a viable tool. However, beginning in the 1990s, many Ripper books have relied on the generic and largely obvious tenets of behavioral profiling to build a case for their respective suspects. This is to be expected in the game of one-upmanship that is suspect Ripperology, but the views of Douglas and his fellow profilers seeped into our wider understanding of the case in large, particularly as to whether or not the Ripper would have communicated with authorities.

In 1984 the *Seattle Post-Intelligencer* received a letter signed 'callmefred' that contained details about the Green River killings that had not been released to the public. Local investigators, believing that it had been written by the killer, sent it off to Douglas for analysis. He immediately replied that the man he was hunting would not communicate with authorities and that they should ignore the letter as relevant. Ridgway, upon his capture, admitted having written the letter. Douglas repeatedly espoused in interviews or in his own published literature his belief that prostitute killers, including Jack the Ripper, would not be moved to communicate with the press or police. This is likely true in most cases, but for many Ripperologists in the 1990s, when serial killer profiling was still considered a science and not an art, such professional opinions somehow solidified

into fact and dramatically impacted our understanding of even historical cases, such as the Whitechapel murders. Applying fresh wisdom to our understanding of history can be helpful, but when it proves wrong we should move quickly to correct the record and not saddle the next generation of researchers with our mistakes.

In the early 1990s, two highly influential Ripper books hit the shelves. Both were bestsellers. *The Lodger*, authored by Stewart P. Evans and Paul Gainey, detailed the discovery of the suspect, Francis Tumblety, and raised the bar for all suspect books to follow. It also helped secure the reputation of its key author, Evans, as an authority on par with Begg and Fido. The other notable offering from this era was *The Diary of Jack the Ripper*, by Shirley Harrison. The subject of the work was a brief confessional of sorts purportedly written by Liverpool cotton merchant and minor true crime personage, James Maybrick.

For books drawing from the same historical well, these two could hardly have been more different. The *Lodger*, though clearly written with the agenda of promoting Tumblety as the Ripper, benefited from newly unearthed source material and the insight of a true Ripper historian. The *Diary*, for all intents and purposes, seemed to most a sensationalized hoax. One of the many ways these works differed was in their handling of the Goulston Street writing. The *Diary* refers to the writing cryptically as the Ripper's 'funny Jewish joke', thus cementing it (for those who believe the Diary legit) as a bona fide Ripper communique. Stewart P. Evans was not swayed, writing: 'It is difficult to imagine that the killer stopped, in pitch darkness, to write a cryptic message on a wall. More likely he simply threw the bloodstained rag into the doorway as he passed.'

In 1995, historian Philip Sugden published the results of his lengthy and seemingly objective study into the Whitechapel murders. *The Complete History of Jack the Ripper* was well-received by Ripperphiles and continues to be one of the most highly recommended tomes by respected researchers. This is spite of the fact that it's not particularly friendly to the Anderson 'Polish Jew' theory, accepts the contemporary view that Liz Stride was a Ripper victim, and has this to say about Goulston Street: 'The trouble with the chalk message is that, like many clues relating to these murders, we can document its existence but do not know enough to interpret its meaning...

Although it seems likely that the graffito was written by the murderer it yields little clue to his identity.' In short, Sugden was no minimalist.

Regardless of Sugden's influence on the field, by 1995 the movement away from accepting Goulston Street as a viable clue had progressed too far to be thwarted by a single work. Here I've the explored the reasons why this ideology took hold and is moving towards a majority. We should expect that any major shift in thought is the result not of a single new revelation or idea, but of multiple alterations in perspective occurring over a relatively short period of time. An objective appraisal of the 'Ripper letters' has revealed that no one letter begs to be accepted as having been written by the murderer of any of the Whitechapel victims. That's not the same as saying they've all been proven a hoax, because they haven't been, but without a specific reason to accept any as legitimate, they cannot be viewed as clues in and of themselves towards identifying the Whitechapel murderer. However, in a possible case of throwing the baby out with the bathwater, it seems the Goulston Street writing has been lumped in with the many hoax letters and summarily set aside.

The 1987 discovery of Anderson's suspect as a man named 'Kozminski' and the promotion of him as a major Ripper suspect also forced reconsideration of the writing, as a person who was assumed to be illiterate in English could not have composed such a message. Coming at the same time was the assessment of a few FBI agents that Jack the Ripper and other prostitute killers would not communicate with authorities. With the most respected voices of the field – Fido, Begg, and Evans – standing in solidarity with the FBI, itself one of the most informed investigative forces in the world, it's at least understandable why so many logical and rational minds turned against the Goulston Street writing, or 'graffito' as it has been dismissively dubbed since Fido coined the term in 1987.

But there's another reason logical minds might refuse to seriously consider that the Ripper himself chalked those words, and that has to do with trends, patterns, and even snobbery. Whereas so many of the more scholarly works of the past generation have dismissed or outright refuted the writing, many others have opened their arms welcomingly to it and, in some cases, built an entire thesis on the grounds that the Ripper – and no one else – could have composed the graffito. The problem here is that nearly all of these books represent the most fanciful and perhaps worst that Ripper scholarship has to offer. Anyone immersed in the case literature will pick up on this and if their tastes tend to the more 'responsible' of the works, then it stands to reason that their forming perspectives and biases will be influenced by the people and sources they respect.

In short, someone might be influenced by factors, other than their own objective case study, to endorse certain conclusions. Factors such as the all-too human need to 'fit in'. That's not to say there's a conspiracy within Ripperology to spread disinformation. There absolutely is not. The handful of people whose work forms the foundation for modern Ripperology have rightfully earned their place at the 'cool kids' table and anything they posit should be seriously considered and not dismissed out of hand.

But what if the opinions of these experts should happen to conflict with another group of experts – the men with badges who were there?

A reader of the works above might be forgiven if he were to conclude that the contemporary police did not take the graffito seriously and, like Stewart P. Evans, thought it little more than a meaningless piece of graffiti under which the apron piece happened to be discarded. But Warren's suspicious resignation coming only a few days after a Home Office inquiry into the erasure of the graffiti should, at the very least, give us pause. Not many of the men involved first hand with the Ripper investigation committed their opinion on Goulston Street to print, but some did, and others said enough to allow us to read between the lines.

Superintendent Arnold did not write a memoir giving his insights, so we do not have a definitive statement on how he regarded the Goulston Street writing. But in later years he omitted the name of Catherine Eddowes from his list of Ripper victims, so by discounting her murder as a Ripper crime, he's effectively dismissing the writing as a Ripper clue.

It would be fair to say that the City Police counterparts to Warren and Arnold on the night of the double event were Acting Commissioner Henry Smith and Inspector James McWilliam. McWilliam was one of the men fighting for the preservation of the writing until a photograph could be taken, so he must have seen probative value in the writing. Twenty years following the murders, Smith published his memoir and had this to say:

Sir Charles Warren was instantly apprised of this discovery, and, coming down himself, ordered the words to be wiped out, alleging as his reason for so doing that he feared a rising against the Jews. This was, I thought, a fatal mistake, as Superintendent McWilliam plainly told Sir Charles when he called about seven o'clock, accompanied by Superintendent Arnold. It is just possible the words, if photographed, might have afforded an important clue. The assassin had evidently wiped his hands with the piece of apron.

Martin Fido was no fan of Smith. For an author wishing to remove the writing of any relevance, a high ranking copper with opposing views had to be dealt with, and one way to do this is by casting doubt on his veracity. Fido quoted from Smith's book and painted a picture of a man who made up stories completely out of whole cloth. Smith claimed, according to Fido, to have chased the Ripper from Mitre Square to a wash fountain where he found blood still gurgling down the drain. Fido correctly pointed out that this would have been impossible given the length of time that passed from when the murder occurred and when Smith arrived on the scene. However, if one were to read down a couple of paragraphs in Smith's memoir it became obvious that the bloody fountain he was referring to was the one outside the bedroom of murder victim Mary Kelly and had nothing to do with the Mitre Square murder. Fido had erred unintentionally in his reading of Smith, but this error has been oft repeated and used to besmirch Smith's veracity wherever he might have voiced an opinion that ran contrary to the popular narrative.

Although an unabashed braggadocio who often claimed personal responsibility for the achievements of his subordinates, Smith is generally reliable in his memory of the facts and possessed the humility necessary to admit that he had no idea who the Ripper had been.

More confounding than Fido's handling of Smith is the stock which he puts in the views of Walter Dew:

He [Warren] has been severely criticized for this prompt action. So it is worth noting the considered judgment of Walter Dew who, at the time, was a Whitechapel Detective Constable, thoroughly familiar with goings-on at street level and the likelihood of any such writing emanating from the Ripper. The message's destruction 'was certainly unfortunate,' he conceded. 'But I doubt if it made a lot of difference anyway. There was no reason, so far as I can see, why this particular message should have proved more useful than many others which Jack the Ripper was supposed to have written.

Dew, as Fido points out, was a constable at the time of the Ripper murders and so was not in a position to receive much information outside that of his own experiences. Unlike Smith, Dew was nowhere near Goulston Street or Mitre Square on the night of the murders. Writing 30 years after Smith, and 50 years following the Whitechapel murders, Dew's memoir is so flawed in its handling of the facts that its value is more academic than practical for the modern researcher. Dew is not dishonest in recording his personal impressions of cases on which he worked, but he cannot be trusted in the details. On matters outside of his personal experience his writings are all but worthless. For instance, Dew believed that the person most likely to have seen the Ripper in person was Fanny Mortimer in Berner Street. Mortimer, as detailed in earlier chapters, was considered a potentially serious witness for only a matter of hours before it was determined that the dark figure she'd watched moving hastily along the street was in fact Leon Goldstein, who presented himself to police and relieved himself of all suspicion.

It's interesting to note that what Dew is saying is not altogether different from what Smith was lamenting. They both agree it was unfortunate that the writing had been erased. They agreed it was not certain that it had been written by the Ripper. The main difference appears to be that Smith felt the clue should have been preserved and utilized, whereas Dew felt there was no clue to follow. Later in his memoir Dew made it clear that his argument was entirely one of logic: 'As I have said before, it is questionable whether these messages were the work of the murderer at all. Why should he fool around chalking things on walls when his life was imperiled by every minute he loitered?' Had Dew been more aware of the details of the murders he might have wondered why the Ripper would have loitered as he did over dead bodies in order to mutilate them; in particular, the mutilation of Catherine Eddowes's face and apron seem more risk than reward, unless there was a purpose to them.

Fido's enthusiasm for dismissing the writing, as suggested earlier, might have had something to do with the suspect he was chasing – Anderson's 'Polish Jew'. Fido may have been unaware of Anderson's own view on the Goulston Street writing and might have made significant alterations to his chapter had he known. In 1910 former Assistant Commissioner Dr. (now Sir) Robert Anderson published his memoirs as a series of articles in *Blackwood's Edinburgh Magazine*. Anderson discussed the Ripper murders but failed to address the actions of his superior in Goulston Street, an omission not lost on Sir Henry Smith, who was preparing his own memoir at the time. Smith fired a bullet: 'How Sir Charles Warren wiped out – I believe with his own hand, but will not speak positively – the writing on the wall, how he came to my office accompanied by Superintendent Arnold about seven o'clock the same morning to get information as to the murder of Catherine Eddowes, I have already stated on p. 153. The facts are indisputable, yet Sir Robert Anderson studiously avoids all allusion to them. Is it because "it would ill become him to violate the unwritten rule of the service," or is he unwilling to put on record the unpardonable blunder of his superior officer? I leave my readers to decide...'

In fact, Anderson was on record with his views a few two years earlier when he was interviewed for a newspaper. He was discussing the Ripper crimes and moments when clues were 'destroyed, wiped out absolutely – clues that might very easily have secured for us proof of the identity of the assassin.' He discussed a clay pipe that was broken and then 'in another case there was writing on the wall – a most valuable clue; handwriting that might have been at once recognised as belonging to a certain individual...'[171]

Following the publication of his memoirs, Smith or someone else wrote to a local paper to vent their frustrations over Anderson's omission. Anderson wrote a letter in response and the text of this letter was preserved by journalist J. Hall Richardson in his memoir, *From City to Fleet Street*, in 1927. It must be noted that the newspaper he's quoting here has not yet been identified, so caution must be recommended until it is, however the 'voice' of the letter and the details force the conclusion that it is indeed the writing of Anderson:

In your notice of my article in this month's Blackwood, you refer back to what I wrote last month about the Whitechapel murders, and you add: In that connection he might have recalled – but did not – the crass stupidity of Scotland Yard men, who wiped out from the wall of the labourer's buildings in Goulstone (sic) Street, the only tangible piece of evidence obtained pointing to the identity of Jack the Ripper.

I beg to assure you that here you do an injustice, not only to me, but to the Criminal Investigation Department. The night on which the murder in question was committed I was on my way home from Paris, and great was my indignation when, next day, I heard of what you rightly call an act of 'crass stupidity'. But the Scotland Yard men were in no way responsible for it – it was done by the officers of the uniform force in the division, upon an order issued by one of my colleagues. The exact words of 'the mural inscription' which the murderer chalked upon the wall were, 'The Jewes are not the men to be blamed for nothing."

May I add that all this was in the MS. of my article, but a wish to avoid what seemed to reflect upon others, led me to strike out the paragraph.

Anderson is clearly indicting the Ripper not only for murder but for graffiti. It is worth noting that although Anderson expressed certainty, there was, in fact, no way for him to have been as certain as he was. So, in other instances where he expresses similar confidence, such as in his finger-pointing of an 'enterprising London journalist' for having penned the infamous 'Dear Boss' letter, or even his identification of a certain unnamed 'Polish Jew' as the murderer himself, we might do well to remember that Anderson's burden of proof might not be nearly as heavy as some of his colleagues; or, for that matter, as our own.

What we can gather from Anderson's point of view is that whoever his Polish Jew suspect was, he was a man capable of having chalked the message. This could prove significant as a number of candidates have been put forth over the years and if any of them were illiterate or incapable of speaking or writing in English, they could not have been Anderson's suspect.

Chief Inspector Donald S. Swanson, Anderson's right hand man, was one of several individuals to submit a report to Home Office about the writing on Nov 6th. This in spite of the fact that he had not visited Goulston Street and had no personal experience of the writing. In the course of his report he gives as Warren's reason for erasing the writing that it purported to 'throw blame upon the Jews'. He does not say for what the writer was blaming the Jews, but as the subject was the Whitechapel murders it should be expected that this was the thinking. This means the writing was not assumed to be some irrelevant piece of graffiti as some modern commentators have suggested. Swanson also made the curious observation that the writing was 'blurred'. It's been suggested this was evidence that the writing was not fresh. However, no one who actually saw the writing mentioned any blurring and Swanson does not qualify the comment. In fact, DC Halse, who spent the most time of anyone in the presence of the writing, remarked that it appeared fresh and would not have survived long in the Jewish neighborhood. Swanson would have seen Superintendent Arnold's report of the same date in which Arnold stated that the writing was in such a position that it would be 'rubbed by the shoulders' of persons coming and going. Arnold was using slang to illustrate that the writing was visible to passersby, but as it was written below waist level it could not have been rubbed by passing shoulders. It is possible Swanson misinterpreted Arnold to mean that it had been blurred by those passing. Also possible is that he was attempting to offer some form of soft protection for his superior (Warren) whom he knew was in hot water.

On October 13th, before he would have known he was in his final few weeks as Police Commissioner, Warren was perhaps more candid than he should have been in an exchange with Permanent Under-Secretary of State at Home Office, Godfrey Lushington. In this rare (and rarely commented upon) insight into Warren's personal Ripper theory, we also learn what the head of the Metropolitan police thought was the Ripper's agenda on the night of the double event:

As Mr. Matthews is aware I have for some time past inclined to the idea that the murders may possibly be done by a secret society, as the only logical solution of the question, but I would not understand this being done by a Socialist because the last murders were obviously done by some one desiring to bring discredit on the Jews and Socialists or Jewish Socialists.

Lushington responded the same day:

I cannot at all agree with the Commr.'s idea that the only logical solution of the question is that the murders may possibly have been done by a Secret Society. He also says he cannot understand this having been done by a Socialist, because the last murders were evidently done by some one desiring to bring discredit on the Jews and Socialists or Jewish Socialists. – It seems to me on the contrary that the last murder was done by a Jew who boasted of it.

First we must deal with Warren's staggeringly random observation that a secret society was behind the murders. In the 21st century we think of a 'secret society' as some sort of global network of rich men banded together for some nefarious world dominating purpose. However, in the 19th century a secret society might have been a group of 8 local barbers who decided to team together under an oath and raise money for the poor. In other words, Warren is probably not thinking of a particularly large group of people and it needn't be a wealthy or influential organization, such as the Freemasons (of which he was a respected member). It is not surprising that Warren would consider the possibility of more than one killer working together as a team; what is surprising is that he would confidently attest that it's the 'only logical solution of the question'. We can only guess at when he came to this revelation and how.

Returning to the subject of Goulston Street, Warren tells us it's 'obvious' that the Ripper wished to bring discredit on the Jews and Socialists or Jewish Socialists. Socialists enter the discussion due to Liz Stride's body being discovered in the passageway next to the Berner Street Socialists club, so the separate mention of 'Jews' could only refer to Goulston Street. This is certainly how Lushington (who had long suspected the Ripper was a Jew) understood as he disagreed and offered that the 'last murder' (Eddowes) was done by a Jew who 'boasted of it'.

None of these men could speak from personal knowledge and say who wrote the strange message. Nevertheless, there appears to have been a near consensus that it was the work of the man who would shortly be christened Jack the Ripper. Even the architect of its destruction and chief naysayer, Supt. Arnold, acknowledged in his report to Home Office that it was a 'clue'. As generations pass and more voices sound off, some louder than others, that consensus gets lost. Whether this represents progress or chaos is, like so much, open for debate.

Jack the Copycat

That Jack the Ripper inspired other killers, both in his own day and into the current era, is a matter of common knowledge and common sense. That some of the Ripper murders were themselves the work of a copycat killer is the source of much speculation and debate. However, what we'll talk about here is the possibility that the Ripper copycatted the myths and misconceptions generated in the press by his own crimes.

In late 2007, researcher and writer, Dan Norder, reached out to me with an angle he'd been looking into for a new article. He had observed that early reports of the Annie Chapman murder mistakenly described her heart as having been removed. He looked around and found other similar mentions and wondered if this was how the Ripper himself had gotten the idea to remove the heart of victim Mary Kelly. I suggested some additional material and the article he composed, entitled 'Heartless: The Evidence for a Copycat Killer', was published in the 28th edition of his journal, *Ripper Notes*, in early 2008. It quickly became one of my favorite pieces of speculative reasoning in the Whitechapel murders.

What resonates the most with me are the curious connections between early press reports following the murder of Annie Chapman and the events of the 'double' event, which occurred just after the inquests into the murders of Chapman and Polly Nichols had been completed. There should be no doubt that the most avid reader of the papers at this time was Jack the Ripper himself. The greatest minds in the country were offering speculation as to his identity, the police were forced to admit defeat, and their most experienced doctor, George Bagster Phillips, testified in awe at the Ripper's swiftness and ability. At no point during the series of murders would the Ripper have felt more empowered and invulnerable than just after these inquests had closed and he realized he'd again beaten one of the most powerful police forces in the world. What he also would have been exposed to were a myriad of actions ascribed to him that he knew to be untrue.

As news of Chapman's murder coursed like lightning through the East End, there followed it a thunderous echo of yet a second murder – another woman found with only her throat cut. The *Evening News* reported: 'Shortly after ten o'clock, this morning, a rumour was current in the East-end, that the body of a young woman with her throat cut, had been found in the graveyard attached to St. Philip's Church, at the back of the London Hospital.' This macabre tale was proved untrue, yet the idea of a 'double event' was now out there in the wind. But this was not the only rumor making the rounds. Word of a message written on a wall circulated with such force that it was covered in numerous newspapers – *'The murderer left a message on the wall in the yard, which was made out to read, Five; fifteen more, and then I give myself up.'* Some presented it as ascertained fact, while others, such as the *Times*, cautioned their readers that the story was uncorroborated. The *Pall Mall Gazette* correctly noted that it simply wasn't true.

But the rumors had caught the imagination of the public. Indeed, less than 48 hours before the double event, the word 'Look' was found chalked on a lamp post. A long line ran from it to a place on the pavement where two stick figures were drawn – one of a woman and the other of a man holding a knife. Written above and beneath the figures were the words 'I am Leather Apron' and 'Five more and I will give myself up.'[172]

Without knowing who the Ripper was it's impossible to quantify what effect all the rumors and misreporting would have had on him. However, it's safe to say that he kept himself in the thick of it and was aware of these stories, as they had made significant press, to say nothing of word of mouth on the street. It's not unreasonable to conclude that what happened on the night of the 'double event' – two women murdered and a mysterious message chalked on a wall – was precisely what he had planned to do when he stepped from his doorway that evening.

Dan Norder, in his research for 'Heartless', developed the even more remarkable suggestion that the Ripper may have copycatted a murder committed by a copycat of his own. On Sept. 23rd, 1888, in the small village of Birtley, 300 miles from the gothic ghettos of the East End, the body of Jane Beadmore is discovered. She had been brutally murdered with a knife, her killer slashing at her throat and abdomen, leaving her intestines protruding, as had been the case with Polly Nichols. There was suspicion that London's boogeyman had taken the train to Birtley. Inspector Roots of the CID and Dr. George Bagster Phillips traveled to Birtley to decide for themselves. However, the police quickly developed a suspect in the person of William Waddell, a 22 year-old man who'd been in a relationship with Beadmore and had fled town following the murder.

Waddell, as might be imagined, was not as sophisticated a killer as Jack the Ripper, who knew how to render a victim unconscious and kill them cleanly. Waddell was a mad slasher. In his attempt to mimic the Ripper, Norder points out, he inflicted injuries to the victim's face, something the Ripper was not known to do. Illustrations appearing in the press in late September show the corpse of Beadmore lying on the ground with facial cuts on her cheeks that look like chevrons with a line running through them. Waddell would not be captured until Oct. 1st, so on the night of the double event, the Ripper would have been aware of Beadmore's murder, the suspicion that it was one of his own crimes, and that no one was under arrest. This might have spurred him to make Eddowes's murder appear more like Beadmore's in order to confuse the police investigation. Or, perhaps, he simply liked what he saw in the papers and chose to add it to his repertoire.

If there is an additional reason why the Ripper found the idea of a chalked message appealing (and there's no reason to suppose there would have been only one), then it's likely the reason proposed by researcher Jeffrey Bloomfield in 1995.[173] Mr. Bloomfield's simple yet immensely sensible suggestion is that Jack the Ripper imagined himself the arch nemesis of Sherlock Holmes. This might at first sound contrived, but upon reflection, it actually clicks into place rather nicely.

The very first Sherlock Holmes tale, 'A Study in Scarlett', made its debut in *Beeton's Christmas Annual* in December of 1887. The novella was illustrated by D.S. Friston and the frontispiece was an illustration of Holmes and cohorts pondering a strange message written on a wall in blood. The message read 'RACHE', which Inspector Lestrade thought pointed to the name 'Rachel', but Holmes knew better.[174] The story was such a sensation that it reinvented the craft of mystery fiction almost overnight. Nine months after its publication, the police stand pondering a confusing message chalked on a wall over a murder victim's bloodied apron. Mr. Bloomfield doesn't believe this was a coincidence and I'm inclined to agree. After all, if the Ripper wrote the message, something influenced him to do so. Was it the recent press attribution of similar writings to him? Or did he fancy himself an arch villain going up against the great Scotland Yard (sans the erstwhile Holmes)? I suspect it was a bit (or a lot) of both.

As discussed earlier, this was the Ripper's peak time. He couldn't have helped but feel invincible following the closure of the Nichols and Chapman inquests when it was announced that the police were stumped and no closer to knocking on his door than they had been the month before. Something that occurred on the night of the double event might have shaken his confidence as he would take his longest hiatus since prior to the Tabram murder.

If crafting a message with a meaning that wasn't immediately obvious was the Ripper's intention, he succeeded better than he could have expected. Unlike with Doyle's tale, there was no Sherlock Holmes nearby to point out the obvious. A photograph likely would have settled the matter, but even that can't be said with certainty.

So what did the Goulston Street message really say? What did it really mean?

The Final Word on the Second Word?

Our understanding of any historical event comes from how we interpret the facts. And we should always assume that we do not have all the facts. In the case of Goulston Street, truth be told, we have none. There were no witnesses to its composition and even those investigating the matter could only offer their best guesses. Any author offering a certainty either that the writing was a worthless clue or that it's the key to the Ripper's true identity is selling you a bill of goods. But even if there are no hard conclusions, we can at least weigh what we do know into a balance of probabilities.

No one living in the building recalled having seen the writing prior to the time of the Eddowes murder and neither PC Long nor DC Halse noticed it as they passed. This indicates (note that I do not say 'proves') that the writing was placed on the wall not long prior to its discovery. Its proximity to the apron portion is not in dispute and is the sole reason the writing is suspected of having been written by Jack the Ripper. Had the apron been disposed of on another street or even one of the many other entryways on Goulston Street, the writing would have passed without notice until its inevitable erasure by an annoyed tenant.

A common argument one hears is that such graffiti was common in the East End. There surely is some truth in that. However, if there had been any graffiti similar in tone, text, or style, anywhere in the vicinity of Goulston Street (or the whole of London, for that matter), it couldn't have escaped the attention of the patrolling constables, all of whom would have been keenly alert when word of the written message made the rounds.

If we look at the message outside of the context of the Ripper murders it makes even less sense. As an anti-Semitic rant it fails miserably. Someone with chalk wishing to rant against the Jewish population could have done so in very colorful language and without ambiguity. We wouldn't expect to see a message intended to inflamed written in small letters on a door jamb; it would be presented 'loud and proud' on the open space of the outer wall for all passersby to see. So, if we accept the graffiti as something separate from the murder of Catherine Eddowes, we're accepting an awful lot on faith, not the least of which is that her torn and bloody apron ended up just below this most unique piece of writing. And if we conclude the writing was a meaningless happenstance and not a 'clue' at all, we are pitting our wisdom against that of virtually all of the men who were there, including the man who ordered its obliteration.

Another fact that would not have missed the attention of the investigators is that the Ripper made his work more difficult and time consuming in Mitre Square by cutting lengthwise through Catherine Eddowes's apron in order procure a section. As discussed earlier, her apron would have been tied to her in only two places. He'd already cut through one string, so why not one more 'snip' and take the whole thing away? That he didn't do this means either that he was out of his mind or else the entire purpose of removing this portion was so that it could be matched to the portion remaining with Eddowes. There's no other reason for this except that the bloodied portion was intended to serve as his 'signature' in Goulston Street. Had he simply needed a rag to make off with her purloined organs, any one of the rags he'd removed from her pocket previously would have sufficed.

So, for the sake of argument, if we assume that the man with chalk on his fingers was also the midnight assassin with blood on his hands, then we must ponder what he was trying to tell us. Commissioner Warren clearly felt that he was a 'they' (secret society), obviously gentile, and trying to cast blame on the Jews of Goulston Street and the socialists of Berner Street. Home Office big wig Godfrey Lushington believed the Ripper a Jew who composed the message to take responsibility. Assistant Commissioner Anderson also believed the Ripper a Jew and so must also have felt the message was a confession.

As much as these suggestions differ, what they have in common is the belief that the message in some way makes references to Jews. This is because of the second word in the sentence. However, one thing we can be certain of is that this word was not 'Jews'. It apparently had more than four letters and was not at all clear or obvious, because multiple variations were offered by those who saw it or those who access to these individuals – Juwes, Jewes, Juewes, Juews, are a few examples.

I'm going to offer a suggestion that some might see as radical and others might think is perfectly sensible. I stress that this is only an idea and not a belief I have. Because no photograph exists the simple fact is that we'll never know what it said. But it occurred to me some years ago that one reason why these alert, intelligent men failed to observe the same word is that it wasn't a word at all.

The Ripper killed two women that night. Elizabeth Stride was the first and she was not mutilated below the neck. The Ripper would have been one of very few people aware of this fact at the time he made his appearance in Goulston Street. He might have been concerned that he wouldn't get the credit for both kills. One way to guarantee against this would be to write a message assuming responsibility for Stride's murder and 'sign' it with an item stained with Eddowes's blood and easily traceable to her.

Crouched in the dark passage of the Wentworth model dwelling, his heart beating with anticipation, and in possession of an item that would guarantee he hangs, the Ripper's best 'chalkmanship' might not have been on display and this could partially account for the difficulty investigators had in understanding the second word. Because it wasn't a word at all.

The Ripper murdered Stride in the yard of the Berner Street club, or, as it's often called in Ripper books, the International Workingmen's Educational Club. But their name as it actually appeared on the front-age of the house was 'INTERNATIONAL WORKING MEN'S EDUCATIONAL SOCIETY'. It occurred to me that if the Ripper was not personally associated with the club, this is the name he would have known them by, and it being so long he may have chosen to reduce the name to its acronym, feeling this was sufficient. In short, I'm suggesting he may have written 'IWMES' instead of 'Juwes'. When written in cursive they are virtually identical. I am aware that the version Commissioner Warren offers has only the first of the letters capitalized, but there's no reason to suppose it was a faithful recreation of the appearance of the writing. In fact, the handwriting does not appear stilted, so it seems its intention was simply to preserve what they believed the message read.

Pareidolia is a fancy word that means seeing something that isn't there because the mind wants or expects to see it. In this case, the men expected to see a word, not an acronym (which were nowhere near as ubiquitous as they are today), and given the already rife speculation that the Ripper was Jewish, the Leather Apron scare, and the murder of Stride next to a Jewish Socialist club, some variation of 'Jews' made the most sense. But had the Ripper actually intended to write the word 'Jews' we might expect to see more accord among the witnesses. After all, they had no trouble making out any of the other words.

If I'm correct – and I have absolutely no idea if I am or not – then what the Ripper was actually telling us was this: 'The International Working

Men's Educational Society are the men who will not be blamed for nothing.' Now, we're back to the conundrum as to whether or not he's saying they're blameless or that they're not blameless. But if this hypothesis makes sense, it settles two ongoing debates at once as it concludes that the Ripper was responsible for the murder of Elizabeth Stride as well as for writing the Goulston Street 'graffito'.

In conclusion, we'll never know for sure what was written or who wrote it. But I hope and believe the above has demonstrated that an objective and thorough consideration of the evidence and the opinions of the men who were there tip the scales dramatically in favor of the Goulston Street message having been the handiwork of the man who killed Elizabeth Stride and Catherine Eddowes. If that man was indeed one and the same as the man who killed Polly Nichols, Annie Chapman, and perhaps the earlier victims, then we almost had a photograph of his handwriting. If only the City Police had gotten their way that night.

THE MCCARTHYS OF DORSET STREET

I N ALL THE puzzles placed before us by the Whitechapel murders, the quest for the woman we know as Mary Jane Kelly must be second only to that of the hunt for the Ripper himself. With so little to go on, and virtually all of that information hearsay, the researcher hopes to find a clue by digging deep into the pasts of those who knew her best. In this regard, Kelly's one-time beau, Joseph Barnett, has rightfully been given precedence.

While much information has surfaced over the years allowing us a better knowledge of the life and times of Barnett, none of this has brought us closer to Mary. The hunt continues, and although different paths are taken, all roads lead to Dorset Street and to the door of #27 wher lived a man named John McCarthy.

Or were there two John McCarthys living at this same address? If so, which one was Kelly's landlord? These are the questions we'll attempt to answer here.

The message boards at *Casebook: Jack the Ripper* have been alive recently with discussion about McCarthy. Chris Scott, A.P. Wolf, Robert Charles Linford, and many others have been posting important new finds and tracking census records in hopes of zeroing in on *the* John McCarthy, ever mindful of the embarrassing blunders of past writers who confidently published their findings on George Hutchinson or Joseph Barnett only to discover they'd been tracking the wrong man all along.

The confusion comes from the fact that

the 1891 census records show two John McCarthys – with the very same age but decidedly different histories – residing at 27 Dorset Street. The census returns for the address read as follows:

McCarthy, John Head Married M 42 General Shopkeeper Spitalfields

Marry Wife Married F 38 Spitalfields

George Son Single M 16 Spitalfields

McCarthy, Daniel Head Married M 27 Grocer Southwark

Ann Wife Married F 23 Southwark

McCarthy, John Head Married M 42 Grocer Dieppe, France

Elizabeth Wife Married F 38 Shoreditch

Margaret Daughter Single F 15 St. George

Elizabeth Daughter Single F 12 St. George

Ann Daughter Single F 6 Spitalfields

Nelly Daughter Single F 0 Spitalfields

Alder, Eliza Domestic Single F 16 Domestic Servant St. Pancras

Alder, Lisa Domestic Widowed F 39 Domestic Servant Lambeth

This census listing is no new find. In fact, it has been recorded in various journals, books, and websites over the years that there were two John McCarthys – one a simple lodging house keeper, the other the landlord of Miller's Court, living in Dorset Street at the same time. It's been suggested that this was an error on the part of an overworked census taker. More often, and perhaps more likely, it's been suggested that the Johns were relatives and one was staying in the rooms of the other.

Separating these individuals and determining which of the two was the man who was Kelly's landlord – and who may have been her pimp or relative (or both) – is crucial if further research is to be undertaken. Here we will evaluate the above census listing, consider a couple of new discoveries, and see if we can find the answer we're looking for.

We should first rid ourselves of the notion that this was all an error of the census taker. While errors in the census records are rampant, they usually pertain to the spelling of the name or age of the individual. There is no reason to assume that in this instance an entire family was invented or that the wrong surname was recorded. We'll accept, then, that we are dealing with two separate John McCarthys and start our evaluation from there.

Drawing from the census reports, we find that one McCarthy was born in Dieppe, France, and that the other was a Spitalfields native.

Tracing the first McCarthy back thirty years to the census records of 1861, we find his family living at 12 Red Cross Square, Southwark. John's age is given as 13 at the time. His parents, Daniel and Margaret, were each 35 years of age and born in Ireland. Of their five children only John was born in France. Daniel's profession, listed only as 'labourer,' suggests that work of some sort had taken the family to France for a short time, circa 1848, where John was born.

John was the oldest of the children and his siblings, as listed in the 1861 census, are: Dennis (10), Jeremiah (7), Timothy (3), and Daniel Jr. (6 mos.). Dennis was born in Hertfordshire, Jeremiah and Timothy in London, and Daniel Jr. in Southwark. Daniel Sr. and Margaret would have their first daughter, Annie. The family made the fortuitous move to London's East End circa 1867 and would grow again with the birth of Ellen McCarthy. From this it is clear that John's early life had been spent on the move. For whatever reason, life there agreed with him, and it is here we still find him in 1891. By contrast, it would appear the other John McCarthy had spent his entire life in the East End.

Turning our attention to their listed professions, the first John is described as 'grocer,' which ties in neatly with the fact that Kelly's landlord owned and operated a grocer's shop. The other John is listed as 'general shopkeeper,' a term that suggests he was in someone else's employ. The Daniel McCarthy residing at 27 Dorset Street is listed as 'grocer' and his age as 27, making him 11 years younger than both Johns. Considering that the first John had a younger brother by this name who was 12 years his junior in the 1861 census (hardly a considerable discrepancy by census standards), it seems possible if not likely that they are one and the same.

Working from the scant information that is afforded us by the census reports, it seems probable that the first John, born in France, is the man we seek. This has long been the favored view of researchers, but up to now has only been an educated assumption, made all the more tantalizing by the "French Connection" it offers. However, recent fids relating to these 'dueling McCarthys' have strengthened this view.

'Jack' McCarthy Takes the Stage

On July 16th, 1901, the *Daily Mail* published a scathing condemnation of Dorset Street, unambiguously titled 'The Worst Street in London.' Even those who've not read the article itself will be familiar with some of its bolder claims from modern Ripper books that have utilized the article as a source. Among these claims are that police constables were loath to venture down the small byway, less they travel in pairs. Needless to say, the residents and business owners in Dorset Street were none too pleased with the piece, nor its author, a Mr. Fred A. McKenzie.

A meeting took place in Dorset Street the next day, but finding that the facilities were too small to accommodate those interested in attending, the gathering was adjourned until Monday, July 22nd. Flyers went up all over the neighborhood announcing the meeting to be held at the Duke of Wellington on Shepherd Street. Although Dorset Street resident Edward Locock was organizer and chairman, only one name appeared on the bill – Mr. Jack McCarthy. 'Jack' took to the podium with only a copy of the offending edition of the *Daily Mail* in hand and spoke for an hour and fifty minutes without the aid of notes. A pamphlet of the proceedings was published, and it languished in obscurity for over a century before being re-discovered by the very productive Richard Jones during one of his searches through the Tower Hamlets archives. Jones graciously donated this find to Stephen Ryder's *Casebook: Jack the Ripper*, where it remains for all to read.

Internal evidence makes clear that the 'Jack' McCarthy s one and the same as Mary Kelly's landlord, and the pamphlet provides many interesting insights and tidbits of information. For our purposes here, we'll consider a few excerpts. The first is McCarthy's introduction, reproduced here for the purpose of displaying McCarthy's impressive oratory skills:

Mr. Chairman and gentlemen, I was very much surprised on

reading the article in the 'Daily Mail,' and I may tell you that I immediately put it in the hands of an eminent council. Now, gentlemen, I intend to take this article, piece by piece, and prove to you that there is not a particle of truth in it from beginning to end. I hope, that in the course of my remarks, I shall not say anything to hurt the feelings of anybody present and I will confine myself solely and wholly to the article in question. I should like you to notice while reading this article, that every time Mr. Mackensie [sic] refers to the lodging houses in Dorset Street, he calls them dosshouses, but when speaking about Glascow or Lord Rowton he describes their lodging houses as admirable homes, although Lord Rowton's houses are simply common registered lodging houses the same as those in Dorset Street. The same medical officers, the same inspectors and the same superficial measure for every bed. Now, gentlemen, I had an idea that Mr. Mackensie, who wrote this article, who knows all about the rickerty tables, who knows everything about crime, etc. would live in a very dismal place himself. After careful enquiry I found out that his business place was Toynbee Hall, and that all letters received there were sent on to his private address, 602, Birkbeck Bank Buildings, Chancery Lane. A friend and myself went last Saturday night to have a look at 602, Birkbeck Bank Buildings, Chancery Lane, facing the street there is a public house and a constable and the potman were persuading a man, who was rather unruly, to leave, of course, had this been in Dorset Street, it would have been said he was drunk and was chucked out, but round by Birkbeck Bank Buildings, it is said he was slightly inebriated and requested to leave. Gentlemen, the language this man this man used was worse than anything I ever heard and in fact, it was impossible to hear worse, even in Dorset Street. We went on further on towards 602, Birkbeck Bank Buildings and at the side of a boarding, saw an officer pushing a lady and gentleman along, had they been near Dorset Street, of course, the lady would have been a prostitute, but they are not to be found near Birkbeck Bank Buildings, but I leave you my friends to infer what they were doing in such a quiet spot. Dorset Street is better lighted than this spot, close to Birkbeck Bank Buildings and thus, "The Worse Street in London," is a credit to the Local Authorities.

John McCarthy was clearly a well-educated man with a more than adequate command of proper English. It was likely for this reason, as well as his prominence in the neighborhood, that he was chosen to speak. This insight is vital in our attempt to distinguish between the two McCarthys.

As mentioned before, internal evidence in the speech points to 'Jack' McCarthy as landlord of the Miller's Court properties. McCarthy was at the top of what might be called a proto-Mafia in the East End. He wanted everyone to have McKenzie's address and so repeated it multiple times. He knew the pamphlet would make its way to McKenzie and so he made sure to point out that he, in company of a 'friend', personally visited the reporter's street.

Another indicator that this is the McCarthy we seek is his prolonged rant against McKenzie's description of the furnished rooms in Dorset Street. To appreciate McCarthy's rebuttal we should first consider the offending paragraph from McKenzie's article:

FURNISHED ROOMS

The lodging-houses are bad, but they are the best side f a bad street. They at least have certain official inspection, and a certain minimum amount of sanitation and decency is there secured. But the furnished rooms so-called are infinitely worse. Farming furnished rooms is exceedingly profitable business. You take seven or eight-roomed houses at a rent of 10s. or 11s a week, you place on each door a padlock, and in each room you put a minimum amount of the oldest furniture to be found in the worst second-hand dealers' in the slums. The fittings of the average furnished room are not worth more than a few shillings. Then you let the rooms out to any corners for 10d. or 1s. a night. No questions asked. The pay the rent, you hand them the key. If by the next night they have not their 10d. or 1s again ready you go round and chuck them out and let a newcomer in.

Now we'll examine McCarthy's rebuttal. Read closely, as the information he gives pertains directly to Miller's Court. Words and phrases in bold are of my emphasis and indicate points to be discussed:

Then taking up THE 'DAILY MAIL' again he went on with the article. Here we have in large type, FURNISHED ROOMS. The lodging-houses, he says, are bad enough, but they are THE BEST SIDE OF A BAD STREET. They have a certain amount of sanitation and decency as well as efficient inspection, while the furnished rooms have neither. Mr. Mackensie says, you take a seven or eight roomed house at a rent of 10s. or 11s. a week. (Cries of "Where are they?", "Is the man mad?" etc., were heard.) He says you put a certain amount of the oldest furniture to be found in the slums in them, and then you let them out to the first-comers at 10d. a night. (Loud and prolonged laughter.) No questions are asked, THEY PAY THE RENT, and you hand them the key. (Laughter.) If b the next night they have not got their 10d. or 1s. ready you go round and CHUCK THEM OUT (IT IS ALWAYS 'CHUCK' in Dorset Street) and let a new-comer in. (Laughter.) McCarthy went on, WHAT A MARVELLOUS MAN this Mackensie is! Why he actually knows where we buy the furniture, what we pay for it, what rent we pay for our houses, and the next time I want any furniture I will commission Mr. Mackensie to get it for me. Anybody might guess we don't GO TO MAPLE'S for it; but what's the matter with Savage's – (loud applause) – and the hundreds of private and public sales THAT TAKE PLACE IN LONDON every week? Mr. Mackensie must have a poor opinion of the BUSINESS ABILITIES of the proprietors of furnished rooms. **For the information of Mr. Mackensie, furnished rooms ARE REGISTERED for poor people who have no homes and yet have one or two children.** There is a medical officer and inspector who hold FIRST CLASS CERTIFICATES for sanitation, etc. These men go through a searching examination, the facsimile of that of the COUNTY COUNCIL INSPECTORS, and they ARE QUITE AS COMPETENT to do their duty. They have the power to visit furnished rooms, NIGHT OR DAY, and, in fact, though under the local authorities, have the same powers as the London County Council inspectors have to visit lodging-houses. (Cheers.) Thus it will be seen that they are A PRESSING NECESSITY to the poorer class of working-men. Mr. Mackensie says we throw the oldest furniture, always, as he says in the "Toynbee Hall Record," A RICKETY TABLE AND ONE CHAIR, into the room, and leave them to put themselves in order. Now, then, I will try to prove that what MR. MACKENSIE INTENDS AS A SLUR is really a compliment to the proprietors of the furnished rooms. Considering what THIS ASPIRANT TO JOUNALISTIC HONOURS has written, they must be very kind-hearted, simple people, for, as Mr. Mackensie tells you, after going ROUND THE SLUMS and buying the worst furniture at the low-est possible price (always a FEW SHILLINGS), he leaves them about, trusting to the honesty of the first person that comes along with 10d. (Loud and prolonged laughter).

It is not my intention to digress too long from the primary intention of this article, but it would hardly be prudent to consider this informa-tion without bringing up a couple of important items touched upon by McCarthy that do not appear to have been discussed up to this point.

The first item in bond is rather self-explanatory; McCarthy states quite clearly that furnished rooms were registered for the purpose of providing shelter to poor people with children. While he clearly didn't always abide by this rule – allowing Barnett and Kelly to live in #13 child-free – this might explain why it was thought by some that Kelly did have a child living with her.

The second excerpt in bold is quite significant in that McCarthy, while speaking in venomous sarcasm, mocks McKenzie's suggestion that he or any other keeper of furnished rooms would spend their time and money purchasing furniture only to "leave them about" in the rooms, trusting that they wouldn't be stolen. McCarthy's words, and the "loud and prolonged laughter" they induced, seem to me to indicate that he took precautions against such theft by somehow affixing the bed and tables (we'll assume the chairs remained free) to either the floor or wall, and that to do otherwise would have been poor practice. Of course, given the area and clientele of his operation, to secure the furniture in this way is only logical, otherwise he'd have been off purchasing replacements each time a lodger skipped out.

It is standard practice today in motel rooms around the world and there's no reason to suppose it was any different in 1888. Although only a minor revelation in the larger scope of things, this indication that Kelly's bed and table were immovable adds to our knowledge of the crime scene and casts serious doubt on the popular (but by no means obvious) notion that Kelly's bed and/or table had been moved in taking the second crime scene photo, which offers a closer view of her mutilations and the items atop her bedside table.

With this brief but enlightening digression of the way, let us regain our focus by stepping out of Miller's Court and saying 'ello to the other John McCarthy.

A Midnight Meeting

Richard Harding Davis is most well-known today for his Van Bibber series of books and his many writings as a foreign war correspondent in the early 20th Century. However, he began his career as a young American journalist in Philadelphia. It was in his role of journalist that 25 year-old Davis set off on a Spring/Summer 1889 tour of London and Ireland with a team of Philadelphia cricketers.

He spent most of his time in London at small universities covering the matches, but nevertheless managed to find the time to take a midnight stroll around Whitechapel with Inspector Henry Moore, who only months before had replaced Inspector Abberline as the man in charge of the Ripper enquiry. Davis's nocturnal sojourn was published later that year in the *Pall Mall Gazette* and comprises chapter 30 of Stewart Evans & Keith Skinner's *The Ultimate Jack the Ripper Companion* (aka *Sourcebook*). Davis describes his visit to 13 Miller's Court, where by then another couple was residing.

I found the interview to be intriguing and provocative and wondered if Davis had written of the murders elsewhere. To satisfy my curiosity I purchased a couple of his books: *Our English Cousins* (1894) and *The Adventures and Letters of Richard Harding Davis* (1917). In *Our English Cousins*, Davis devotes a good amount of space to his observations in the East End, by which time he'd visited repeatedly. Most intriguing of his tales is a little episode from his walk with Inspector Moore that did not make it into his *Pall Mall Gazette* article. This is a brief dialogue with a common lodging house attendant named McCarthy, the man who emerges from history as the other 'John'.

> One night an inspector of police woke fifty of these men in McCarthy's lodging-house on Dorset Street, off the Commercial Road, to exhibit them, and I felt as though I had walked into a cage with the keeper. They lay on strips of canvas naked to the waist, for it was a warm, close night, and as the ray from the policeman's lantern slid from cot to cot, it showed the sunken chests and ribs of some half-starved wrecks of the wharves, or the broad torso of a "docker" or a sailor's hairy breast marked with tattooing, and the throats of two men scarred with long, dull red lines where some one had drawn a knife. Some of them tossed and woke cursing and muttering, and then rested on their elbows, cowering before the officers and blinking at the light, or sat erect and glared at them defiantly, and hailed them with drunken bravado.
>
> "The beds seem comfortable," I said to McCarthy, by way of being civil.
>
> "Oh, yes, sir," he answered, "comfor'ble enough, only it ain't proper, after paying twopence for your bed, to 'ave a policeman a-waking you up with a lamp in your face. It 'urts the 'ouse, that's wot it does." He added, gloomily, "It drives away trade."

I would argue that the man Davis met was not the same McCarthy who would later be chosen by his peers as the voice of Dorset Street when its reputation came under attack, and thus it's logical to conclude he was the 'other' John McCarthy present at the time in Dorset Street managing a common lodging house.

The Final Answer?

Linguistically speaking, we must conclude that the better-spoken "Jack" McCarthy was the fellow born in Dieppe, France, with connections to the London stage, who traveled around with his family before settling in the East End to become a successful business owner, while the cockney-tongued gentleman whose clientele was so rudely disturbed by a brash Inspector Moore and wide-eyed young Richard Davis would most likely be the John McCarthy born and bred in Spitalfields.

This leaves us with only one other question: were the two Johns kin to one another? While it's hard to say for sure, 'Jack' McCarthy gives us good reason to believe they were not. During his speech to his fellow Dorset Street regulars, McCarthy observed:

> There are four shops – one fish shops and three general shops – and it is a remarkable coincidence that the three shops are all of that same historical name, 'McCarthy.' Though this is the case, they belong to three separate and distinct families.

Is the evidence presented here conclusive and irrefutable? No, it is not. But until the day should come when such proof is found, I'd say to all researchers following the trail of 'John McCarthy, grocer', to keep doing so with confidence as it seems you're on the right track.

AUTHOR'S NOTE: This article originally appeared in the 26th issue of *Ripper Notes* magazine. Editor Dan Norder informed me that he was publishing an excellent piece by Don Souden entitled 'Time Is on My Side' about Mary Kelly's landlord, John McCarthy. The same issue would also feature an article by himself on a painting he thought might have been on the wall of Kelly's room. I'd had some material saved up from my own researches on McCarthy and decided to write this to fit into the theme that Norder was loosely going for in the issue. This was years before my research would force me to take a more intensive interest in the doings of the 'Lords of Spitalfields' discussed in *The Bank Holiday Murders*. With the better understanding we now have of the criminalistics tendencies of the East End lodging house keepers, the thinly veiled threats by McCarthy against journalist Fred McKenzie are glaringly apparent. I also find very relevant McCarthy's public statements to the effect that his Miller's Court rooms were let only to women with children, as this might explain the early myths that Kelly had a child living with her.

MARY KELLY AND THE DECADENTS

IN THE LONDON of the 1880s and 90s there existed a group of bohemian poets, writers, and artists often referred to as the 'Decadents', more so for their wild and careless lifestyles than their literary output, only some of which could be termed 'revolutionary'.

Oscar Wilde is arguably the most famous name of the bunch, but also circling in orbit around Wilde were, among others, Ernest Dowson, John Barlas, Walter Sickert, Francis Thompson, and Frank Miles. The remarkable fact about these acquaintances is that each one of them have been pointed to as Jack the Ripper in the century-plus since the Whitechapel murders of 1888. No less astonishing is the fact that this is the first time this extraordinary coincidence is being discussed. No doubt this is because the respective cases against each of these men has to date been unimpressive at best, nonexistent at worst; nevertheless, three of these *artistes* have books arguing for their candidacy, and the fact that *any* five suspects personally knew each other must give a researcher reason to pause.

Just for good measure, I'll mention that a friend and travel partner of Sickert and Dowson was Charles Conder, the anarchic cousin of Claude Reignier Conder, the man handed the Ripper crown by author Tom Slemen in his recent book, *Jack the Ripper: British Intelligence Agent?*. Charles Conder would die of Syphilis at age 40, Ernest Dowson of alcoholism at age 32, while John Barlas and artist Frank Miles eventually expired in insane asylums.

Clearly, this group were as disturbed as they were gifted.

But were any of these men Jack the Ripper? The best we can say is that we don't have any true reason to believe so. But our purpose here isn't to determine guilt, but to discover why a small group of friends have drawn such suspicion, from so many people, across numerous generations.

We need not spend much time with Francis Thompson and Frank Miles, both modern suspects with little or no support outside of their dedicated accusers (although a pending book by dogged Thompson-as-Ripper devotee, Richard Patterson, threatens to change that). Miles was even in an asylum throughout the run of the Ripper murders, and Thompson is provably guilty of nothing more than being yet another opium-addicted poet with associations to prostitutes.

Our focus here is on the trio of artist Walter Sickert and the poets Dowson and Barlas.

Jack the Blue-blooded Bard?

John Barlas was discussed at some length in David A. Green's excellent 'In Hours of Red Desire', published in *Ripper Notes* #26 in 2006, and more recently in my own, 'The Cattleman, The Lunatic, and the Doctor: The Three Suspects of Jabez Spencer Balfour', in *Casebook Examiner* #4. Barlas was born in 1860 and wrote under the *nom de plume* of Evelyn Douglas, publishing eight volumes of verse between 1884 and 1893, including 1885's evocatively titled *The Bloody Heart* and 1887's *Phantasmagoria: Dream Fugues*. His verse drew some attention and he gained a minor celebrity, primarily through his associations with Oscar Wilde and Ernest Dowson. Barlas was a devoted socialist, serving as an organizer for the Social Democratic Federation and writing for William Morris' socialist paper *Commonweal*. He was demonstrating in Trafalgar Square in 1886 when he was beaten badly by the police; an apocryphal tale that may or may not be true has him falling, bloodied, at the feet of Eleanor Marx-Aveling, youngest daughter of Karl Marx and co-founder of the Socialist League. Many sources, even reputable ones, erroneously attribute this event to 1887's 'Bloody Sunday.'

The Berner Street club was a branch of the Socialist League, with William Morris a regular speaker (and occasional renter of space when needed) and Eleanor Marx an infrequent attendee. Barlas' socialist ties and activism make it unavoidable that he would have been quite familiar to the members of the club at Berner Street.

Barlas was briefly associated with the famous Rhymer's Club, having been sponsored by his friend, Ernest Dowson. His mental health was fragile, pushed to unstable, some say, by the head injuries sustained in Trafalgar Square. On the morning of New Year's Eve, 1891, he stood and fired three shots at the House of Commons, suffering under the delusion that he was an important figure from the Bible.

Long-time friend Oscar Wilde bailed Barlas out, but eventually there was no choice but to readmit him, and he would spend his later years in Gartnavel Asylum, Glasgow, where he would die at age 54 in 1914. During his years in incarceration, Barlas wrote an autobiography, which has unfortunately not survived.

Some attribute his madness to syphilis, obtained from a prostitute he took in as a lover after leaving his wife, whom he habitually abused. If indeed he suffered from syphilis in 1891, one would not have expected him to have lived so many more years. However, if the stories handed down from those who knew him are true, then Barlas was unstable from at least 1886. Of all the 'decadent' suspects discussed here, he is the first to have had suspicions published about him regarding the Ripper murders.

The following first appeared in the *New York Times* of October 23rd, 1897, and was discovered by Wolf Vanderlinden, who published it in *Ripper Notes* #23.

I have been informed on perfectly trustworthy authority that the perpetrator of the Whitechapel murders is known to the police, having been finally identified with a certain lunatic, who is now confined in a madhouse in Scotland. The murderer is an Oxford graduate, and made a certain reputation some ten years ago as a minor poet. He bears a distinguished name, which has been repeated to me, and is famous in Scottish history in connection with a young woman who saved a King's life in a heroic way. The 'Ripper' had a wife who was descended from a very famous English Admiral. His latest delusion is that he is the grandson of Napoleon the Great.

The details presented in this clipping could apply only to John Barlas, who was an Oxford graduate, and poet of some repute, who married the great-grandniece of Admiral Lord Nelson, and was descended from Catherine Douglas, later Barlass, who attempted but failed to save the life of King James I of Scotland. Who the 'perfectly trustworthy authority' was who suspected Barlas and why he was suspected, can only be guessed at, but as he appears to have suffered from delusions that he was important historical personages, it's possible that he lapsed into periods where he thought he was Jack the Ripper and made confessions to the crimes. But false and delusional confessions were in no shortage in the decade following the Ripper crimes, so what else might have set Barlas apart and made him seem a worthy suspect? The answer to this question might be found in statements made regarding his friends.

'Mr. Moring,' a Suspect No More

In 1935, memoirist R. Thurston Hopkins published *Life and Death at the Old Bailey*, a work that has drawn considerable comment in recent years in numerous works on the Ripper, primarily for his description of a whimsical figure haunting Fleet Street whom he suspected of having written the Jack the Ripper letters. Hopkins also described an acquaintance he shared with Ripper victim Mary Kelly.

> One of Mary Kelly's friends was a poor devil-driven poet who often haunted the taverns around the East End. I will call him "Mr. Moring," but of course that was not his real name. Moring would often walk about all night and I had many long talks with him as together we paced the gloomy courts and alleys. Of externals Moring was utterly heedless. He wore a blue pea-jacket, baggy trousers (much like the modern Oxford bags) and pointed button boots. His collar was, I distinctly remember, tied together with a bow of wide black moiré ribbon, and like his boots, seemed to be crumpled into folds of sympathetic irregularity. He was what the Victorians called a ne'er-do-well, and a bard. It was said that his father – a prosperous tradesman in the East End – had

disowned him because he had become a drug addict. Occasionally he returned home and begged money from his parents, and on his return to old haunts he would enjoy a short period of luxury and sartorial rehabilitation. Moring, who knew every opium den in the East End, although at that time they were not counted in with the sights of London, often gave himself up to long spells of opium smoking.

Many of the drinking dens of London were open all night during those days, and I can still see Moring sitting at a tavern table, surrounded by a villainous company as he lectured on the merits of opium. "Alcohol for fools; opium for poets," was a phrase which recurred constantly in his talk. "To-morrow one dies," was his motto, and he would sometimes add "and who cares – will it stop the traffic on London Bridge?"

In looking up this case in an old newspaper published at the time, I read that a man named George Hutchinson came up with a statement the day after the inquest on Mary Kelly.

From the details provided by Hopkins, author Martin Fido identified 'Mr. Moring' as the poet Ernest Dowson and published his findings in *Ripperana* #29 (1999). The identification is considered accurate by most researchers but has come under fire from author Richard Patterson, who suggests the suspect is Francis Thompson.

Dowson was born in 1867 and is described by biographer, Jad Adams, as '...the purest representative of the literary movement of the 1890's referred to as the 'Decadence.' His life of exquisite verse, classical learning, French travel, dissolution, blighted love and Catholic Conversion made him the archetypal 1890's character even before he set the sea on his iconic status with an early death.'[175] Adams also tells us that Dowson had a 'fascination with girl children' and became obsessed with the 11 year-old daughter of a Soho restaurant owner. Six years later, Dowson's parents died within a very short time of each other, probably both from suicide, and the object of Dowson's affections (now 17) became engaged to another man. This precipitated Dowson's decline and he would die in 1900 at the home of R.H. Sherard in Catford from tuberculosis exacerbated by depression and alcoholism. He was only 32 years old.

Whenever considering Hopkins' writings on the Ripper, it must be remembered that he was born in 1884, making him only four years old at the time of the murders, and but a lad of 16 when Dowson died. Hopkins was a prolific writer on many topics, and it would make perfect sense for a young man in his teens to seek out professionals such as Ernest Dowson to learn from. Incidentally, Hopkins also came to know John Barlas, spending evenings drinking with him in taverns, apparently during one of the brief periods Barlas was at liberty.

Ernest Dowson, who has achieved immortality by providing us prose that has left us with memorable phrases such as 'these are the days of wine and roses,' and 'gone with the wind', strikes a very tragic but also harmless figure. Because of Hopkins' innocent remark that George Hutchinson's suspect dressed eccentrically as did 'Mr. Moring', it has caused many writers to assume that Hopkins was pointing the finger of suspicion at 'Moring', and by association, Ernest Dowson. However, Hopkins was very clear that he entertained no suspicion at all against 'Moring,' stating 'but I could not connect a man of such extraordinary gentleness committing such a dreadful series of outrages.'

So Ernest Dowson a.k.a 'Mr. Moring' can now be struck from all suspect lists, and we can view Hopkins' tale with a fresh perspective. He was not trying to 'beef up' his Ripper chapter by offering his own suspect, but instead was simply sharing the story of an old friend who had a tangential, but perhaps significant, connection to the Ripper case.

Dowson was 'one of Mary Kelly's friends.'

Re-evaluating Walter Sickert's Place in Ripperology

Walter Sickert is without doubt one of the most controversial suspects in recent years. Although the two best-selling Ripper books of all time owe themselves largely to his name, he, unlike Barlas, does not appear to have fallen under any suspicion in the early years following the murders, but instead entered the picture in the 1970s courtesy of Joseph Gorman, who took the artist's name, claiming to be his son. Gorman's tales became weirder and weirder as the years went on, with Sickert being promoted from inside source, to accomplice, to the Ripper himself. The general consensus today is that there might well have been some kernel of truth to the story, but that the vast majority of information emanating from Gorman was of his own creation and has no historical value whatsoever. However, the one detail that remained consistent throughout the decades as Gorman told and retold his tale was that his alleged father (Walter Sickert) knew Mary Kelly.

In 1990, Jean Overton Fuller published *Sickert and the Ripper Crimes*, which in many respects was more of a memoir than a research work. As a child Fuller would listen to the stories of her mother's friend, Florence Pash, who claimed to have known Mary Kelly and even brought her into Walter Sickert's hire as a nanny. From this point, Fuller's tale takes the usual turn with an illegitimate royal child, the murders, and hidden clues in Sickert's art regarding the Ripper's identity.

Although Florence Pash was certainly a friend of Sickert, much of Fuller's remembered claims do not hold up to scrutiny and lack corroboration. Nevertheless, in Fuller we have a source that claims to have discussed the crimes with someone who was alive at the time, knew Walter Sickert and his friends, and claimed that both she and Sickert knew Mary Kelly.

Mary Kelly – The Tie That Binds?

There is certainly a lot of smoke, but does that necessarily mean we should expect fire? On the one hand, we have three friends, all writers or artists, one of whom made the papers within the first decade following the murders as a possible Ripper suspect, the other two described by people who knew them as friends or associates of Mary Kelly.

On the other hand, Hopkins, Gorman, and Fuller are all second hand sources at best, and individually have not enjoyed a reputation for credibility within the Ripper community, and deservedly so.

But Hopkins lived much closer to the time of the murders, and appears to have personally known Ernest Dowson, who told Hopkins he was a friend of Mary Kelly. Hopkins made no attempt to ring any sensation out of his story, so we can assume it was the truth as he knew it, and as Dowson and his friends frequented prostitutes, there is no real reason to suppose he didn't know Mary Kelly as he allegedly claimed. Ergo, if Dowson knew Mary Kelly, it's reasonable to suppose that some of his friends might also have done, lending support to the claims that Sickert knew Mary Kelly, and this fact could be what gave birth to the myriad of conspiracy theories attached to Sickert's name.

Regarding Barlas, just such an association with a Ripper victim may have been the factor that set him apart from other mad confessors and attracted genuine suspicion from a source the *New York Times* dubbed "perfectly trustworthy."

Mary Kelly allegedly boasted of having a relative on the stage. Might this have been a point of contact between herself and Sickert, who was an avid admirer of theatre? Considering her position as West End and later East End prostitute, it is not necessary for us to look too hard for a point of contact, considering at least Dowson (and probably many of his associates) was a habitual user of prostitutes. Nevertheless, an intriguing report appeared in the *Hull Daily Mail* on November 12th, 1888, only a few days after Kelly's murder, that suggests it might have been she who sought out the creative 'decadents', instead of vice versa.

> Further inquiries during the night have thrown little fresh light on the circumstances of the Whitechapel murder. There is good reason to believe that the unhappy woman Kelly was a native of Cardiff, where her family, according to her statement, were well-to-do people. She is stated to have been very well educated, and an artist of some pretensions.

As tantalizing as this is, it is merely one report among hundreds that appeared in the press within the weeks following the murder in Miller's Court, many of which were riddled with errors or demonstrably false. Therefore, we cannot take for granted that the information in this report is accurate. Regrettably, this is the case with every clue we've considered in the thread that makes up the central thesis of this essay – that Mary Kelly was personally associated with a group of artists and writers at some point in the few years prior to her death. Individually, these pieces of information hold little value and hold no currency with modern researchers.

But when placed together like this, they each lend the other just enough strength to allow for the possibility that another chapter in the life of Jack the Ripper's most enigmatic victim might yet be written.

AUTHOR'S NOTE: This article first appeared in *Casebook Examiner* #5 (December 2010). There's not much of a story behind it other than I observed that there was some connection between a number of men who at different times have been pointed out as Jack the Ripper. Today, Walter Sickert is the most well-known, largely because of the efforts of popular fiction novelist Patricia Cornwell. He is not and never has been a serious suspect and likely was in Paris during at the time the murders of Polly Nichols and Annie Chapman occurred. If he has any historical connection at all to the Ripper saga, it would only be a claimed acquaintanceship with victim, Mary Kelly.

Section 1: The Buck's Row Murder
3:40am, Friday, August 31st, 1888

1. His true surname was Lechmere but he opted for his stepfather's name.

2. The street is presently named Valance Road.

3. Evening News, Sept. 3rd, 1888.

4. It was allowed for constables to supplement their income by acting as human alarm clocks for residents on their beat who were willing to pay for the service of a knock at the door when it was time to rise for work.

5. East London Observer, Sept. 8th, 1888.

6. Evening Post Sept. 1st 1888.

7. Lloyd's Weekly Newspaper, Sept. 2nd, 1888.

8. The Standard, Oct. 26th, 1888. Discovered by researcher David James, who also found the Daily News report of the same date, and posted them to jtrforums.com on Sept. 12th, 2010.

9. Spelling and punctuation are Polly's.

10. Item discovered by Debra Arif and posted to jtrforums.com.

11. Sheffield Evening Telegraph, Sept. 11th, 1888, discovered by Howard Brown.

12. People, Sept. 9th, 1888.

13. East London Observer, Sept. 28th, 1888.

Sifting the Medical Evidence

14. Inspector Spratling bio at Casebook.org.

15. Daily News, Sept. 3rd, 1888.

16. Sept. 4th, 1888.

17. 'Flash' was slang for rings of cheap make.

18. Daily Telegraph, Sept. 3rd, and East London Advertiser, Sept. 8. The Daily News of Sept. 3rd recorded this as 'strong-bladed' as opposed to 'long-bladed'.

19. People, Sept. 2nd 1888.

20. Sept. 3rd 1888.

21. Edition of Sept. 8th. The Daily News of Sept. 3rd published the same observation with the word 'seven' in place of 'severe'.

22. For more information and discussion about the weapon used on Tabram, see The Bank Holiday Murders by Tom Wescott.

23. Evening Post & City Chronicle, Sept. 3rd, 1888.

24. As reported, in similar or identical language, in the Star, Evening Post, Evening Standard, and Illustrated Police News.

25. Evening News, Sept. 3rd, 1888.

26. Daily News Sept. 4th, 1888.

27. The Daily News of Sept. 3rd gave the time as 10am and mentioned that Llewellyn's assistant was present for the post mortem. The Echo of Sept. 1st provides the name of Seccombe and further suggests

he may have joined Llewellyn in Buck's Row and was present after the body was removed and before the blood was washed away. Further research by Debra Arif confirmed this identity and gave us his Christian and middle name. According to the 1891 medical directory he shared the address of 152 Whitechapel Road with Dr. Llewellyn.

28. Evening Post, Sept. 1st, 1888. The two witnesses were a coffee stall keeper who had served a man and a woman, who fit Polly's description, a half hour before the murder, and a butcher's salesman named Mr. Scorer, who thought the woman might be his estranged wife. Neither witness recognized Polly.

29. Daily News of Sept. 18th, 1888.

30. Ibid.

31. Or '9 feet from the gateway' as reported by the Star of Sept. 1st, 1888.

32. Star, Sept. 5th, 1888.

33. Evening News, Sept. 3rd, 1888.

The Brady Street Puzzle

34. This name might be a corruption of Handley's mews, located between 51 and 53 Brady Street and owned and operated by William Handley. Research courtesy of David Gates and Robert Linford.

35. Lloyd's Weekly Newspaper, Sept. 2nd.

36. Ibid.

37. Daily News, Sept. 4th, 1888.

38. Daily News, Sept. 3rd, 1888.

39. Daily News, Sept. 4th, 1888.

40. The family's surname is erroneously rendered as 'Celville' and 'Colwell'

in the contemporary press and she's attributed (incorrectly) the Christian name 'Sarah' in modern literature on the case. The correct identities for the Coldwell family comes courtesy of researcher David Gates who posted his research at Casebook.org on January 8th, 2015.

41. Research courtesy of David Gates and Robert Charles Linford.

42. Lloyd's Weekly Newspaper, Sept. 2nd, 1888.

43. The Echo, Sept. 1st, 1888, and Lloyd's Weekly Newspaper, Sept. 2nd, 1888.

44. Evening Standard, Sept. 1st, 1888.

45. East London Advertiser, Sept. 1st, 1888.

The One That Got Away

46. I reached out to researchers Robert Linford and Debra Arif and they independently suggested 'Millhouse' as her true name. They each also turned up information relating to a Margaret Millhouse who, in 1868, at the age of 12, accused her cousin, Stephen Millhouse, of raping her. He was not charged with the crime. It's not known for certain if this Margaret Millhouse and Margaret Millous were one the same. Her describing herself as married certainly makes it possible that she married into the name, in which case the 12 year-old Margaret Millhouse would be someone completely different. But given the nature of her injury and how it may have come about (prostitution) she may have chosen to use her maiden name.

47. All information pertaining to the trial of William Hopkins courtesy of oldbaileyonline.org.

48. Discovered by Debra Arif and posted to Casebook.org in 2008.

49. 'Leather Apron; Or, the Horrors of Whitechapel, London', Samuel E. Hudson, Philadelphia, PA, published December, 1888.

Lost Clues & Missed Opportunities

50. Sept. 3rd edition.

51. Morning Advertiser Sept. 18th, 1888.

52. The Times Sept. 18th, 1888.

53. 1891 census – Casebook.org.

54. East London Advertiser, Sept. 8th, 1888.

The Great Ripper Hunt

55. The Star Sept. 3rd, 1888.

56. East London Observer, Sept. 8th, 1888.

57. The Star, September 3rd, 1888.

58. The Echo Sept. 1st, 1888.

59. Glasgow Herald, Sept. 10th, 1888, discovered by Howard Brown.

60. Irish Times, Sept. 6th, 1888, also the East London Advertiser of Sept 8th remarks that 'a mysterious individual in the character of a seaman has been dragged into the affair, but with what foundation in fact has not yet transpired'.

61. Daily Telegraph, Sept. 4th, 1888.

62. Illinois Daily Register, August 31st, 1888.

Buck's Row – A New Perspective

63. Evening News, Sept. 6th, 1888.

64. Samuel, Raphael, East End Underworld: Chapters in the Life of Arthur Harding (1980).

Section 2: The Berner Street Mystery
Jack and the Grape Stalk

65. See also the Irish Times of Oct. 1st for some minor details not present in the Evening News edition of that day.

66. Other papers have his name as 'Kozebrodsky'.

67. Some sources state that Diemshitz used a match upon coming back into the yard from the club, but this is not so. He used a match prior to going in, and his wife handed him a candle for better light before he went back out.

68. Papers have his name variously as 'Heshberg', 'Hoshburg', and 'Heahbury' and/or incorrectly give his address as '20 Berner Street'.

69. Dr. Blackwell, in his first statements to the press, described a 'box of cachous' and gave the erroneous information that Stride had nearly been decapitated. He may have been misquoted.

70. Presumably Dr. Kay was not at home at the time the constable called.

71. Fanny Mortimer also mentioned grapes in her Oct. 1st statement to the press, though she was reporting hearsay. See the essay on Fanny Mortimer's evidence elsewhere in this book.

72. The fact that Dr. Phillips mentions there were no grape seeds in Stride's stomach is important in light of constable (later inspector) Walter Dew's unfounded assertion that grape skins had been found in the yard and the postulations of some modern authors, such as A.P. Wolf, that Stride may have swallowed the meat of the grape and spit out the skins. Had she done so, she would likely have swallowed some of the seeds as well.

A Murder in the Neighborhood

73. Information courtesy of Christopher-Michael DiGrazia, 'The Whitechapel Dossier No. 2: Berner Street,' Ripper Notes Vol. 3 #3, January 2002.

74. The 1891 census for Berner Street lists a Harstein family living at #40, in the stable yard.

75. This is not the George Yard in which Martha Tabram was murdered.

76. Paul Daniel, 'The Streets of Whitechapel', Ripperologist #7, September, 1996.

77. Charles had two older sisters, Florence (28) and Martha (26), but given their ages, they'd likely have married and moved out by 1888. His youngest sister, Mary, would have been 11 in 1888 but may have died or gone into service by that date, as she's not to be found in the 1891 census.

78. See Evans, Stewart P. and Paul Gainey, 'The Lodger: The Arrest and Escape of Jack the Ripper' by Stewart Evans and Paul Gainey, titled 'Jack the Ripper: First American Serial Killer' for U.S. publication.

79. 'Lipski' is, of course, more known to Ripperologists from the witness testimony of Israel Schwartz. See Stewart P. Evans and Keith Skinner's 'The Ultimate Jack the Ripper Sourcebook.' For more on the Lipski case, see Martin L. Friedland's 'The Trials of Israel Lipski.'

80. My thanks to Rob Clack for providing this reference.

81. The Star, Oct 1st, 1888. Author Paul Begg describes it as the 'left gate'. This is correct from the vantage point of standing in the gateway and facing the street. I prefer to refer to it as being on our right viewing the gate from the street. This avoids confusion as Stride is referred to as lying on the right side of the passageway.

82. Daily Telegraph, Oct 2nd, 1888. Clubman William Wess testified: "In the kitchen is a window which faces the door opening into the

yard. The intervening passage is illuminated by means of a fanlight over the door."

83. Ripper Notes #20, 'Dutfield's Yard: A Change in Methodology?'

84. For an opposing view see 'Considerable Doubt' and the Death of Annie Chapman' by Wolf Vanderlinden, Ripper Notes #22 (April 2005).

85. Morning Advertiser Oct. 4th, 1888.

86. Dundee.ac.uk/forensicmedicine/notes/woundsdjp.pdf.

Exonerating Michael Kidney

87. On his August and October, 1889 trips to the Whitechapel Workhouse, he gave his age as 40, which would have made him 39 at the time of the murder.

88. A painful condition of the lower back, as one resulting from muscle strain or a slipped disk. From Anwers.com.

89. Dyspepsia can be defined as painful, difficult, or disturbed digestion, which may be accompanied by symptoms such as nausea and vomiting, heartburn, bloating, and stomach discomfort. From Answers.com.

90. Daily News, Oct. 3rd, 1888.

91. Yost, Dave, 'Elizabeth Stride and Jack the Ripper: The Life and Death of the Reputed Third Victim', McFarland, 2008.

92. Evans, Stewart P. & Keith Skinner, The Ultimate Jack the Ripper Companion, Pg. 129-130, Carroll & Graff Publishers, Inc. 2000.

93. Since this article was originally published, Wolf has had the text of his book removed from Casebook.org, so it is no longer available there.

94. From the Daily Telegraph, condensed here for only the relevant portions.

A Berner Street Rogues Gallery

95. Papers accessed were all from Oct. 29th, 1888, and were The Daily Telegraph, Evening Standard, Irish Times, Freeman's Journal and Daily Commercial Advertiser, and The Evening News.

96. The Boston Daily Globe, Dec. 10th, 1888.

97. He viewed the body on Oct. 1st, less than 24 hours after he witnessed the couple in Berner Street. The Daily News, Oct. 6th, 1888.

98. By 'opposite No. 58', Marshall means that the couple was standing outside its door, on the pavement, just three doors away from where he was standing.

99. The Times of Oct. 6th adds that this lamp was over 70 Berner Street.

100. This must be in reference to the George IV pub at 68 Berner Street, only two doors from Marshall and five doors from where the couple was standing.

101. 1996 edition, the most recent at the time of writing (Feb. 2010).

102. Official description circulated to the various police departments in October.

103. Evening News, Oct. 1st, 1888.

104. Yost takes the view that all witnesses, including and especially the discredited Matthew Packer, were telling the truth. He struggles to make all the men witnessed with Stride to be young, like the man Packer described. In reference to Marshall's man, he makes the delightful observation that "the young man was middle-aged" and, on the next page, "the young man seemed middle-aged".

Bachert on Berner Street

105. Evans, Stewart P. and Keith Skinner, Jack the Ripper: 'Letters From Hell', Sutton Publishing, (2001).

106. Scott, Chris, Editor, Ripperologist 101, April 2009, citing the Pall Mall Gazette of 24 November 1885.

107. Spryder, Stephen P., Editor, 'Public Reactions To Jack The Ripper, Letters To The Editor: August-December 1888', Inklings Press, (2006).

108. Evans, Stewart P. and Keith Skinner, 'Jack the Ripper: Letters From Hell', Sutton Publishing, (2001).

109. Posted to the Casebook.org on Sept. 3rd, 2008, by researcher Chris Scott.

110. For more on Haynes see 'The Bank Holiday Murders: The True Story of the First Whitechapel Murders' by Tom Wescott (2014).

111. Eastern Post & City Chronicle, April 14th, 1888.

112. The majority of the press excerpts referenced in this article are from the e-book, 'Jack the Ripper: A Cast of Thousands' (2004) by Christopher Scott. Also consulted was 'Albert Bachert', an essay by David O'Flaherty. Both of these works may be found at Casebook. org simply by typing 'Bachert' into the search engine.

113. 'Amateur Detectives at Work' feature in *the East London Observer*, Oct. 13th, 1888.

Matthew Packer: The (Not So) Simple Truth

114. Previous to this, the WVC/IWMES connection was discussed in 'Jack and the Grape Stalk: The Berner Street Mystery Pt. 1' in Ripper Notes #25 January 2006.

115. Morning Advertiser, Oct 3rd, 1888. The article mentions three private detectives under hire of the WVC. The identity of the third man is unknown. Assuming he ever existed, he was no longer in their employ by Oct 13th when the East London Observer published their feature on the committee and described only two detectives.

116. 'Amateur Detectives at Work' feature in the East London Observer, Oct. 13th, 1888.

117. Unless otherwise noted, all quotations from police reports are credited to authors Stewart P. Evans and Keith Skinner, 'The Ultimate Jack the Ripper Companion', Carroll & Graf (2000).

118. Packer was 59 years old, but likely appeared older.

119. 'Mrs. Kuer's Lodger', Ripperologist #81, July, 2007 and 'Is There an Echo Around Here? An Addendum to 'Mrs. Kuer's Lodger", Ripperologist #83, Sept. 2007.

120. 'Jack the Ripper and the Case for Scotland Yard's Prime Suspect' (2011).

121. North-Eastern Daily Gazette, Wednesday, Oct. 10th, 1888.

122. I'm obliged to Maria Birbili for making this comparison on a Jtrforums.com thread. For those not aware, Kaelin was a witness in the OJ Simpson case and was noted as being good for a sound bite or a bit of comic relief.

123. See Section 1, Chapter 6, for 'Henry Birch & the Cambridge Heath Road Incident'.

124. See Section 2, essay 'Bachert in Berner Street', for more on this intriguing character.

125. See Section 2, essay 'A Berner Street Rogues Gallery, chapter 'Berner Street Club Member/Attendee for my ideas on the man PC Smith saw talking with Stride, as well as the following essays on Fanny Mortimer and Israel Schwartz for more discussion of Smith's evidence.

126. East London Advertiser, Oct. 13th, 1888.

127. Birmingham Daily Post, Oct. 8th, 1888. Discovered by Howard Brown.

128. Evening News, Oct. 31st, 1888.

129. Evening News, November 15th, 1888.

130. Not one and the same as PS White from Packer's first folly.

131. Sheffield & Rotherham Independent, November 16th, 1888.

132. Discovered by Howard Brown and posted to Jtrforums.com.

133. On November 21st, Annie Farmer, a prostitute, claimed to have been attacked by a client she'd escorted back to 19 George Street. Her throat was cut, but only superficially so, and it's possible she had stolen from the man and been caught out, then accused him of being the Ripper so he'd run away, which he managed to do successfully.

134. The Sheffield & Rotherham Independent, Sept. 14th, 1889. Discovered by Debra Arif.

135. Information shared by Debra Arif on the Casebook.org message boards.

What Fanny Didn't See

136. Lloyd's Weekly Newspaper, Sept. 30th, 1888, courtesy of Howard Brown. Or see oldbaileyonline.com and search 'James Stephens' for that date.

137. Researcher Chris Scott discovered William's death notice and posted it to jtrforums.com. All it tells us is that he died sometime in the first quarter of 1889.

138. I utilized the Daily News for this excerpt, but the report appeared identically in other papers.

139. The Star, Oct. 2nd, 1888.

140. Identified by researcher Chris Scott in the 1891 census and posted to Casebook.org.

141. Daily News, Oct. 3rd, 1888.

142. 'I Caught Crippen: Memoirs of Ex-Chief Inspector Walter Dew CID' (1938).

143. From Smith's inquest testimony, Evening News, Oct. 06th, 1888.

144. Although probably unrelated, it's worth noting an overlooked piece of information provided to the police the next day and potentially relating to the murder of Catherine Eddowes in Mitre Square. A Mrs. Lindsay, living at 11 Duke Street, which overlooked Church Passage leading into Mitre Square, recalled being woken up in the middle of the night (she couldn't say the exact time) by the sound of two people talking. She heard a man say, angrily, "I am not the murderer." Surprised by this, she attracted her husband's attention and they both looked out the window in time to see a man of average height, dressed in dark clothes, and carrying an umbrella and a small parcel, walking in the direction of Aldgate. – The Star, Oct. 1st, 1888. The East London Observer of Oct. 6th noted that another resident of the street, a Miss Solomon, corroborated the story.

145. Evening News, Oct 1st, 1888.

146. There must have been a measure of question about even this, as some papers reported 39 Fairclough Street.

147. Daily Telegraph, Oct. 6th, 1888.

148. Echo, Oct. 1st, 1888.

149. Daily Telegraph, Oct. 6th, 1888.

150. In fact, it was Edward Spooner who was standing on the corner at this time, so it was he that Brown took for a policeman.

Israel Schwartz – A Critical Analysis

151. Evans, Stewart P. and Keith Skinner, 'The Ultimate Jack the Ripper Companion', page 133 (2000).

152. Anderson is counting Martha Tabram among the Ripper's tally.

153. Begg, Paul, 'Jack the Ripper: The Facts', 2006.

154. Following is the complete text of the Oct. 3rd, 1888 Star editorial:

'A few words here as to the general system adopted in setting about the investigation of a murder mystery, such as the latest Whitechapel one and the others that have preceded it, may not be out of place.

'The detectives from Scotland-yard go down to the station in the locality of the crime, and they and the chiefs and detectives of the police whom they have come to assist have a consultation. Each suggests what is the best way to set to work, and finally a theory is adopted and acted upon. People who are supposed to know something bearing on the case are invited to give evidence, and everything they say is taken down – sometimes openly, sometimes by a concealed shorthand writer. If they are suspected of knowing more than they care to disclose, they are treated in a friendly manner, and pleasantly invited to come again. Meanwhile their movements are closely watched.

'The services of "noses" – that is to say, people who are hand in glove with persons of indifferent character, are frequently called into play, and they are deputed to go to the low lodging-houses and other places that are the resort of low characters, and keep their eyes and ears open for anything likely to give a clue to the individual or individuals wanted. Women often act as "noses."

'In investigating a crime, detectives proceed very quietly – often too quietly, it might be thought – and frequently through the agency of too credulous reporters lead the really suspected person to believe that the scent lies quite in another quarter, while in reality his every movement is being closely watched. In some instances, the reluctance of witnesses to come forward with evidence is a great stumbling block in the way of success.

'The police are generally held responsible for the particular kind of evidence that is brought against a person charged with committing a crime when the case goes for trial, but it seems they are not responsible for the line adopted by the prosecution.

'The duties of detectives sometimes cast their lines in pleasant places. At noblemen's balls helmeted policemen keep the doors, but the detective, in dress coat and kid gloves, enters with the company. It is not generally known that even at balls given by the highest nobility, by Ambassadors, and the most exclusive of the "Upper Ten," a detective in evening dress, with a bland smile on his face, and his moustache curled in the most aggravating fashion, stalks about and makes note of diverse things.'

155. The Text of this valuable resource is available for free at Casebook. org.

156. 2010 edition.

157. See 'Murder in the Neighborhood: The Berner Street Mystery Pt. 2' elsewhere in this book for a tour of the street.

158. Eyges, Thomas G., 'Beyond the Horizon: The Story of a Radical Emigrant', by Thomas G. Eyges (1944). This is the autobiography of Eyges who was himself a member of the Berner Street Club in the late 1880s.

159. It must be pointed out that the club was not the only possible residence for the Schwartz family on Berner Street. Many of the residents took in lodgers, including Matthew Packer and the Mortimers. In fact, the 1881 census records a family very similar to the Schwartz's residing with William and Fanny Mortimer. Henry Morris, a tailor, and his wife, Jane, were both 25 years old and from Poland.

160. For more on Violina see Wescott, Tom, 'The Bank Holiday Murders: The True Story of the First Whitechapel Murders' (2014).

161. The Penny Illustrated Paper, Sept. 15th, 1888.

162. Harry Harris, who along with Joseph Levy had been with Lawende when they say the mystery couple, informed the press that 'he is of the opinion that [Joseph Lawende] saw no more than he did,

and that was only the back of the man' – Evening News, Oct. 9th, 1888.

163. "We never in one single instance found a person who had seen a man with any of the murdered women on the evenings they were murdered, so we never had a description of him." - Northeastern Daily Gazette, April 15, 1896

'As no one ever saw the man except his victims, not the slightest evidence could be obtained as to his description.' – East London Observer, June 1st, 1901

'No description of Jack the Ripper was ever obtained.' – Morning Advertiser, March 1st, 1903.

164. Daily Telegraph, February 18th, 1891.

165. Schwartz's description of BS Man was circulated to police stations immediately and published in the Police Gazette on Oct. 19th, so it would have been futile if not impossible to keep it secret from coroner Baxter.

Section 3: Curios & Oddities
The Ghoul of Goulston Street

166. Begg, Paul, with Martin Fido and Keith Skinner, 'The Complete Jack the Ripper A-Z' (2010).

167. Sir Henry Smith, 'From Constable to Commissioner,' 1910.

168. 'Eddowes's Apron', Ripperologist Magazine No. 57, January 2005.

169. 'The Complete Jack the Ripper A-Z', (2010).

170. East London Observer, Nov. 10th, 1888.

171. The Daily Chronicle, Sept. 1st, 1908.

172. For more on this episode see 'James Johnson' entry in the essay 'The Berner Street Rogues Gallery' in this book.

173. Mr. Bloomfield's brief essay 'On the Danger of Writing Graffiti Too Cleverly' appeared in the anthology 'Who Was Jack the Ripper', compiled by Camille Wolff.

174. Holmes correctly deduced that 'Rache' was German for 'revenge'.

Mary Kelly and the Decadents

175. From Ernestdowson.com.

Index

A

B

C

D

E

F

G

H

Holmes, Sherlock, 298-299

Hopkins, George, 48-50

Hopkins, R. Thurston, 319-322

Horsnell, Emily, 43

Hudson, Elizabeth, 150-152

Hummerston, Henry, 41, 71

Hutchinson, George, 134-135, 160, 202, 210, 304, 320, 321

J

Johnson, James, 149-152

Johnston, Edward, 86, 87, 89-94, 108, 224, 225

K

Kay, Dr. John, 90

Kelly, John, 145

Kelly, Mary, 316-324, 61, 83, 105, 106, 168, 184, 191, 210, 211, 283, 290, 296, 304, 305, 307, 311, 312

Kent, James, 119

Kentorrich, Barnett, 100, 156

Kidney, Michael, 105, 110, 121-148, 155, 163, 168, 175, 192

Killeen, Dr. Thomas, 25, 28

King James 1, 319

Kosminski, Maurice, 102

Kozebrodski, Isaac, 84-86, 89-93, 108, 156, 177, 225

'Kozminski' suspect, 260, 288

Kozminski, Aaron, 204

Krantz, Philip, 104, 107, 156, 157

N

Neil, John (PC), 13, 14, 26, 54, 55, 56, 62

Nelson, Admiral Lord, 319

Nichols, Mary Ann (Polly), 12-80, (Discovery of murder) 11-13, (marriage to William) 14, (October 1887 arrest, 'worst woman in the square') 15-17, (attempted stabbing of workhouse official) 18, (resided at 35 Dorset Street) 20, (rings stolen from her) 22, (murder similar to Smith and Tabram) 24-28, (blood pool under legs) 27, (eyewitness account of post mortem) 28-30, (possibility of missing organ) 28-35, (same killer as Emma Smith) 77, (use of carotid chokehold aka 'garroting') 79, 83, 110, 114, 120, 124, 151-152, 179, 275, 296, 299

Nichols, William, 14, 18-19

Norman, Henry, 190

Norris, Henry, 101

Nue, PC, 150

O

Ostrog, Michael, 260

P

Packer, Matthew, 72, 84, 94, 97, 98, 100, 129, 131, 195-213, 228, 241, 245, 248, 256

Packer, Rose Ann, 100, 128, 129

Pash, Florence, 322

Paul, Robert, 12-13, 26, 54, 58

Phillips, Dr. George Bagster, 28, 86, 89, 90, 93, 114, 115, 119, 120, 123, 131, 239, 272, 297-298

T